Library of
Davidson College

THE POETRY OF CLOUGH

THE POETRY OF CLOUGH

An Essay in Revaluation

by Walter E. Houghton

OCTAGON BOOKS
A DIVISION OF FARRAR, STRAUS AND GIROUX

New York   1979

Copyright © 1963 by Yale University

Reprinted 1979
by special arrangement with Yale University Press

OCTAGON BOOKS
A DIVISION OF FARRAR, STRAUS & GIROUX, INC.
19 Union Square West
New York, N.Y. 10003

Library of Congress Cataloging in Publication Data

Houghton, Walter Edwards, 1904-
  The poetry of Clough.

  Reprint of the ed. published by Yale University Press, New Haven.
  Bibliography: p.
  Includes index.
  1. Clough, Arthur Hugh, 1819-1861—Criticism and interpretation.
PR4459.H6 1979   821'.8   78-27119
ISBN 0-374-93982-9

Manufactured by Braun-Brumfield, Inc.
Ann Arbor, Michigan
Printed in the United States of America

To my daughters
Nancy and Esther Edwards

ACKNOWLEDGMENTS

I WISH TO EXPRESS my gratitude to Gordon Haight of Yale for a perceptive criticism of the manuscript that provoked some important revisions; to Robert Stange of Minnesota for reading and discussing Chapter 1; to my former student, Vicki Hahn Weisberg, now at Radcliffe, for similar help on Chapter 6; to Julee Stone MacGowan of the Yale University Press for editing the text; to Frederick Mulhauser of Pomona for loaning me microfilms of the unpublished letters; to Richard Gollen of Rochester for so often giving me the benefit of his wide knowledge of Clough's work; and to my wife, Esther Rhoads Houghton, for assistance of every kind, including the burdens of proofreading and indexing.

I also wish to thank the following publishers for permission to quote from books on which they hold the copyright: the Clarendon Press for quotations from *The Poems of Arthur Hugh Clough*, ed. H. F. Lowry, A. L. P. Norrington, and F. L. Mulhauser, and from *The Correspondence of Arthur Hugh Clough*, ed. F. L. Mulhauser; the Oxford Press for quotations from *The Letters of Matthew Arnold to Arthur Hugh Clough*, ed. H. F. Lowry, and from *The Poetical Works of Matthew Arnold*, ed. H. F. Lowry and C. B. Tinker.

Finally, I am especially grateful to Katherine Duff (Clough's grandniece), F. L. Mulhauser, and the Bodleian Library for permission to quote from the manuscripts of Clough now in the Bodley; to the Harvard Library, and to William A. Jackson, librarian of the Houghton Library, for similar permission to quote from the collection there.

Note

For clarity, a distinction is made in the volume between the titles of Clough's longer poems, which are set in italics, and those of his shorter works and unfinished fragments, which appear in quotation marks.

CONTENTS

Acknowledgments   vii

Preface   xi

1. THE CRITICAL TRADITION   1
    1. The "Failure" of Clough, 1848–70   2
    2. Victorian Preconceptions   8
    3. The Nadir, 1870–1930   19
    4. New Insights and Old Assumptions, 1930–60   21

2. THE SHORTER POEMS   27
    1. Was Clough an Artist?   27
    2. Neoclassical Foundations   38
    3. The Metaphysical Strain   49
    4. Romanticism   55
    5. Objectivity   68

3. *ADAM AND EVE*   80
    1. Christian Guilt and the Moral Conscience: The Fall of Man   83
    2. Christian Atonement and the Moral Conscience: The Murder of Abel   88

4. *THE BOTHIE OF TOBER-NA-VUOLICH*   92
    1. The Modern Poem   93
    2. Narrative Synthesis   100
    3. Range and Variety   112
    4. Charm   116

5. *AMOURS DE VOYAGE* 119
   1. The Oxonian at Rome   119
   2. The Ennuyé   125
   3. The Anti-Hero   128
   4. The Intellectual in Love   135

6. *DIPSYCHUS* 156
   1. Lyric Drama   159
   2. Dipsychus   160
   3. The Spirit   163
   4. Background   172
   5. The Action: Scenes I–VII   177
   6. The Action: Scenes VIII–XIII   192
   7. Emphasis   206

7. *MARI MAGNO* 208
   1. A New Departure   211
   2. Distinction   218

A Final Word   225

Bibliography   229

Index   231

PREFACE

> *It is not our purpose to dwell upon the biography of Mr. Clough, but rather to examine his works, and to show in what their real and vital excellence consists.*
> —John Addington Symonds, 1868

I AM NOT CONCERNED in this book with Clough's poetry as a biographical document, or as a record of his thought, or as an index to the age. The poetry itself is the end in view, and this is a work of criticism—more exactly, of historical criticism. Though the chronological arrangement, despite some overlapping, makes it possible to chart Clough's development, my intention is to increase the understanding of his art by combining technical analysis with whatever insight can be gained from a knowledge of his ideas, especially on aesthetics, and of his environment.

The time is ripe for such a critical effort. For one thing, all the scholarly equipment that is needed, except for his journals, is now available, so that the disabilities that plagued the only previous books on the poetry, by Samuel Waddington (1883) and James Osborne (1919), are gone. Since much of Clough's verse was unpublished when he died and much of it was left in various states of revision, a scholarly edition was a necessity for any study of his work in depth. In the *Poems* of 1951, Howard Lowry, A. L. P. Norrington, and Frederick Mulhauser gave us a text based on a careful examination of the manuscripts. Six years later came the two-volume selection from the *Correspondence*, edited by Mulhauser; and almost all of the unpublished letters, conveniently catalogued in his Appendix III, are now open to inspection at Oxford or at Harvard. Finally, in 1959, Clough's grandniece, Katherine Duff, presented the Bodleian Library with a large number of prose essays that had not been seen before, except by a few favored scholars, and had never been used—indeed, had remained largely unknown until they were described in July 1960, in the *Bulletin of the New York Public Library*. To these prerequisites may be added two other advantages: the historical knowledge of Victorian thought that we now possess, which provides the background needed for the right perspective on many poems, and the methods of close analysis first initiated thirty years ago by Eliot, Richards, and Leavis. One could scarcely ask for a better set of tools for the study of Clough's poetry.

Furthermore, such a study leads, we find, to some exciting discoveries. As I show in Chapter 1, Clough has had a bad press. Even from able critics like Arnold, Swinburne, and Lionel Trilling, he has received much less than his due, and since 1910 he has had few readers. The fact is, however, that on fresh examination in the 1960s, much of his poetry turns out to be sophisticated and alive. A remark about Clough in Graham Greene's *The Quiet American* ("He was an adult poet in the nineteenth century. There weren't so many of them.") points to qualities in his work that have led some recent critics to compare him not only with Auden and MacNeice, but also with Laforgue, Pound, and Eliot. Yet his modernity, let alone something far more important, his intrinsic success as a poet, remain unknown outside a small circle of discoverers.

It is therefore time for a revaluation that will underscore his achievement, and in particular will give the three narrative poems that are his major work—*The Bothie of Tober-na-Vuolich, Amours de Voyage,* and *Dipsychus*—the recognition their very genre has often denied them. This emphasis need not mean neglecting his limitations, which I take up at various points, but it calls for a primary concern with his "real and vital excellence." What is wanted at the moment is to persuade Victorian students and everyone who cares for poetry to read the neglected work of a fine artist.

W. E. H.

Wellesley, Massachusetts
July 1962

1

THE CRITICAL TRADITION[1]

WHEN GEOFFREY TILLOTSON remarked not long ago that "when we are concerned with a poet of Clough's status, we are concerned with English poetry," the readers of the *Times Literary Supplement* on both sides of the Atlantic must have been startled and incredulous. For everyone—except the handful of critics described by one exasperated writer as Cloughomaniacs—knows that Clough was a failure. Shortly after Tillotson's eccentric judgment, Stephen Spender reaffirmed the conventional opinion with a new twist: "In a sense, Matthew Arnold was right in saying that Clough was no artist. What he did was create his own failure and leave a record of it. He effectively expresses ineffectiveness through being ineffective, expresses failure through often failing." In the same year, 1957, Hoxie Fairchild spoke for the Victorian scholars: "It is perhaps unfortunate that Arthur Hugh Clough chose verse as the vehicle for his perplexities: although he desired to write 'poetry' he was not sufficiently an artist to be much interested in making poems."[2]

---

[1]. An earlier draft of this chapter was published in *Studies in English Literature, 1500–1900*, 1 (1961) 25–61, as "Arthur Hugh Clough: A Hundred Years of Disparagement."

[2]. Tillotson's remark appeared in the issue for June 18, 1954, p. 400; the Cloughomaniacs in the *Saturday Review*, 66 (July 7, 1888), 26; Spender in the *Sunday Times* (London, Nov. 3, 1957), under the ironic title—not his own, I assume—of "Great Writers Rediscovered"; and Fairchild in his chapter on Clough in *Religious Trends in English Poetry: Volume IV: 1830–1880* (New York, 1957), p. 505. Here and throughout this chapter my quotations have been selected to show Clough's reputation and should not be read as summing up a critic's entire opinion. A list of nearly everything ever written about Clough, including letters as well as essays and books, will be found in Part III of the *Bibliography of Arthur Hugh Clough*, to be edited by the present writer in collaboration with Richard M. Gollin and Michael Timko.

2   THE CRITICAL TRADITION

There is nothing novel about this disparagement, nor about the dogmatic tone of voice with which it is pronounced. The same injustice, as I think, has been done to Clough from the beginning. Though often praised for a character of great beauty and purity, he has suffered, early and late, from the same kind of stigma. In the 1860s, critics were already deploring the " 'wasted genius,' 'baffled intellect,' 'unfulfilled purpose,' and 'disappointed life' of Mr. Clough."[3] Some of them were his friends: indeed, perhaps only Lytton Strachey has done more to denigrate the man and the poetry than Francis Palgrave, Mrs. Clough, and Matthew Arnold.

1. The "Failure" of Clough, 1848–70

No one for whom a brilliant future was predicted has ever deserved that confidence more than Clough, or paid for it more dearly. To his teachers and contemporaries he seemed the most highly endowed person of his generation, and his combination of intellectual gifts and moral qualities pointed to a distinguished career. And what happened? After winning every prize at Rugby and the Balliol scholarship, he "failed," as he said himself, in the schools, where he received only a second (1841);[4] in the same year lost a Balliol fellowship; and after being elected at Oriel in 1842, a great distinction at the time, was rejected for a professorship in Ireland (1847) and for one in Australia (1851); resigned his Oriel fellowship in 1848, and was forced to resign his headship of University Hall in 1852; sought his fortune as a teacher in America (1852–53) but did not find it; returned home to marry and take a laborious post in the Education Office at small pay; and died in 1861 at the age of forty-two.

Nor did the work he published during his lifetime do anything to relieve the embarrassed feeling of his friends that he had failed to realize his enormous potentialities. Half a volume of short poems, only twenty-nine in all, in *Ambarvalia* (printed with the mediocre

---

3. Reported by J. A. Symonds, "Arthur Hugh Clough," *Fortnightly Review*, 10 (1868), 589, reprinted in *Last and First* (London, 1919), p. 65.
4. Thomas Arnold, Jr., "Arthur Hugh Clough: A Sketch," *Nineteenth Century*, 43 (1898), 106.

verse of Thomas Burbidge in 1849); a narrative poem with the uninviting title of *The Bothie of Tober-na-Vuolich* (1848) and another called *Amours de Voyage*, published only in the *Atlantic Monthly* (1858) and not in England; and apart from some juvenile work in *The Rugby Magazine*, six poems in periodicals, one being "Say not the struggle nought availeth," but that, too, buried in an American journal—this was the total output. It amounted to less than five thousand lines and to only about thirty-five hundred published in England. However, when the whole body of Clough's work appeared in 1869, it proved to be almost as large as Arnold's, and much larger than Herbert's, Goldsmith's, or half a dozen other English poets of distinction. Nevertheless, Clough's friends and critics had become so imbued with the notion of his "broken life" that they continued to excuse him—or to blame him—for the scantiness of his production.[5]

But the major error was their blindness to the quality of the work. While in private, Froude was telling Carlyle that Clough's poems might survive "as an evidence of what he might have been," and Carlyle was telling Froude that he had "expected very considerable things" of "poor Clough," and Arnold was saying that now that "poor Clough" had died, people would stop thinking "he never would do anything" and start focussing on "what there was of extraordinary promise and interest in him when young, and of unique and imposing even as he grew older without fulfilling people's expectations"—while all this was being said, a public la-

---

5. Henry Sidgwick, *Westminster Review*, 92 (1869), 364, reprinted in his *Miscellaneous Essays and Addresses* (London and New York, 1904), p. 61, explained that one reason why Clough's friends tended to dwell on "unrealised possibilities" was that "he produced very little." Cf. Mrs. Clough's "Memoir," *The Poems and Prose Remains of Arthur Hugh Clough* (2 vols. London, 1869), *1*, 41, or *Prose Remains* (London, 1888), pp. 41–42. Though J. A. Symonds helped Mrs. Clough with this edition, she herself apparently wrote the "Memoir," for in the preface she thanked him for his assistance only "in making these selections and in arranging these volumes." Hereafter I refer to both volumes as *Prose* and in each case give a double reference.

In the definitive editions, Clough's *Poems*, ed. H. F. Lowry, A. L. P. Norrington, and F. L. Mulhauser (Oxford, 1951), and the *Poetical Works* of Arnold, ed. C. B. Tinker and H. F. Lowry (London and New York, 1950), I find 13,578 lines by Clough and 14,023 by Arnold.

ment to the same effect was initiated in the journals.[6] *Blackwood's* thought a higher court of appeal would have to decide whether or not Clough's life had been a failure; the *Daily News,* admitting that his poems were not "what they might have been," found consolation in the fact that they showed "what *he* might have been"; and the *Cornhill* was quite certain there was "some supreme excellence which Clough *might* have achieved, *ought* to have achieved, but somehow *did not*," which made him "one of the prospectuses which never become works."[7]

This was the vein expanded and established in the authoritative memoirs of Francis Palgrave and Mrs. Clough; and which naturally led, in all who admired the man and thought the poetry a failure, to the conclusion that his real achievement was not aesthetic but moral. "His poems," wrote his wife, "tell us of his perplexities, his divided thoughts, his uncertainties; those who remember him will think *rather* of his simple directness of speech and action, the clearness of his judgment on any moot point; above all . . . his entire nobleness, his utter purity of character." Palgrave, indeed, praising his beautifully unselfish life, had already discouraged the potential readers of the first edition by adding, "It might be truly said, that he rather lived than wrote his poem."[8]

---

6. J. A. Froude, *Thomas Carlyle: A History of His Life in London, 1834–1881* (2 vols. London, 1884), 2, chap. 25, 243–44. Strictly speaking, Froude's remarks were made as he was writing, but Carlyle's were in reply to a letter of Froude's in 1861 and begin, "I quite agree in what you say." Arnold's letter to his mother, Nov. 20, 1861, is in *The Letters of Matthew Arnold to Arthur Hugh Clough,* ed. H. F. Lowry (London and New York, 1932), p. 157.

7. W. Lucas Collins, according to "Blackwood's Contributors' Book," in *Blackwood's Magazine,* 92 (1862), 586; A. P. Stanley in the *Daily News* (Jan. 9, 1862), p. 2 (the italics are mine); the *Cornhill Magazine,* 6 (1862), 398, is assigned to G. H. Lewes on a publisher's list.

8. Mrs. Clough, *Prose, 1,* 49, or p. 51 (the italics are mine); Palgrave, "Memoir" prefixed to *Poems* (Cambridge and London, 1862), p. xxi.

Henry Sidgwick, *Miscellaneous Essays,* p. 61, remarked that the tone which many of his friends "have adopted in speaking of the author and his writings has, though partly the result, been also partly the cause of the slow growth of their popularity."

Complementing the shift of praise from the poetry to the man is the praise of the poetry as history. That line of apologetics received its classic statement from James Russell Lowell, "Swinburne's Tragedies" (1866), *My Study Windows* (Boston

Arnold himself, for all his greater intelligence, continued the strain of apology with a wistful condescension. As he concluded his "Last Words" on Homer from the chair of poetry at Oxford, where his voice would carry special authority, he singled out "two invaluable literary qualities" that Mr. Clough had possessed, but both, it turned out, were *moral* qualities: the disinterested love of literature and complete freedom from the arts of flattery and servility. Of the poetry Arnold would say only that phrases from *The Bothie* came back to his ear "with the true Homeric ring"! But he added at once: "That in him of which I think oftenest is the Homeric simplicity of his literary life."[9]

It was "Thyrsis," however, quoted by so many critics, read by so many people who knew nothing else about Clough, that spread the damaging view of his poetry which is still being repeated:

It irk'd him to be here, he could not rest.
  He loved each simple joy the country yields,
    He loved his mates; but yet he could not keep,
  For that a shadow lour'd on the fields,
    Here with the shepherds and the silly sheep.
      Some life of men unblest
  He knew, which made him droop, and fill'd his head.
    He went; his piping took a troubled sound
  Of storms that rage outside our happy ground;
  He could not wait their passing, he is dead.

         .   .   .   (41–50)

But Thyrsis never more we swains shall see;
  See him come back, and cut a smoother reed,
  And blow a strain the world at last shall heed—

         .   .   .   (77–79)

---

and New York, 1899), p. 211. "We have a foreboding that Clough, imperfect as he was in many respects, and dying before he had subdued his sensitive temperament to the sterner requirements of his art, will be thought a hundred years hence to have been the truest expression in verse of the moral and intellectual tendencies, the doubt and struggle towards settled convictions, of the period in which he lived."

9. *On the Study of Celtic Literature and On Translating Homer* (New York, 1883), p. 300.

> And this rude Cumner ground,
>   Its fir-topped Hurst, its farms, its quiet fields,
>   Here cam'st thou in thy jocund youthful time,
>   Here was thine height of strength, thy golden prime!
>
> . . .   (216–19)
>
> What though the music of thy rustic flute
>   Kept not for long its happy, country tone;
>   Lost it too soon, and learnt a stormy note
> Of men contention-tost, of men who groan,
>   Which task'd thy pipe too sore, and tired thy throat—
>   It fail'd, and thou wast mute!
>
>   (221–26)

It is hard to imagine anything more misleading: In his happy youth at Oxford Clough attained his greatest artistic strength; but unfortunately his knowledge of the suffering and oppression of the poor called him away from the Cumner Hills; whereupon he turned to subjects or styles which were too much for his poetic gift, so that it failed and he became silent; but if only he could come back, he would sing more smoothly and then the world would listen. Anyone who has read the troubled and satiric poetry Clough wrote *at* Oxford, or who knows that most of his verse—and almost all that makes him a distinguished poet—was written *after* he left Oxford, can only feel astonished by this reading of his life, and dismayed that "Thyrsis" should have been a major vehicle of Clough's reputation.

It is true that in private Arnold admitted there was much in Clough "which one cannot deal with in this way," so much that he would not send the poem to Clough's wife. "Still," he added, "Clough *had* this idyllic side, too; to deal with this suited my desire to deal again with that Cumner country."[10] That is half the explanation. Arnold wanted to write "The Scholar-Gipsy, Part II." He did not want to write about Clough. And he would never have done so had his conscience let him alone, but some tribute of some sort had to be written by Clough's closest friend and fellow poet.

---

10. C. B. Tinker and H. F. Lowry, *The Poetry of Matthew Arnold: a Commentary* (London and New York, 1940), p. 216.

The new "Scholar-Gipsy" would have to be a pastoral elegy. That convention, of course, has freedoms and demands which absolve the poet from any strict adherence to biography. But even within its pattern, Arnold could have treated Clough more fairly, and he would have done so if he had liked the poetry.[11]

Implicit in all the talk about failure is the basic assumption that Clough was not really an artist and that, barring a few poems, his work was second-rate. Before 1930 we can count the critics who praised his poetry *as poetry* on our fingers. The party line was laid down by Palgrave in his "Memoir" of 1862: "Viewed critically, Clough's work [*The Bothie*] is wanting in art; the language and the thought are often unequal and incomplete; the poetical fusion into a harmonious whole, imperfect. Here, and in his other writings, one feels a doubt whether in verse he chose the right vehicle, the truly natural mode of utterance."[12] In defining this charge more fully, Arnold added a second explanation of his failure, privately in letters to Clough written during 1848–49, and publicly, so to speak, in 1932 when their publication reinforced the old contention with the weight of his authority. The crucial passages are these:

> A growing sense of the deficiency of the *beautiful* in your poems, and of this alone being properly *poetical* as distinguished from rhetorical, devotional or metaphysical, made me speak as I did. . . .
> No—I doubt your being an *artist:* but have you read Novalis? He certainly is not one either: but in the way of direct communication, insight, and report, his tendency has often reminded me of yours.

---

11. Cf. H. F. Lowry's discussion of "Thyrsis" in Arnold's *Letters to Clough*, pp. 21–22. Mrs. Clough (letter to Henry Sidgwick, Sept. 19 [1869], in the Bodleian Library) found the poem "offensive" because "he denies his friend's greatness."

12. *Poems* (1862), p. xi. Cf. the very first public notice, a review of *The Bothie* in the *Spectator*, *21* (Dec. 2, 1848), 1166, dismissing the poem as "prosaic verse," and the *Saturday Review*, *12* (Nov. 30, 1861), 564, talking of the lack of genius needed to give his ideas "intelligible and attractive versification."

> Many persons with far lower gifts than yours yet seem to find their natural mode of expression in poetry, and tho: the contents may not be very valuable they appeal with justice from the judgement of the mere thinker to the world's general appreciation of naturalness—i.e.—an absolute propriety—of form, as the sole *necessary* of Poetry as such: whereas the greatest wealth and depth of matter is merely a superfluity in the Poet *as such*.
>
> I often think that even a slight gift of poetical expression which in a common person might have developed itself easily and naturally, is overlaid and crushed in a profound thinker so as to be of no use to him to help him to express himself. —The trying to go into and to the bottom of an object instead of grouping *objects* is as fatal to the sensuousness of poetry as the mere painting . . . is to its airy and rapidly moving life.
>
> Consider whether you attain the *beautiful*, and whether your product gives PLEASURE, not excites curiosity and reflexion.[13]

In short, Clough was not an artist because (1) he was mainly occupied with ideas as such and getting them expressed directly as autobiography, or else rhetorically, as in philosophical essays or public speeches, whereas the artist is concerned above all with form—grouping objects into a unified pattern and finding the precise words that will articulate them, through sound as well as sense; and because (2) his poetry is not beautiful.

2. Victorian Preconceptions

Though no one would claim that Clough's form was always adequate, he succeeded so often in fusing language and thought into an organic whole that one must suppose the depreciation of his art arose from something more basic, something only half realized —because never clearly formulated in Victorian criticism—about

---

13. *Letters to Clough*, pp. 66, 98–99; also cf. p. 81. In his later criticism the stress on substance brought Arnold closer to Clough's position: see Michael Timko, "Corydon Had a Rival," *Victorian Newsletter*, no. 19 (1961), 5–11.

VICTORIAN PRECONCEPTIONS 9

the very nature of poetry, something covered, however loosely, by the charge that his poetry lacked "beauty."[14] For plainly and in various ways, Clough's work failed to meet the preconceived notions of what poetry should be, not only in his own time but through the later Victorian and Georgian periods. Only today, when these assumptions are being challenged, have we begun to look at his poems with open minds. Yet even now, in the very period that has revived the work of Donne and Dryden and praised the satire of Byron, most critics remain oblivious to a poetry that follows along the lines those men laid down. For with Clough's usual bad luck, the advantage of a new age sympathetic with his art has been offset by the long tradition of disparagement and the influence of Arnold's letters.

To begin with the broadest description, the Victorians wanted poetry to be "poetic." Under Romantic influence they associated the word with sensuous diction and imagery, an affective rhythm that was melodic, and a syntax sufficiently straightforward to make the verse understandable at one reading. They thought that poetry should be simple, sensuous, and, if not always passionate, at any rate emotional.[15] It might, of course, contain ideas, but it should not be intellectual: it should not be witty or dialectical or difficult. It should express "states of feeling" or of "thought coloured by feeling, under the excitement of beauty."[16] Its ideal form, therefore—the form best representing its character—was the lyric. Browning is a striking exception, but Browning was never recog-

14. Clough's failure and success in the control of form is described below, in chap. 2, sec. 1.

15. In "Emerson," *Discourses in America* (London, 1885), p. 154, Arnold specifically adopted Milton's principle "that poetry ought to be simple, sensuous, impassioned."

16. J. S. Mill, describing what he admired in Wordsworth, *Autobiography*, ed. Harold Laski (London, 1924), p. 125. Cf. his statement in "What is Poetry?" *Early Essays*, ed. J. W. M. Gibbs (London, 1897), pp. 208–09: "Poetry is feeling, confessing itself to itself in moments of solitude, and embodying itself in symbols, which are the nearest possible representations of the feeling in the exact shape in which it exists in the poet's mind." This is almost exactly the line adopted by Arthur Henry Hallam in the review of Tennyson called "On Some of the Characteristics of Modern Poetry" (1831), reprinted in *The Writings of Arthur Hallam*, ed. T. H. Vail Motter (New York and London, 1943): see especially, pp. 184–95.

nized by the older Victorians; his vogue came in the seventies and eighties.

This definition of poetry can be sharpened and historically placed by remembering the dichotomy that first appeared, I think, in Addison's famous essay on genius. There the natural genius, relying on his own inspiration (Shakespeare), was differentiated from the artificial genius who knew his classics and followed the "rules" (Milton). This distinction passed through various metamorphoses until it emerged, in a final and influential form, in the *Biographia Literaria* (1817). The difference emphasized by Coleridge was that between a "poetic" or "organic" structure, analogous to the creation of nature, in which the several parts were blended and fused, each into each, "by that synthetic and magical power . . . imagination," and a "prosaic" or "inorganic" structure where they were related but discrete, and bound together by the fancy, which is the intellectual faculty of choice and control. The former was the work of genius, the latter merely of talent. Though in theory this allowed for two kinds of poetry—and Coleridge once admitted that "with the presumption of youth" he had undervalued the kind of poetry written by the neoclassical school and "withheld from its masters the legitimate name of poets"—nevertheless, he often spoke as though romantic, imaginative art were alone worthy of the name. "A poem of any length," he said, "neither can be, or ought to be, all poetry," which is to say that elements of analytic or "prose" structure will be present in passages which have been "preserved *in keeping* with the poetry" by "a studied selection and artificial arrangement." Remarks of this kind led Victorian critics like Julius Hare to assume that *all* true works of art had the organic type of structure. Poems that did not were not poetry; they were verse.[17]

This too, and perhaps under the same influence, is the principle adopted by Arnold. In a well-known passage of his essay on Gray

17. Addison's essay is in the *Spectator*, No. 160 (Sept. 3, 1711). For Coleridge I am using the *Biographia Literaria*, ed. J. Shawcross (2 vols. Oxford, 1907), chaps. 1–2, 4, the end of 13, 14–15; and quoting *1*, 11 and *2*, 11, 12. Robert Preyer, "Julius Hare and Coleridgean Criticism," *Journal of Aesthetics and Art Criticism*, *15* (1957), 449–60, provides an interesting view of Victorian aesthetics from a novel source. I am indebted to his summary of Coleridge's theory, pp. 454–55.

he spoke of "the poetic language of our eighteenth century" being in general "language merely recalling the object, as the common language of prose does," that is to say, referring to it rather than giving its impact on the poet's sensibility. "The evolution of the poetry of our eighteenth century," he continued, "is . . . intellectual; it proceeds by ratiocination, antithesis, ingenious turns and conceits. This poetry is often eloquent, and always, in the hands of such masters as Dryden and Pope, clever; but it does not take us much below the surface of things, it does not give us the emotion of seeing things in their truth and beauty." It is not "the language of genuine poetry." Consequently, as he says elsewhere, "Dryden and Pope are not classics of our poetry, they are classics of our prose."[18]

We scarcely need to know that Clough was working within the neoclassical tradition to recognize the connection between these passages and Arnold's criticism of his poetry.[19] For Clough's work is also too intellectual in content and method, too lacking in sensuousness, and therefore deficient in beauty. And if Arnold denies that Dryden is a true poet, no wonder he doubts that Clough is a true artist. "The difference between genuine poetry and the poetry of Dryden, Pope, and all their school, is briefly this: their poetry is conceived and composed in their wits, genuine poetry is conceived and composed in the soul." Or in Coleridge's terms, their "poetry" is composed by the fancy, genuine poetry (Romantic-Symbolist poetry) by the imagination.[20] The specific application of this stand-

18. "Thomas Gray" and "The Study of Poetry," *Essays in Criticism, Second Series* (London and New York, 1891), pp. 95-96, 41-42.

19. Chap. 2, sec. 2, below, deals with the neoclassical influence on Clough's style.

20. Arnold, *Essays, Second Series,* p. 95; and on p. 39 he brings in the imagination by saying that in the eighteenth century a fit prose could not be established "without some touch of frost to the imaginative life of the soul." In "Maurice de Guérin" (1863), *Essays in Criticism, First Series* (London, 1875), p. 93, Arnold's definition of a poetry of natural interpretation is a perfect definition of Romantic-Symbolist intention, namely that it should so deal with things "as to awaken in us a wonderfully full, new, and intimate sense of them, and of our relations with them," and thus to make us feel "in contact with the essential nature of those objects." The other type of poetry, of moral interpretation, is related to neoclassical verse, for the examples on p. 128 are statements of ideas. Arnold goes on to say that great poets write in both modes, which is true of himself; indeed, some of his work is closer to Clough in style than his letters would suggest.

ard to Clough was made as early as 1849 in a review of *Ambarvalia:* "Especially in Mr. Clough's half of the book there is often an obscurity of thought, and a careless roughness of form, which ... more exertion given to throwing his thoughts into *a concrete and truly imaginative form,* might easily have remedied"; which leads, naturally enough, to the conclusion that "he is meant to be an earnest thinker and prose writer upon some of the deepest questions of our day."[21]

Think of a Victorian with preconceptions like these opening Clough's poems and reading the conclusion of "Look you, my simple friend":

>   And can it be, you ask me, that a man,
>   With the strong arm, the cunning faculties,
>   And keenest forethought gifted, and, within,
>   Longings unspeakable, the lingering echoes
>   Responsive to the still-still-calling voice
>   Of God Most High,—should disregard all these,
>   And half-employ all those for such an aim
>   As the light sympathy of successful wit,
>   Vain titillation of a moment's praise?
>   Why, so is good no longer good, but crime
>   Our truest, best advantage, since it lifts us
>   Out of the stifling gas of men's opinion
>   Into the vital atmosphere of Truth,
>   Where He again is visible, tho' in anger.

How could we expect a reader in 1849 to appreciate an idiom and rhythm so far from "poetic," a diction so logically precise and so lacking in sensuous connotation, a ratiocinative evolution demanding close attention to the syntax (and probably a second reading to grasp the antecedents of "these" and "those" and the force of the antithesis), and least of all the final touch of paradoxical wit when crime is made a means to the recovery of God? Though any one or

---

21. *Fraser's Magazine, 39* (1849), 580–81 (the italics are mine). The author was probably John Conington: see Charles Kingsley, *Letters and Memories of His Life,* edited by his wife (2 vols. London, 1877), *1,* chap. 7, 191.

even two of these liabilities could have been tolerated, and all can be found at one point or another in Victorian verse, it is their combination in Clough—it is the whole intellectual and non-"poetic" cast of his work—that for the most part made his poetry seem devoid of art.

But there were other disabilities too. Before the seventies and eighties it was not enough for a poet to be "poetic," he also had to be a prophet. This too was partly a Romantic inheritance, from Wordsworth and Shelley especially; and then, starting in the early thirties with the pronouncements of Carlyle, Henry Taylor, and the Cambridge Apostles, it became a platitude to say that in an age when traditional creeds were shaky or crumbling and a new democracy was emerging, the writer was a priest whose duty it was "by wise teaching [to] guide the souls of men."[22] Certainly it was *not* his duty to stand indecisive between opposite theories, still less to pour out the worry and dismay already too much felt in the face of science, biblical criticism, and the increasingly secular and commercial atmosphere of the nineteenth century. Rather, he should "enter deeply into the struggles of his own time, and do his utmost to raise men out of confusion and dissonance into harmony and order."[23] To do this, a poet might instruct by preaching doctrine or, more commonly, he might create an ideal image, of nature or of man, that would quicken the moral sensibility. While Clough was at Rugby, Dr. Arnold himself had advocated the theory of poetic inspiration:

> Our common temper ... which is but too generally cold, and selfish, and worldly, is altogether unpoetical; but let anything occur to put us above ourselves, anything to awaken our devotion, our admiration, or our love—any danger to call forth our courage, any distress to awaken our pity, any great emer-

---

22. See my *Victorian Frame of Mind, 1830–1870* (New Haven, 1959), pp. 152–54, and cf. pp. 101–02, 227–28, 247. Henry Taylor's preface to *Philip van Artevelde* appeared in 1834. The quotation is from Carlyle's important lecture, "The Hero as Man of Letters," *On Heroes, Hero-Worship, and the Heroic in History* (1841; London, 1897), p. 162.

23. Daniel Macmillan in a letter to George Brimley, Feb. 24, 1855, quoted in Thomas Hughes, *Memoir of Daniel Macmillan* (London, 1882), p. 256.

gency to demand the sacrifice of our own comfort, or interest, or credit, for the sake of others, then we experience for the time a *poetical temper,* and *poetical feelings;* for the very essence of poetry is, that it exalts and ennobles us, and puts us into a higher state of mind than that which we are commonly living in.

A few years later, Frederic Rogers, the friend of Newman, developed this aesthetic in another form. "A *poetical* way of viewing things," he wrote, "is that which is opposed to a matter-of-fact one; it is poetical so far as it does not rest in the mere phenomena which it handles, but aims at informing them with something spiritual, ideal, unearthly." Consequently, "the poetical element" that distinguishes characters like Hamlet, Miranda, Shylock, or Caliban from the "prose" characters of Jane Austen is the "glowing elevation of tone which runs alike through all, and seems alike to lift us off the ground and make us tread in air. . . . Poetry is essentially an aspiration."[24]

This conception, reinforced by the desire for positive and hopeful attitudes, created the Victorian prejudice against literature that was negative or depressing. An artist was not to criticize anything that was not patently evil; he was not to be realistic if that meant stressing the darker sides of human nature; and he was not, of course, to be a pessimist—certainly not if he were a poet. The threshold of tolerance was lower in fiction, but Matthew Arnold, besides finding Wordsworth's view of life "healthful and true, whereas Leopardi's pessimism is not," agreed with Sainte-Beuve that Flaubert was inferior to George Sand because in him "the ideal has ceased, the lyric vein is dried up" (the world of *Madame Bovary* is one of "bitterness, irony, impotence; not a personage in the book to rejoice or console us"), and he regretted the publication of Dowden's *Shelley* because, by revealing the seamy side of his life, it had tarnished the former image of the "delightful" Shelley, the "ideal"

---

24. Thomas Arnold, preface to *Poetry of Common Life* (1831), reprinted in his *Miscellaneous Works* (London, 1845), p. 253; Rogers, the *British Critic,* 24 (1838), 277–78. The attribution of this essay to Rogers is made by Clough, *The Correspondence of Arthur Hugh Clough,* ed. F. L. Mulhauser (2 vols. Oxford, 1957), *1,* 85.

Shelley, the "beautiful and lovable Shelley."[25] When the master critic talked this way, woe to the poet who wrote in a critical, realistic, or melancholy temper. Poor Clough![26]

Many of his virtues from our point of view—the realism and the skepticism, the refusal of evasion, the recognition of ambivalence, the strain of irony and ridicule, sometimes of bitter sarcasm, and the subtle exploration of the doubt, frustration, and despair that swept through the Victorian mind—these virtues, under the prevailing conditions of taste, became liabilities. Nor was his plain style, based on the idioms and rhythms of living speech, any recommendation. Try as he might (and he did try, since he was only partly in revolt against Victorian poetics, and only partly aware of his revolt) Clough simply could not, like Tennyson, submit to "the requirements of the age." Some of his work is sensuous, even sentimental, and some of it prophetic, but most of it was broadcast on a wave length for which there was no adequate receiver between 1850 and 1930.

The contemporary distaste for his particular virtues colors the apologetics of his friends. Mrs. Clough, in the widely read "Memoir" of 1869, was happy to report that after his marriage "the humour which in solitude had been inclined to take the hue of irony and sarcasm, now found *its natural and healthy outlet";* and that since his thought was passing from the speculative to the constructive stage, "he would have expressed his mature convictions in *works of a more positive and substantial kind.*"[27] In the contemporary reviews, the standard pattern was to praise *The Bothie* as the work in which Clough approached "most nearly to that realisation of the joy and beauty of life" which some critics feel is an "essential feature of true poetry," and then to see deterioration in its great successors. The *Amours de Voyage* lacks "the healthy tone and

25. *Essays, Second Series,* pp. 192, 253, 276, 213, 245, from the essays on Byron, Tolstoi, and Shelley. The general subject is treated in a section of the *Victorian Frame of Mind* called "Moral Optimism," pp. 297-304; and cf. another on Victorian evasion, pp. 413-24.
26. Cf. his "Review of Some Poems by Alexander Smith and Matthew Arnold," *Prose, 1,* 361, or p. 357, where Clough pleads for poetry not to "content itself merely with talking of what may be better elsewhere, but seek also to deal with what *is* here."
27. *Prose, 1,* 45, or pp. 46-47. The italics are mine.

sunny cheerfulness of 'The Bothie.'" Its power is "the power of insight into the under-side of human nature—into the doubts, weakness, and self-deception which underlie that aspect of things on which it is most pleasant, and perhaps most profitable, to dwell. There is often a jar produced on the feeling of the reader by some bitter or weary expression of despondency or self-distrust."[28] The ending, in which the lovers separate and do not, like good Victorians, marry and live happily ever after, could be shocking even to an admirer of Clough like Emerson. And the ending of *Dipsychus*, with the submission of the idealist to the hard demands of the world, was "no conclusion fitted to satisfy either the artist or the moralist, and, after a series of powerful but discordant utterances, leaves a sense of deep dissatisfaction behind." So it does, and in one meaning of the word, was meant to.[29]

In this aesthetic milieu the place of satire is obvious: it has no place—not in poetry. A Victorian novelist might be a satirist (or, more precisely, he might combine satire with love and pathos) but not a Victorian poet; for once the poet-prophet donned his singing robes, he was committed to beautiful or exalted themes and a lofty style. Indeed, Victorian taste was not prepared to consider satire a significant form of art in any medium. The general aura of optimism, the sentimental stress on the goodness of human nature and the virtues of sympathy and benevolence, along with the concomitant dislike for critical, mocking, or pessimistic attitudes, combined to make the writing of satire difficult and the reputation of a satirist dubious. One Victorian, speaking in the very decade when Clough's satires were published, thought it was vain to expect a "History of Satirical Literature," much as it was needed, "during the ascendancy of the prevailing taste for twaddle," and felt that

---

28. The *Guardian* (Oct. 6, 1869), p. 1111; W. Y. Sellar, *North British Review*, 37 (1862), 340–41. Sellar's authorship of this anonymous article is given in a letter of W. G. Blaikie, the editor, to A. C. Fraser, Sept. 25, 1862, in the Fraser Papers (privately owned).

29. Emerson's protest is in Clough's *Correspondence*, 2, 548; the *Guardian* (Oct. 6, 1869), p. 1112. J. A. Symonds, *Last and First*, p. 107, asked, "Ought a poet not rather to lead the world, and to show the ultimate truth, than to represent the waverings of a discontented spirit ill at ease?"

he had to begin his sketch of the subject with a defense of the form because "we are all so sham-amiable in these 'gushing' days."[30]

There was nothing "sham-amiable" about Arnold, but also nothing in his aesthetics to surprise us by the omission, in his summary estimates of Dryden and Pope, of any reference to their satires. Though he praised Byron's personality for "its ever-welling force, its satire, its energy," what he had in mind was Byron's fine attack on the corruptions of the old order rather than the artistic quality of his satire as such. Nor was he much attracted to comedy, for "Comedy ... escapes ... the test of entire seriousness; it remains, by the law of its being, in a region of comparative lightness and of irony." But, alas, the characters of Claude in *Amours de Voyage* and the Spirit in *Dipsychus* are masterpieces of comic art, and the Scotch Lords and Oxford undergraduates of *The Bothie* less subtle but equally deft achievements in the same mode. And perhaps Clough's greatest gift as an artist was irony. It is hardly surprising, then, that Arnold spoke unfavorably of both the Scotch and Roman poems, and would probably have disliked *Dipsychus*. But Chaucer, too, we remember, as well as Burns, failed to meet the test of high seriousness.[31]

Laughter and humor were all very well in their proper place (light verse, light opera, and the novel) *and* if they were clearly innocent, but otherwise not. J. M. Robertson, the first critic to recognize the sophisticated art of Clough's longer poems, was care-

---

30. James Hannay, "The Literature of Satire," *Temple Bar*, 22 (1868), 190. The background of the antisatiric influences mentioned can be found in the *Victorian Frame of Mind*, pp. 273–81 in a section called "Sympathy and Benevolence," and pp. 416–19 on the goodness of human nature. In Hannay's *Satire and Satirists* (1854; New York, 1855), he says, p. 229, "We are told sometimes, that the day of Satire is past; that literature is disgraced by such fighting; and that we must all be friendly, and peaceable, and respectable." He goes on to protest (p. 231) against "the nonsense about the blackness and morbidity of the satirist," but his own reply, significantly enough, is to argue that for the most part satirists are "kindly, and good, and warm-hearted men."

31. Arnold's "The French Play in London" (1879), is in his *Irish Essays*, in *Mixed Essays, Irish Essays, and Others* (New York, 1896), pp. 440–41. The other remarks are in "Byron" and "The Study of Poetry," *Essays, Second Series*, pp. 197, 34, 49. His poor opinion of Clough's long poems is in *Letters to Clough*, pp. 95, 132, 147, but it rests primarily on other grounds, discussed below, p. 96.

ful to explain that he praised them as fiction. Because they were pervaded by humor, they were "not to be classed as poetry proper," if indeed they were "to be called poetry at all." But what if the humor were tainted, if comedy dealt lightly with anything evil, or laughed at something noble or sacred? That was "levity," and levity was something Queen Victoria found "not amusing" and Dr. Arnold checked immediately with "startling earnestness." Evangelical morality and the cult of enthusiasm for what is beautiful and heroic combined to make the alliance of levity and seriousness, common enough in seventeenth- and twentieth-century poetry, simply impossible. When Blanche Smith balked at publishing various poems and passages *pro pudore,* and was shocked to find "that good men were so rough and coarse" (so shocked she wished the world had been made "all women"), and when even George Eliot was disturbed by laughter directed at any "sacred, heroic, and pathetic theme which serves to make up the treasure of human admiration, hope, and love," Clough, to say the least, was at a disadvantage. Even Walter Bagehot was embarrassed because Claude did not reflect "in a very dignified or heroic manner."[32]

It should not be supposed that there were no critics or readers who were able to transcend the limiting criteria of Victorian taste. Bagehot, R. H. Hutton, J. A. Symonds, and Henry Sidgwick produced a body of perceptive criticism in the 1860s that is still superior to anything else one can read about Clough. But the task of establishing a tradition of balance and insight was beyond their powers. The odds against it were enormous. For no other Victorian poet ran foul of contemporary taste *at so many points* (and I have not mentioned how his English hexameters outraged ears that were too much tuned to the classical meter); let alone the fact that all the other critics, including Arnold himself, were talking failure,

---

32. Robertson, "Clough" (1887), *New Essays towards a Critical Method* (London and New York, 1897), pp. 308–09. Blanche Smith is quoted in Clough's *Correspondence, 2,* 402 n. *The Bothie* was sharply censured at Oxford, according to Clough (*Correspondence, 1,* 240), for being "indecent and profane." George Eliot's "Debasing the Moral Currency" was published in *Impressions of Theophrastus Such* (1879), and is quoted from her *Works* (Illustrated Cabinet Edition, 24 vols. New York, n.d.), *11,* 104; Bagehot, "Mr. Clough's Poems" (1862), *Literary Studies* (3 vols. London, 1898), *2,* 275.

that is, criticizing the poetry, or praising the man instead, or—if defending the poetry—defending it as history.[33]

3. The Nadir, 1870–1930

As the aesthetic movement developed, looking back to Keats, Shelley, and the early Tennyson for artistic ideals, and creating a poetry permeated by Greek and Medieval reconstructions in which the form was highly wrought, delicate, and stressed at the expense of content, Clough's reputation was bound to decline further (at the least his verse would seem "harsh and unadorned").[34] It was also weakened in a period when agnosticism first became common enough and acceptable enough to make religious distress seem silly or cowardly. One could predict an attack from Swinburne, though its sharpness is unexpected. "Literary history," he remarked with fine condescension, "will hardly care to remember or to register the fact that there was a bad poet named Clough, whom his friends found it useless to puff: for the public, if dull, has not quite such a skull as belongs to believers in Clough."[35] This was too much for Saintsbury. In his *History of Nineteenth Century Literature* (1896),

---

33. William Whewell, "English Hexameters," *Macmillan's Magazine*, 5 (1862), 488, is a good example of the hostility on grounds of metrics: Many lines in *The Bothie* are "of a most barbarous and dissonant kind, suggested apparently by the author's love of the grotesque." John Rickards Mozley, the *Quarterly Review*, 126 (1869), 352, thought that the hexameters had definitely hindered the popularity of *The Bothie* and *Amours de Voyage*.

34. Symonds, *Last and First,* p. 132, thought this would be the case. In *Four Victorian Poets* (London and New York, 1908), p. 55, Stopford Brooke remarks that "unlike a true artist" Clough was "indifferent to beauty, to excellence, to delicate choice and arrangement of words and music." According to W. M. Rossetti, *PræRaphaelite Diaries and Letters* (London, 1900), p. 239, Tennyson found the language of *The Bothie* to be "execrable English." Samuel Waddington's introduction to his *Arthur Hugh Clough: A Monograph* (London, 1883) is a long defense of the school of poetry and criticism which stresses "thought and subject-matter" against the school that is concerned solely with "form and manner."

35. In "Social Verse" (1891), *Complete Works,* ed. Sir Edmund Gosse and Thomas J. Wise (20 vols. London and New York, 1925–27), *15,* 283; and cf. Desmond MacCarthy's first essay on Clough, reprinted in *Portraits* (London, 1931), p. 65, "The critic who did more than any other to damage Clough's reputation as a poet was Swinburne. He never wrote about him; but from time to time he directed a destructive comment at him."

he rose to the defense. "Clough," he said, "has been called by persons of distinction a 'bad poet' "; but this is "a rather bad joke." There was "a distinct vein of poetry in Clough" and "not a few" good things among the shorter poems, and some "fine passages" in the longer ones. Of course his hexameters were wretched, and some of his work brought him close to the Spasmodic School, and besides, he had "neither the strength to believe [in God] nor the courage to disbelieve 'and have done with it'." After which Saintsbury himself comes to the conclusion that "on the whole" Clough *was* "a failure." But the failure, he hastily adds, fearing to be identified with obtuse persons of distinction, "of a considerable poet, and some fragments of success chequer him." The slim praise, the fault-finding, the qualifications that give the case away—this is the familiar strategy of Clough's "friends."36

As for his enemies, there was also Strachey, with his devastating picture of the man with "the weak ankles and the solemn face," soaking up moral priggishness at Rugby and losing his faith at Oxford, only to spend the rest of his life lamenting the loss in prose and verse, when he wasn't tying up brown paper parcels for Florence Nightingale. Strachey's vogue has been so great, especially through the anti-Victorian reaction, that even today this picture is what many people think of when, and if, they think of Clough at all. In any event, the standard authorities—Edmund Gosse, Stopford Brooke, Charles Whibley—kept his name rolling downhill; and even the editor of a volume of selections, Sir Humphrey Milford, warned his potential readers: "Clough was not primarily an artist; he was more interested in getting his thoughts and doubts expressed somehow than in the poetic expression of them. . . . Much of the material of the *Bothie*—and this is even more true of the *Amours de Voyage*—is almost intractable in poetry."37

36. Pages 308–09.
37. Strachey's sketch is in "Dr. Arnold," *Eminent Victorians* (New York, 1918), pp. 234–36; and cf. "Florence Nightingale," pp. 174–75. See Gosse, *Books on the Table* (London, 1921), pp. 129–35; Brooke, *Four Victorian Poets*, p. 55; Whibley, *Poems of Arthur Hugh Clough* (London, 1913), p. xxii; Milford, *Poems of Clough* (London, 1910), p. xi.
It should be noted, however, that despite critical opinion, Clough continued to be read. Between 1870–1900 there were at least thirteen printings of his poems by

or even on Pegasus"; and then closed his case by noticing how much Clough dreaded the loose, emotional splurge of a man like Swinburne. The circle was coming round. A year later Humbert Wolfe argued that the real Clough was a satirical genius thwarted by moral earnestness, and he struck out at the ridiculous picture Clough's friends had created of the dreamer and the "shadowy Pierrot of a scholar-gipsy." At the same moment, Howard Lowry was finding that vigor of mind and love of life were the essence of Clough's character, not weakness of will or morbid introversion. Then, as he was protesting against the distortions of "Thyrsis," Lowry made a revolutionary remark: "We have forgotten that Corydon once *had* a rival, and a very good one!" After this, the only thing a Cloughomaniac could have asked for was supplied a few years later, again by MacCarthy. "To ask why Clough failed," he wrote, "would be absurd, for he did not; his contribution to English poetry is unique and valuable."[38]

Twenty years later Clough was received at the Clarendon Press and given a handsome edition of his *Poems* (1951) and another of his *Correspondence* (1957), both evidence of a new appreciation, and cause in turn for some critics to "consider it again." The best tribute came from V. S. Pritchett. Clough, he said, like Bagehot, was "one of the few Victorians who seem to belong to our time rather than their own. The lack of the histrionic air, the lack of that invoked and obligatory sense of greatness . . . makes these two writers at once accessible to us." After defending him from Strachey, and by implication from all the other critics who have taxed him with indecision ("his doubts suggest not vacillation but modesty, hardness of mind, the strength of integrity and candour"), Pritchett summed up the new critical perspective:

38. Since MacCarthy's first essay was reprinted in 1931, the "breakthrough" must have come earlier, but I have not been able to trace its periodical publication. My quotations are in *Portraits*, 65–66. A reference to Strachey makes 1918 the earliest possible date. Wolfe's vigorous but exaggerated and sometimes inaccurate essay was in *The Eighteen-Sixties: Essays by Fellows of the Royal Society of Literature*, ed. John Drinkwater (New York and Cambridge, Eng., 1932), pp. 20–50. Lowry's introduction to his edition of Arnold's *Letters to Clough* (1932) deals with Clough on pp. 6–23; the quotation is on p. 22. MacCarthy's second essay was a review of Goldie Levy's biography of Clough (London, 1938), in the *Sunday Times* (London, Dec. 25, 1938).

4. New Insights and Old Assumptions, 1930–60

Although the Clough tradition has continued on its plausible way, it has lost its supreme authority. No one has challenged it formally, but dissenters have been appearing and Clough is being recognized at long last, here and there at least, as a fine poet and a "modern" poet. The breakthrough came with the publication of Desmond MacCarthy's essay, reprinted in *Portraits* (1931). Though imagining that Clough's preference for truth rather than beauty spoiled his chance to be "a great poet," MacCarthy insisted that his fidelity to life as he saw it and his refusal to heighten his own feeling had made him "a unique poet." He meant in his own time, for he added pointedly: "We ought to be thankful he did not ride off like his contemporaries on the high horse of some prophetic cause,

---

Macmillan and Co., and two volumes of selections; between 1900–30, two printings (1903, 1909), and two selections (1906, 1910). The next volume to appear was the *Poems* of 1951. We see, therefore, that even his readers had departed about 1910.

In this period (1870–1930) three books on Clough were published. The first, by Samuel Waddington, *Clough: A Monograph,* was written by a moralist and not a critic. The second, by Edouard Guyot, *Essai sur la formation philosophique du poète Arthur Hugh Clough: pragmatisme et intellectualisme* (Paris, 1913), is an attempt to bring Clough's thought within the categories of formal philosophy, but since Clough was not a philosopher the result is unsatisfactory. In any event, the essay has had no influence. The third book, though superficial by present standards of analysis, was the work of a genuine critic, James Osborne, *Arthur Hugh Clough* (London, 1919), and marked a step forward in perspective and appreciation. However, in his "Conclusion," pp. 190–91, Osborne was unable to disengage himself from the Clough tradition. After apparently saying what needed so badly to be said, that it was "graceless to be asking so insistently why this man did not accomplish more, instead of marvelling that he accomplished so much as he did," he went on, within a few sentences, to admit that readers would "keep on finding him something of a failure" and to agree with this himself. "Lack of determination, inadequate opportunity, limited comprehension—here are the causes of failure"; and though Clough had his virtues, we feel "some unescapable limitation in the man's physical nature. He was not sufficiently sensuous. He did the best he could with a nervous system that was simply not finely enough organized, not delicate enough, to delight and gloriously to succeed in creative effort." These are the final words of the best book written on Clough before the 1960s.

Two notable exceptions to the critical drift in this period were an anonymous essay in the *Contemporary Review, 105* (1914), 285–88, where Whibley was attacked and Clough called a "great poet," and "The Clough Centenary: His *Dipsychus,*" *Sewanee Review,* 27 (1919), 401–10, by Martha Hale Shackford, where the praise of Clough's satire and the recognition of his ironical method were a radical innovation.

His unofficial manner, his truthfulness about personal feeling, his nonchalance, his curiosity, even his bitterness and his use of anti-climax, are closer to the poets of the Thirties than they were to his contemporaries. His line is clean. His lack of pretense is austere.

It looks as though the time were ripe for a Clough revival.[39]

Or does it? Unhappily, most of the comment on *Poems* and *Correspondence* demonstrated the tenacity of the Clough tradition. When reviewers are rushed, as they normally are, they skim a poet they have looked at before and rely on what they "know." Harold Nicolson put the old charge of failure into new phrases: "total inability to cope with life," "sense of fatuity," lack of vitality "to develop into a complete adult." Stephen Spender, finding none of the graces in Clough that "one attaches even to minor poets," was prepared to let Swinburne's limerick "pass unchallenged"—but not unquoted. Less famous names talked again of "his meager literary achievement and his frustrated career"; of his gaining "tenuous literary fame by writing one (and only one) deservedly memorable poem"; of his "timidity and weakness" destroying his great promise; and with a touch of novelty—the novelty of a new injustice—of "his incapacity for accurately comprehending his perceptions."[40]

---

39. Pritchett's essay was reprinted from the *New Statesman and Nation* in his *Books in General* (London, 1953), pp. 1–6. Other recognitions of Clough's accomplishment and its modern parallels are by H. W. Garrod, "Clough," *Poetry and the Criticism of Life* (Cambridge, Mass., 1931); Michael Roberts, *The Faber Book of Modern Verse* (London, 1936), pp. 11–14; Patric Dickinson, *New Statesman and Nation*, 26 (Oct. 23, 1943), 271; J. D. Jump, "Clough's *Amours de Voyage*," *English*, 9 (1953), 176–78; the *Times Literary Supplement* (Nov. 18, 1949, a letter on p. 751, Nov. 23, 1951, and Dec. 6, 1957); John Heath-Stubbs, *The Darkling Plain* (London, 1950), pp. 108–11, which stress Clough's virtues as a "social-realist" poet; and F. L. Mulhauser's introduction to Clough's *Correspondence* (1957), *1*, xxiii. On the general topic, see Paul Veyriras, "Un Regain d'intérêt pour Arthur Hugh Clough," *Etudes Anglaises*, *11* (1958), 226–28.

40. Nicolson's review of the *Correspondence* was in the *Observer* (Dec. 15, 1957); Spender's in the *Sunday Times* (London, Nov. 3, 1957). The "less famous names" are Lawrance Thompson, in the *New York Times Book Review* (Jan. 26, 1958), and Thomas Parkinson, *Victorian Studies*, *1* (1958), 367–69. Much the same tiresome com-

24   THE CRITICAL TRADITION

These are ephemeral pieces, indicative of contemporary opinion but of little influence. Unfortunately the same cannot be said of the damaging estimate published by a prominent critic in 1939, which was the more regrettable because it occurred in a book about Arnold that has been widely read and respected. In using the attack on Clough's poetry in the *Letters* to define Arnold's own poetics, Lionel Trilling did not indicate its limitations as criticism. After citing the main charges, he went on to say, justly enough, that Arnold was thinking of "the antagonism between the creative imagination and the critical intellect," or between the "whole being" thinking in images and the head alone thinking without them, and concluded: "So far as Arnold can see, Clough is simply not a poet." But because he did not indicate that the definition of poetry was loaded—on the romantic-imaginative side—he therefore seemed to give it his approval. A moment later, indeed, after quoting a stanza from Coleridge's "Dejection" to describe the joy of artistic creation, Trilling remarked categorically:

> But poor Clough, however eloquent and sincere his mind, does not have eloquent blood; however great his capacity for high spirits, he does not have the deep power of joy. "We in ourselves rejoice"—but Clough did not rejoice in himself.

Poor Clough! He was the boy who was so excited at Rugby that he felt he was living too fast, and the young man at Oxford who, an hour after midnight, "his defences down and his head overflowing with ideas . . . charmed his listeners with a magical power peculiarly his own."

> Mute and exuberant by turns, a fountain at intervals
>   playing,
> Mute and abstracted, or strong and abundant as rain
>   in the tropics.

---

plaints have been made by H. V. Routh, *Towards the Twentieth Century* (New York and Cambridge, 1937), pp. 167–70; E. K. Brown, *Victorian Poetry* (New York, 1942), 381, where almost every cliché is repeated; and Frances J. Woodward, *The Doctor's Disciples: A Study of Four Pupils of Arnold of Rugby* (London and New York, 1954), pp. 175–79 on the failure of "a second-rate talent."

In intervals like the spring of 1849 at Rome or the summer of 1850 at Venice, could Clough have written poetry like *Amours de Voyage* or *Dipsychus* without a deep sense of joy—as deep, surely, as Coleridge's when he too was writing about dejection? Can we be sure there is no eloquent blood in a poet who wrote lines like these on the social life:

> To herd with people that one owns no care for;
> Friend it with strangers that one sees but once;
> To drain the heart with endless complaisance;
> To warp the unfashioned diction on the lip,
> And twist one's mouth to counterfeit; enforce
> Reluctant looks to falsehoods; base-alloy
> The ingenuous golden frankness of the past.

Clough too, it would seem, was capable of thinking in images, though that was not his normal method, nor Dryden's either. Had Trilling brought out the neoclassical and satiric virtues of Clough's art, his readers would have qualified Arnold's criticism by recognizing its latent hostility to another conception of poetry.[41]

As a matter of fact, Arnold himself, so far as the longer poems were concerned, emphasized their difference in kind from his own aesthetics rather than their failings per se. "I confess," he wrote to Clough, "that productions like your Adam and Eve are not suited to me at present," but he felt no confidence that they might not be "quite right and calculated to suit others." He defended his rejection of *The Bothie* on the ground that he wanted to bar all influences that "I felt troubled without advancing me." Or again, "As to the Italian poem [*Amours de Voyage*], if I forbore to comment it was that I had nothing special to say—what is to be said when a thing does not suit you—suiting and not suiting is a subjective affair and only time determines, by the colour a thing takes

---

41. The evidence for Clough's creative excitement is taken from contemporary sources quoted by Howard Lowry in Arnold's *Letters to Clough*, p. 8, and from *The Bothie*, Canto II, 126–27, *Poems*, p. 126, which are applied to Clough by his wife, *Prose, 1*, 47–48, or p. 49. The lines on social life are from *Dipsychus*, Scene III, 34–40, *Poems*, p. 235. Trilling's main discussion of Clough is in the first chapter of his *Matthew Arnold* (New York, 1939), pp. 23–33; and cf. pp. 67, 72.

with years, whether it *ought* to have suited or no." Of this poem and *The Bothie*, as well as of Tennyson's "Maud," with which he links them both—and all three by implication with the Spasmodics—he simply says, in key with the 1853 preface, "That manner, as you know, I do not like: but certainly, if it is to be used, you use it with far more freedom vigour and abundance than he does."[42] It is clear, then, that while no one should dismiss Arnold's criticism of Clough as simply personal bias, neither should he take it at face value.

The snake has been scotched but not killed. Clough is beginning to emerge from the shadow of a long disparagement, but he will not be free of it—*we* will not be free of it and able to read him freshly—until we ask a new question: not "Why was Clough a failure?" but "Was Clough a success?" From that unusual approach we can expect an analysis of his work which will arrive at a more just estimate, and demonstrate, I think, the high if uneven quality of his achievement.

42. *Letters to Clough,* pp. 86, 95, 129, 132, 147. In general, however, what Arnold wrote to Clough, apropos of the latter's criticism of "Sohrab and Rustum," ibid., p. 145, could better be reversed: "I think you are sometimes—with regard to *me* especially—a little cross and wilful."

2

THE SHORTER POEMS

1. Was Clough an Artist?

THE LONG DISPARAGEMENT of Clough has been nourished by the denial or the doubt that he was an artist. So far as this meant that his poetry lacked what may be broadly called "beauty," the charge can be dismissed, for the Victorians identified the term with a particular kind of art: the sensuous embodiment of felt experience grasped by the imagination, and shaped toward its ideal potentiality. Such a conception ruled out the critical, witty, or ambivalent attitudes that find expression in satire, comedy, and introspective realism. Since most of Clough's work failed to meet this special definition, and indeed often ran counter to it, it was certain to be found deficient in art. But the other interpretation of the charge, that he did not recognize the importance of poetic form and therefore sacrificed its attainment, in word and rhythm, image and rhyme, to the bald expression of thought, needs examination. For the answer is "yes" and "no."

In the place of honor at the close of his part of *Ambarvalia*, the volume he published with Thomas Burbidge, Clough printed a poem that shows his characteristic achievement in the intellectual lyric. The subject is the Victorian awareness that reason was arriving at mechanistic explanations of phenomena once attributed to an autonomous soul or mind, and that these explanations could be destructive of values inherent in the older view. In the present case the example is the poetic imagination:

> Is it true, ye gods, who treat us
> As the gambling fool is treated,
> O ye, who ever cheat us,

And let us feel we're cheated!
Is it true that poetical power, 5
The gift of heaven, the dower
Of Apollo and the Nine,
The inborn sense, "the vision and the faculty divine,"
All we glorify and bless
In our rapturous exaltation, 10
All invention, and creation,
Exuberance of fancy, and sublime imagination,
All a poet's fame is built on,
The fame of Shakespeare, Milton,
Of Wordsworth, Byron, Shelley, 15
Is in reason's grave precision,
Nothing more, nothing less,
Than a peculiar conformation,
Constitution, and condition
Of the brain and of the belly? 20
Is it true, ye gods who cheat us?
And that's the way ye treat us?

Oh say it, all who think it,
Look straight, and never blink it!
If it is so, let it be so, 25
And we will all agree so;
But the plot has counterplot,
It may be, and yet be not.

In a logical structure that is remarkably faithful to the "facts" as they then appeared (reason might, and yet it might not, be telling the truth), Clough has brought together a wide range of emotional response: the bitterness of having been cheated into an idealistic view of poetical power, the excitement of contemplating the soaring imagination and the glories of fame (the roll call of names turns the poets into heroes), the incredulous and exasperated disillusionment, passing again into the initial bitterness (lines 21–22), and finally the sudden gravity of judicial summation in which the resolve to face the worst is juxtaposed against the hope that all may yet be well.

To express such a complex reaction, Clough had to use the poetic medium with skill. The piling up of appositions to "poetical power" as its glories are enumerated, thereby holding back the main verb "is," produces a mounting effect in speed and pitch until line 16. Then, as the grammatical conclusion—and the contrary truth—begin to emerge, the voice starts falling and slowing until it reaches the end of line 20 with disgusted finality. This impassioned reversal is underlined by the use of rhyme to sharpen the contrast:

> All we glorify and bless . . .
> Nothing more, nothing less;
and the imagination on which was built the fame
> Of Wordsworth, Byron, Shelley,
nothing but a condition
> Of the brain and of the belly.

Indeed, even the "b" alliteration has this effect of bathos: all we *b*less, all fame is *b*uilt on, the fame of *B*yron—nothing but the physical action of *b*rain and *b*elly; and the final "b's" explode with irritation. The use of a vulgar word like "belly" in a lyric poem of 1842 is amazing. It testifies to Clough's insistence on absolute fidelity to his inner feelings, regardless of literary fashions. Besides the striking reduction of what had been thought divine to the level of the animal, the word carries just the right tone of outraged disillusion.

Everywhere, the diction is simple, clear, and technically precise. Clough meant brain, not mind; he wanted conformation and constitution and condition; he allowed for both invention and creation; he chose five poets who represented almost the full range of English poetry; he used "and," not "or," in the last line to capture the feeling of "and yet on the other hand. . . ." This exact and often abstract language is conspicuous in the final lines, along with other characteristic techniques—the dialectical movement, the studied use of antithesis, the employment of rhyme and alliteration for sharper communication rather than musical effect (the "b" alliteration in "never blink it" is a functional link back to line 20), and the general lack of imagery, giving the little that is used added force.[1]

This is the intellectual lyric at its best, written by a master of poetic form. Indeed, we can adopt Arnold's own critical test and say that here we see "the true artist's fine passion for the correct use and consummate management of words."[2]

But no one would suppose that a hundred years of disparagement, however unjust, had no foundation in fact, or that a critic of Arnold's intelligence had been entirely mad when he charged Clough with sacrificing form to thought or to direct communication (personal report).[3] Indeed, these are the reasons why some of Clough's work is bad and a good deal of it is uneven.

The explanation is not, as some critics have supposed, that he would not correct and revise; he worked hard on his poetry, as the manuscripts prove. It is true that he had no great gift for either rhyme or metrics, but the success of both techniques in "Is it true, ye gods" is warning that the trouble goes deeper. The fact is that Clough lacked the power of self-criticism, and what he said of Wordsworth is partly true of himself: that he could not tell when his inspiration failed, so that he allowed "his bad" to remain side by side with "his good," and only occasionally wrote "a complete poem, good throughout, and good as a whole."[4]

Certainly, in Clough's case there are far more successes than one would guess from the critical tradition, and many "near misses." But the unevenness is apparent. Here is an example:

---

1. By using a passage in "Notes on the Religious Tradition" (*Prose, 1,* 422–23, or pp. 416–17), and noting the title given the poem by Symonds or Mrs. Clough in 1869—a quotation from Goethe, *Wen Gott betrügt ist wohl betrogen* (Whom God deludes is well deluded)—it is possible to argue that the gods are trying to make one believe, not that the creative power is a spiritual entity when it isn't, but that reason is telling the truth when it isn't; when, in fact, reason's conclusion on the physical level (the plot) may be the exact opposite of the real truth (the counterplot). It seems to me, however, that Clough's choice of "gods" rather than God, of "cheated," not deluded, and his tone of irritation and disillusion—besides the fact that the prose passage is at least ten years later—make such a reading less likely than the one I give.
2. In "Byron," *Essays in Criticism, Second Series,* p. 175.
3. The quotations are given above, pp. 7–8.
4. *Prose, 1,* 318–19, or p. 315; cf. *1,* 25, or p. 26.

> How often sit I, poring o'er
>   My strange distorted youth,
> Seeking in vain, in all my store,
>   One feeling based on truth;
> Amid the maze of petty life
>   A clue whereby to move,
> A spot whereon in toil and strife
>   To dare to rest and love.
> So constant as my heart would be,
>   So fickle as it must,
> 'Twere well for others as for me
>   'Twere dry as summer dust.
> Excitements come, and act and speech
>   Flow freely forth;—but no,
> Nor they, nor ought beside can reach
>   The buried world below.[5]

Though, when compared with "Is it true ...," this looks like much earlier work, both poems were written at the same time. Yet here the precision is gone: Why "strange"? In what sense "distorted"? How can the heart that is dry for him not be so for others? What exactly are the "excitements" that come and how are they connected—if they are—with "act and speech"? The "ought beside" in line 15 looks like sheer padding to eke out the meter; and because "reach" (used apparently for the sake of the rhyme) seems to reverse the meaning of "flow," the final metaphor of a life-giving source is blurred. (The comparison with Arnold, who must have remembered the last line when he wrote "The Buried Life," is plainly to Clough's disadvantage.) Some of the diction, especially in the metaphors, is conventional and flat: the "clue," the "petty life," "toil and strife" (here a rhyme makes bad worse instead of good better, as in "Is it true ..."); and elsewhere in his verse we run into "blue skies," the "cold gray dawn," the "golden glow of sunset," "life's day declining," and sometimes, though he *can* use them well, the loose employment of large abstractions like Reason, Life, or the Right. Finally, the integration is not so close as it might

---

5. *Poems*, p. 30.

be. The several figures remain largely discrete, so that one must quickly relate the sense of insincerity to searching in vain for something in a supply of things stored up, for a clue to a maze, for a spot on which to rest, and for a river flowing from a spring. In particular, the disparateness of the opening and closing images (lines 3 and 16) blunts the poem.

Clough's use of poetic diction can be trying to a modern reader, and the more painful when it is combined, as it often is, with the striking use of original and unconventional, even "vulgar," language. The poems are full of poetic contractions (o'er, 'twere, i', whene'er, 'gan, e'en), of archaisms (wist, wot, agone, athwart, meseems, poesy, dost, thou, thoust), of a too liberal use of "Oh's" and "Ah's," and a far too frequent reliance on exclamation points to lift the emotional level. That these artifices are found as often in Tennyson and Arnold does not make them more acceptable. I may be wrong, but, to my ear and eye, if

> Hope evermore and believe, O man, for e'en as
>   thy thought
> So are the things that thou see'st; e'en as
>   thy hope and belief,[6]

had been written:

> Hope evermore and believe, O man, for just as
>   your thought
> So are the things that you see; even as
>   your hope and belief,

I could have begun this fine poem free of the initial distaste for what looks literary and dated.

More characteristic of Clough's unevenness than "How often sit I," which is nearly a failure, is the second poem in *Ambarvalia:*

>   Ah, what is love, our love, she said,
>   Ah, what is human love?
>   A fire, of earthly fuel fed,
>   Full fain to soar above.

---

6. Ibid., p. 62.

> With lambent flame the void it lips,
>   And of the impassive air
> Would frame for its ambitious steps
>   A heaven-attaining stair.
> It wrestles and it climbs—Ah me,
>   Go look in little space,
> White ash on blackened earth will be
>   Sole record of its place.[7]

Here the image of fire integrates the poem and allows the meaning of "blackened," in Hopkins' phrase, to explode. The expanding movement upward into a larger and heavenly realm is skillfully reversed in the reduction to a "little space"; and the pattern is repeated in the ironic suggestion that what is fed on "earthly" fuel must eventually fall back to "earth," and in the shifting color from red to white and black. Nevertheless, there are the liabilities: the overuse of the "f" alliteration, especially in lines 3–4, the reliance on "Ah's," the padding of "full" and "go look," the inadequacy of the final word ("wrestles" is saved because, in alliance with "stair," it elicits the faint suggestion of Jacob), and above all, perhaps, the curious shift from an immediate dramatic situation in the initial question to an impersonal statement in the philosophic answer. This is the average Clough of the shorter poems, the writer of good but not distinguished verse.

It is not necessary for the critic to account for the uneven character of Clough's work. Perhaps it cannot be done even by the biographer, but there are two explanations worth considering.

In Clough, as in Wordsworth, the normal process of rectifying or burning the second-rate was sometimes thwarted by the excessive estimate placed on the autobiographical. Clough had none of Wordsworth's egotism nor his need, after philosophy had failed him, to turn back to personal experience for a foundation of values. In Clough's case, the emphasis came from the Evangelical demand for "self-examination," that is, for the Christian to keep constant watch on the state of his soul, with a particular eye to any disparity

---

7. Ibid., p. 2.

between the inner life and the outer action. It was this that persuaded Clough by moments, I dare say unconsciously, to accept what was artistically inferior so long as it faithfully expressed his personal emotions. Or, to approach the matter from the negative side, the excessive fear of insincerity (apparent in the search he mentions "for one feeling based on truth")[8] might make a man hesitate to adopt the self-conscious and "calculating" role of the craftsman.

There is no doubt that earnest Victorians were uncomfortably aware that their motivations were ambiguous, since it was but too easy to do the right thing for the selfish reason (which means to do the wrong thing): to be good because it was prudent, or to fulfill an obligation because it was pleasurable. Phyllis Bottome remembered how often the Victorian cult of duty became a smoke screen for personal desires: "I thought, or I believed that I thought because I *wished,* that it was my duty to stay at Swanscombe, helping my father and mother."[9] In a person like Clough, so sensitive, so honest, so committed to the moral earnestness of Dr. Arnold, the fear of such insincerities became acute. This is reflected in the portrait of Claude, who remarks:

> I do not like being moved: for the will is excited; and action
> Is a most dangerous thing; I tremble for something factitious,
> Some malpractice of heart and illegitimate process;
> We are so prone to these things with our terrible notions
>   of duty.[10]

Even more than actions, the spoken word was exposed to this malpractice of heart; and the man who saw "the dangers of unreality and self-delusion with which *vocal* prayers were beset" was likely to look askance at poetic speech.[11] He was reluctant, Clough said, to enter upon a literary career because he thought it "replete with

---

    8. In the poem quoted above, p. 31.
    9. *Search for a Soul* (New York, 1948), p. 301. Cf. *Victorian Frame of Mind,* pp. 410–13.
    10. From *Amours de Voyage,* Canto II, 272–75, *Poems,* p. 195.
    11. Thomas Arnold, Jr., quoted in Clough's *Poems,* p. 465.

temptations and probable mischief for me"· and he explained, in another letter:

> People who have got at all accustomed to write as authors are so incapable of writing, or even speaking, except "in character," and will run through a whole list of dramatis personæ as occasion occurs, without giving you a chance of seeing what they really are off the stage; if they try to be sincere, it often makes bad worse. There! that is one of the mischiefs and miseries of authorship which deters me.

It is scarcely surprising that Clough accused Arnold of not being himself in his writing.[12]

In one sense, of course, sincerity is an artistic virtue—a necessity for significant achievement. The day when Yeats resolved no longer to disguise his thoughts or change his emotions to make them more beautiful, and said to himself, " 'If I can be sincere and make my language natural . . . [I may] be a great poet,' " was a turning point in his development. The same capacity to make his art a genuine expression of his imaginative vision, disguising nothing, heightening nothing, is found in Clough, but he did not always distinguish between poetic and personal sincerity. "I tried from that on," said Yeats, "to write out of my emotions exactly as they came to me in life."[13] The "of" is all important: a poet should not write *out* his emotions but write poems out *of* his emotions. The distinction is one which the Romantic cult of subjectivity tended to blur, and Evangelical piety to overlook or view with suspicion. Where both these influences acted together, they might induce a poet to forego the act of imaginative recreation and the artificial shaping of word and line into an integrated whole. They might dissuade him from trying to speak, as the artist must, in character. Or they might blind him to the artistic weakness of lines he knew to be the literal truth. Fortunately, as his criticism shows no less than his verse, Clough was committed to the creative process by learning and instinct, and

---

12. *Correspondence*, *1*, 303; *Prose*, *1*, 173, or p. 178; Arnold, *Letters to Clough*, p. 135. Clough often complained of the affectations of professional wits and writers: see *Correspondence*, *2*, 341; *Prose*, *1*, 97, or p. 99; *Poems*, pp. 25–26, 75–76.

13. *Autobiography* (New York, 1938), p. 91.

in any event, he had his reservations about Romantic theory and moral earnestness. Nonetheless, he was not impervious to such influences, and they left their mark on his work.

The other explanation of Clough's unevenness is also a function of his environment. It was an age of crisis. The decline of Christian orthodoxy, and indeed of religious faith itself, created a desperate need for new spiritual and ethical creeds. At the same moment, increasing wealth and intense competition demanded a counter emphasis on moral principles. Under these pressures, which affected a good deal of Clough's work, a poet might sometimes stress his message to the neglect of his form. In the midst of "convulsive agonies and wild revolutionary overturnings," what was needed, Carlyle argued, was "intelligible word of command, not musical psalmody and fiddling . . . your wise meaning in the shortest . . . way."[14] He meant to rule out all poetry, but a writer like Clough, though sticking to verse, might well take the advice (Carlyle was one of his heroes). To do so, however, is to substitute rhetoric for art, and to prefer the sincerity of the prophet to the sincerity of the poet.

In these ways, I suspect, Clough was persuaded by moments, no doubt often unconsciously, to make direct communication of his personal experience or the rhetorical expression of abstract thought too central in the creative process, to the detriment of his form. The first failing was noted by Henry Sidgwick, who knew Clough personally:

> His work is so sincere and independent that even when the result is least interesting it does not disappoint, while his production is always so rigidly in accordance with the inner laws of his nature, and expresses so faithfully the working of his mind, that nothing we have here could have been spared, *without a loss of at least biographical completeness*.[15]

This is complemented by Arnold's warning, apropos of Clough's being "a mere d—d depth hunter in poetry," that "when you

---

14. *The Life of John Sterling* (New York, 1900), Part III, chap. 1, p. 196.
15. *Miscellaneous Essays*, p. 59. The italics are mine.

adopt this or that form you must sacrifice much to the ensemble, and that form in return for admirable effects demands immense sacrifices *and precisely in that quarter where your nature will not allow you to make them.*"[16]

Since then, both failings have been loosely fused by a succession of critics telling us that Clough was "not primarily an artist" because "he was more interested in getting his thoughts and doubts expressed than in the poetic expression of them," that he could make no "separation of the man and poet," or that he was "not sufficiently an artist to be much interested in making *poems.*"[17]

But is it true, ye men who cheat us, and that's the way ye treat us, by leaving out the counterplot? Even a glance at Clough's criticism is enough to make one suspicious. He censured Browning for his "reckless, de-composite manner" and Whitman for tapping the tree and not leaving it "to bear flower and fruit in perfect form as it should." He called "a bad style as bad as bad manners," and asked if one would "forgive bad music because it was *well-meant.*" In a period when the organic nature of style was often forgotten, and Arnold himself talked of choosing which of various forms would best embody a given idea, it was Clough who wrote:

> People talk about style as if it were a mere accessory, the unneeded but pleasing ornament, the mere put-on dress of the substantial being, who without it is much the same as with it. Yet is it not intelligible that by a change of intonation, accent, or it may be mere accompanying gesture, the same words may be made to bear most different meanings? What is the difference between good and bad acting but style? and yet how different good acting is from bad. On the contrary, it may really be affirmed that *some of the highest truths are only expressible to us by style, only appreciable as indicated by manner.*[18]

16. *Letters to Clough,* p. 81. The italics are mine.
17. Sir Humphrey Milford and Charles Whibley (above, Chap. 1, n. 37); Hoxie Fairchild, quoted above, p. 1.
18. *Correspondence, 2,* 514 and 520; *1,* 307; *Prose, 1,* 317, or pp. 313–14. The last italics are mine. Also, cf. his praise of Wordsworth, *Prose, 1,* 317, on p. 313, for achieving "that permanent beauty of expression, that harmony between thought and word, which is the condition of '*immortal* verse.' "

This is the creed of an artist—and of modern criticism. Clough did not forget it in "Is it true, ye gods." Nor did he sacrifice his art to nonaesthetic ends in "Qui Laborat, Orat," "Epi-Strauss-ium," "Jacob," "Uranus," the first "Easter Day," "The Latest Decalogue," the "Seven Sonnets," the Old Testament pastorals, "Natura Naturans," "Qua Cursum Ventus," "Say not the struggle nought availeth," and a score of other shorter poems, not to mention the major narratives.

2. Neoclassical Foundations

In a recent broadcast May Sarton called a poem the result of a powerful flood of emotion colliding with an image. Clough would have snorted—or, more politely, made a face. This is the language of symbolist criticism, rephrasing an assumption ultimately derived from Romantic theory and practice. For if the poet perceives an "intuited, creative reality" different from what is grasped by the discursive reason, and if poetry springs from a "spontaneous overflow of powerful feeling," a poem may well be thought of as "an image composed of images," and it will utilize metaphor and symbol in their richest multiplicity of meaning. By contrast, the mode of neoclassical poetry, with its stress on syntax, denotation, and logical order, will be associated with prose—or, rather, with mere verse.[19]

Clough belonged to the latter tradition and its nineteenth-century succession. What may be called the "minority" or "classical" movement in Victorian poetics emerged in the 1830s and achieved something like a manifesto in the preface to *Philip van Artevelde* (1834). There the leading poet of the decade, Henry Taylor, fearing that his work would disappoint "the admirers of that highly-coloured poetry which has been popular in these later years," and aware, I think, of Arthur Hallam's review of Tennyson praising his early verse (1831), felt the need for a counterstatement. Taylor granted that the writers of this poetry "were characterized by great sensibility and fervour, by a profusion of imagery, by force and

---

[19]. For a recent discussion of this distinction see Frank Kermode, *Romantic Image* (London, 1957), chap. 8.

NEOCLASSICAL FOUNDATIONS

beauty of language, and by a versification peculiarly easy and adroit and abounding in . . . melody." Nevertheless, they had important deficiencies:

> They wanted, in the first place, subject-matter. A feeling came more easily to them than a reflection, and an image was always at hand when a thought was not forthcoming. . . . It did not belong to poetry, in their apprehension, to thread the mazes of life in all its classes and under all its circumstances, common as well as romantic, and, seeing all things, to infer and to instruct: on the contrary, it was to stand aloof from everything that is plain and true; to have little concern with what is rational or wise; it was to be, like music, a moving and enchanting art, acting upon the fancy, the affections, the passions, but scarcely connected with the exercise of the intellectual faculties. . . .
>
> Poetry over which the passionate reason of Man does not preside in all its strength as well as all its ardours,—though it may be excellent of its kind, will not long be reputed to be poetry of the highest order. It may move the feelings and charm the fancy; but failing to satisfy the understanding, it will not take permanent possession of the strongholds of fame.

Though Taylor had Keats and Shelley mainly in view, he goes on to include Byron, the poet of wild passions and unreal characters. But he cites Wordsworth in his own cause, and when he denies "the strange opinion" which now prevails among poets and readers, "that reason stands in a species of antagonism to poetical genius," and argues, "Poetry is Reason's self sublimed," he echoes *The Excursion* in sentiment and style.[20]

If Clough read this essay, he must have admired it. For the young poet whom William Allingham met in the forties was shaped in the same mold as Taylor himself:

---

20. *Works* (5 vols. London, 1877–78), *1*, v–ix, xi, xiv–xv. Cf. the favorable review of *Philip van Artevelde* by T. H. Lister in the *Edinburgh Review*, 60 (1834), 1–24 (the authorship is given in the Napier Papers, British Museum, Add. MS. 34616, fol. 363); and see R. G. Cox, "Victorian Criticism of Poetry: The Minority Tradition," *Scrutiny*, *18* (1951), 2–17.

First and last, Wordsworth was for him the chief among modern poets. He had also much liking for Crabbe, and but little for the rich aërial colourists, such as Keats and Shelley, being always uneasy when he felt his legs taken off the ground. He required a tangible intellectual basis, and was rather suspicious of sentiment and imagination.[21]

Another critic, failing to find any analogue for *Dipsychus* in either Tennyson or Browning, compared it with *Philip van Artevelde,* and went on to say that both Taylor and Clough desired "first of all to be understood," and were alike distinguished for "pure and forcible English."[22]

Clough would have welcomed the compliment. He thought diction the central consideration for a poet, and would have associated "pure and forcible" with a tradition he greatly admired, that of English literature from the Restoration to the Romantics. If he first learned the "plain style" from Wordsworth, he soon found its origin in Dryden and came to prefer its classical form. In the first course he chose to give as professor of English at University College, called "English Poetry from Dryden to Cowper," he complained that the earlier writers of the seventeenth century composed English as though it were Latin, and employed the "elaborated diction of learned and religious men." In reading their scholastic works we are never "charmed," as we should be, "by finding our ordinary everyday speech rounded into grace and smoothed into polish, chastened to simplicity and brevity without losing its expressiveness, and raised into dignity and force without ceasing to be familiar." That is the charm of Dryden—and of Clough. For it was Dryden, as he goes on to say, who almost singlehanded converted our old language into this "new birth and renovation," and made it a "living instrument" adequate not only to the requirements of his own time but to those of the whole eighteenth century. By the close of that period, the young Wordsworth was reading a con-

21. *Fraser's Magazine,* 74 (1866), 526–27.
22. *Macmillan's Magazine, 15* (1866), 100. This review of *Dipsychus* was written by William Henry Smith (1808–72): see George S. Merriam, *The Story of William and Lucy Smith* (New York and Boston, 1889), preface, where a passage from this article is quoted as Smith's.

temporary poetry, culminating in Cowper, that was "deficient, perhaps, in force and fertility," but "remarkable for justness and propriety and elegance of diction"—a remark that shows Clough well aware that for all Wordsworth's reaction against certain phases of eighteenth-century convention, his style had its roots in the same tradition.[23] Even today, Clough thought, some familiarity with the prose writers of the eighteenth century was almost essential "to obtain a real command of the language"; in fact, a daily task of writing out "passages, for example, of Goldsmith, would do a verse-composer of the nineteenth century as much good, we believe, as the study of Beaumont and Fletcher."[24]

Clough was not advocating an imitation of neoclassical style in 1850. On the contrary, he saw that a new style was needed to define the more complex perceptions of the nineteenth century. But no writer had come forward, like Dryden, "to re-unite and re-vivify" the language. "We have something new to say, but do not know how to say it." We have found no one to speak "for our day as justly and appropriately as Dryden did for his." In the meanwhile, however, one might do well to utilize, with appropriate modifications, the great style the master had forged.[25]

In all this there is much that Arnold would have accepted, for he too belonged, in theory at least, to the classical school. More than once he criticized the "poetic" verse of Keats, Shelley, and Tennyson for its profusion of imagery, its Elizabethan diction, or its lack of substance; and he argued that "the language, style, and general proceedings" of modern poetry must be "very plain direct

---

23. *Prose, 1,* 330–32 and 313, or pp. 326–28 and 309. Cf. F. W. Bateson, *Wordsworth: a Re-interpretation* (London, 1954), pp. 10–11: "The reason why most of the Victorian critics . . . were not able to recognise the merit of Wordsworth's earlier manner was not simply defective literary taste. They were the victims of their historical position. The Victorian critics were too near the eighteenth century. Their hatred of Pope and all his works made it difficult for them to be fair to a poetry that was, in spite of important differences, basically Augustan. A realisation of the eighteenth-century nature of Wordsworth's early manner is, indeed, the clue to its proper understanding." Cf. "Victorian Preconceptions," above, pp. 10–13.

24. *Prose, 1,* 383, or p. 378. In the same passage he criticizes Alexander Smith because "his diction feels to us as if between Milton and Burns he had not read, and between Shakespeare and Keats had seldom admired."

25. Ibid., *1,* 332–33, or p. 329.

and severe." But he did not mean plain, direct, or severe in the manner of Dryden, for Dryden's style he called the style of an age that called forth "men's powers of understanding, wit and cleverness, rather than their deepest powers of mind and soul."[26]

With that last remark, Clough was by no means in complete disagreement. He confessed that the eighteenth century was a period "rather of the senses & the understanding than of the spirit & the imagination"—an age when "too much of mere every day common sense" was unfavorable to the "exercise of the Vision & the faculty divine." Indeed, even for Dryden he did not claim "a very high place as a great poet."[27] Nevertheless, Clough's real position is different from Arnold's, and for two reasons: because he had more respect for the understanding as such, and because, as a result, he was prepared to recognize what may be called a poetry of the intelligence. He would have protested, therefore, against Arnold's denigration of Dryden in much the same way Hopkins did in his remonstrance to Bridges:

> I can scarcely think of you not admiring Dryden without, I may say, exasperation. And my style tends always more towards Dryden. What is there in Dryden? Much, but above all this: he is the most masculine of our poets; his style and his rhythms lay the strongest stress of all our literature on the naked thew and sinew of the English language, the praise that with certain qualifications one would give in Greek to Demosthenes, to be the greatest master of bare Greek.[28]

The same stress on the naked syntax of the language gives to Clough's style the same kind of force, though the degree is less.

---

26. *Letters to Clough*, pp. 63, 65, 97, 124; *On the Study of Celtic Literature*, pp. 129–30; *Essays, Second Series*, pp. 91–92.

27. "Dryden and his times," six lectures in MS. at Harvard University [bMS Eng 1036 (8)], Lecture VI, fol. 13; a lecture on the period following Swift, in MS. at Harvard University [bMS Eng 1036 (7)], fol. 8. Specifically, the first comment refers to the Restoration, the second to the age of Anne. Cf. *Prose, 1*, 345, or pp. 341–42.

28. Letter of Nov. 6, 1887, *The Letters of Gerard Manley Hopkins to Robert Bridges*, ed. C. C. Abbott (London, 1935), pp. 267–68. Cf. Clough, Lecture VI on Dryden (above, n. 27), fol. 16, saying that "in vigour of mere writing, in manliness & force of style," none of Dryden's followers outdid him.

QUI LABORAT, ORAT

O only Source of all our light and life,
   Whom as our truth, our strength, we see and feel,
But whom the hours of mortal moral strife
   Alone aright reveal!

Mine inmost soul, before Thee inly brought,
   Thy presence owns ineffable, divine;
Chastised each rebel self-encentered thought,
   My will adoreth Thine.

With eye down-dropt, if then this earthly mind
   Speechless remain, or speechless e'en depart;
Nor seek to see—for what of earthly kind
   Can see Thee as Thou art?—

If well-assured 'tis but profanely bold
   In thought's abstractest forms to seem to see,
It dare not dare the dread communion hold
   In ways unworthy Thee,

O not unowned, Thou shalt unnamed forgive,
   In worldly walks the prayerless heart prepare;
And if in work its life it seem to live,
   Shalt make that work be prayer.

Nor times shall lack, when while the work it plies,
   Unsummoned powers the blinding film shall part,
And scarce by happy tears made dim, the eyes
   In recognition start.

But, as thou willest, give or e'en forbear
   The beatific supersensual sight,
So, with Thy blessing blest, that humbler prayer
   Approach Thee morn and night.

A poem like this, so firm in its evolution, so dignified and forceful in its diction without ceasing to be familiar, and in its music so severe and eloquent, has a solidity, a "purity," that wears well. Though more packed and psychological, it reminds us of Pope's

"Universal Prayer." In both poems "the lack of suggestiveness is compensated by the satisfying completeness of the statement."[29] Poets who can command such a style will find recognition among readers who are able to pass beyond the boundaries of the Romantic-Symbolist tradition. Indeed, it is because that tradition is losing its supremacy that a sympathetic reading of Clough is now possible.[30]

Arnold thought "Qui Laborat, Orat" the best poem in *Ambarvalia*, but only because in it "man, his deepest personal feelings being in play, finds poetical expression as *man* only, not as artist"; and he begged Clough to "consider whether you attain the *beautiful*, and whether your product gives PLEASURE, not excites curiosity and reflexion."[31] When the one man to whom Clough turned for artistic guidance and encouragement talked this way about a poem like that, we can only be thankful that underneath Clough's pliable manner lay a hard core of independence and self-confidence.[32]

More to the point, perhaps, there lay a temperament for which the neoclassical mode, to a large extent, provided a natural expression. Clough implied as much when he followed his praise of English style from Dryden to Cowper by a passage on British philosophy from Locke to Hume. He saw that its point of view might be called narrow and material, and that "intimations of a spiritual world of which we cannot be rigidly . . . certified" were elements as essential for our inner life as plain matter of fact. "But it is certain also that without that matter of fact, nothing can be done, and, moreover very little can be thought."

---

29. T. S. Eliot, referring specifically to Dryden's elegy on Mr. Oldham, *Selected Essays, 1917–1932* (London, 1932), p. 302.

30. Critics like Ivor Winters, Donald Davie, and Frank Kermode are closer to Henry Taylor than to Arthur Hallam. Davie's *Purity of Diction in English Verse* (London, 1952), is, in part, a sympathetic study of Augustan verse from Dryden and Pope to Goldsmith and Cowper.

31. *Letters to Clough*, p. 99. Arnold's reference is simply to "the hymn," but the only other possibility, Clough's "Hymnos ahymnos," was not written until two years later.

32. See his own claims in *Correspondence, 1,* 109, 301; also W. G. Ward's and Mrs. Clough's remarks in *Prose, 1,* 18, 21, or pp. 19, 21.

This austere love of truth; this righteous abhorrence of illusion; this rigorous uncompromising rejection of the vague, the untestified, the merely probable; this stern conscientious determination without paltering and prevarication to admit, *if* things are bad, that they are so: this resolute, upright purpose, as of some transcendental man of business, to go thoroughly into the accounts of the world and make out once for all how they stand; such a spirit as this, I may say, I think, claims more than our attention—claims our reverence.

We must not lose it—we must hold fast by it, precious to us as Shakespeare's intellectual, or Milton's moral sublimities; while our eyes look up with them, our feet must stay themselves firmly here. Such I believe *is* the strong feeling of the English nation; the spirit of Newton and of Locke possesses us at least in as full measure as that of any one of their predecessors.[33]

It would be impossible to exaggerate the importance of that passage. It is spoken from the very center of Clough's being. It is the rock on which everything credible had to be built.

This stand made him in some ways anti-Romantic. He was fearful of believing what he wanted to believe, afraid to

> Fix perfect homes in the unsubstantial sky,
> And say, what is not, will be by-and-by.[34]

He dreaded the sentimentalities of love, and all but wrecked his relationship with Blanche Smith because he would not talk like a lover. "As for everlasting unions, and ties that no change can modify, do not dream of them." And again, "But for heaven's sake do not expect too much either of life, or love, or marriage or anything." He once told Shairp to read the *Inferno:* "It will burn out your rose-water, old boy."[35] In art he came more and more to reject

---

33. *Prose, 1,* 350–51 (and cf. pp. 339, 345, 422), or pp. 347–48 (and cf. pp. 335, 341, 416).
34. *Dipsychus,* Scene IV, 97–98, *Poems,* p. 241; and see Sonnet 4, ibid., p. 398.
35. The remarks to Blanche Smith are in *Correspondence, 1,* 301, and in an unprinted part of the letter on p. 300; to Shairp, ibid., *1,* 245.

"the beauties of Nature" and to demand that the modern poem, no less than the modern novel, should deal with those "positive matters of fact, which people, who are not verse-writers, are obliged to have to do with." He was acutely suspicious of what he called mysticism—"letting feeling[s] run on, without thinking of the reality of their object."[36] A poet who held such opinions would naturally be drawn away from the sensuousness of Romantic style and attracted to something plainer.

Moreover, Clough found another element in Augustan verse that appealed to him, its ratiocination. Arriving at Oxford already dedicated, under Dr. Arnold's influence, to a rational search for truth, he was plunged into "the vortex of Philosophism and Discussion" that was simply an intensification of the turmoil of conflicting theories in Victorian society.[37] He could hardly escape it when W. G. Ward, the master debater, became his tutor and soon a close friend. In a small discussion group called The Decade, which met informally in the members' rooms (the counterpart of Cambridge's Apostles), the training of Arnold and Ward in logical analysis was strengthened by public exercise:

> We discussed all things, human and divine. We thought we stripped things to the very bone, we believed we dragged recondite truths into the light of common day and subjected them to the scrutiny of what we were pleased to call our minds. We fought to the very stumps of our intellects.[38]

It would be foolish to argue that Clough's intellectual character could have found expression only in a neoclassical form. He himself would have denied it. But given the bias of his temperament and the environment of Oxford, it is not surprising that he adopted its major characteristics. He discarded the couplets, used a more modern idiom, and in some ways a more subtle diction, but he preserved the plain style and the argumentative structure:

---

36. *Prose, 1,* 324–25, 361, or pp. 320–21, 357; *Correspondence, 2,* 398.
37. The quoted phrase is in *Correspondence, 1,* 97.
38. John Duke Lord Coleridge, *Life and Correspondence,* ed. E. H. Coleridge (2 vols. New York, 1904), *1,* 77.

In controversial foul impureness
    The peace that is thy light to thee
Quench not: in faith and inner sureness
    Possess thy soul and let it be.

No violence—perverse, persistent—
    What cannot be can bring to be,
No zeal what is make more existent,
    And strife but blinds the eyes that see.

What though in blood their souls embruing,
    The [great,] the good, and wise they curse,
Still sinning, what they know not doing;
    Stand still, forbear, nor make it worse.

By cursing, by denunciation,
    [The coming fate] they cannot stay;
Nor thou, by fiery indignation,
    Though just, accelerate the day.

While circling, chasing, unescaping,
    The waters here these eddies tease,
Unconscious, far its free course shaping,
    The great stream silent seeks the seas.

While here, to nooks and shallows drifted,
    Leaf, stick, and foam dispute the shore,
The boatman there his sail has lifted
    Or plies his unimpeded oar.

This unfinished poem complements the more famous "Say not the struggle nought availeth," written in the same year. If they urge opposite doctrine, withdrawal and action respectively, they are both arguments, appealing for a conscious recognition that elsewhere things are better, or will be, and in style they not only use similar analogies with stream and sea, but rely mainly on the prosaic exactness which T. S. Eliot so much admired in Johnson. This kind of precision depends partly on eliciting, by juxtaposition or syntactical connection, the primary meanings of words; and since those meanings have often become blurred through metaphorical extension, the words take on unexpected life as they are freshly used in an exact sense.[39] One should possess his soul in faith (faith in the good "fate," the stream of things, mentioned later) and in inner sureness (Latin *securus*), free from anxiety about the final outcome. A perverse violence does not mean one that is obstinate or willful, but simply *per-versus,* turned from what is right, that is, from moving with the stream of fate. In similar ways the discrete meanings of "stand still" and "forbear," "cursing" and "denunciation," "nooks" and "shallows" are forced on one's attention by their juxtaposition. Near the end, "dispute" means "to contend for or contest a prize" (in this case, the shore), and though a modern reader will also find the connotation of argument and link the word to line 1, thus reading it as an ambiguity, it is unlikely that Clough thought of such a thing.

For he often sought, like the neoclassical poets he admired, to exclude multiple meanings for the sake of clarity of definition rather than to utilize them for richness of implication. In his unpublished lecture "On Language," he described his linguistic goals:

> Since the time of our Charles I theologians, we have certainly struggled after precision and simplicity, and explicitness.... The true rule for distinctness in the use of the vocabulary is to use such words as have been primo applied to visible and tangible objects or images and secundo *in a single sense.* To draw a tooth is a better expression than to extract a tooth; because to draw is more plainspoken an image than to extract. But it cannot be denied that to extract is more precise, because the word draw has a host of applications. It is not one image, but a great many.... Play is a good word; but drama is more exact.[40]

Clough, then, has three criteria for good diction: the word should be concrete; it should be "plainspoken," that is, commonly used in daily life; and it should have one explicit meaning. In practice, of

---

39. Cf. Donald Davie, *Purity of Diction,* p. 65. Eliot's essay on Johnson's poetry is reprinted in *English Critical Essays, Twentieth Century,* ed. P. M. Jones (London, 1933).

40. Bodleian MS., pp. 47, 50–51, 52. The italics are mine.

course, he did not expect to find all these virtues in the same word, but he did intend to use only words that had at least one—especially the last.

3. *The Metaphysical Strain*

Apart from some passages in *Dipsychus,* the condensed metaphor rarely appears in Clough's verse. His characteristic figure is simile, especially the extended simile. This might connect him with the metaphysicals, but Clough himself would have demurred. Certainly by his own definition he was not a metaphysical poet:

> During the 50 years before the Restoration, the style called by Dr Johnson, not very correctly perhaps, the metaphysical, was prevalent, I may say virulent. George Herbert is a great example, Donne the satirist another. Shakespeare was too facile not to let himself be carried away by the taste of his age, & there is only too much of it found defacing his inspirations. I take it to consist mainly in the thinking of the words rather than of the thought, & running off upon the casualties of the form of an expression instead of moving on with the essential tendency of the thought. You are led on per saltum from word to word, & word again after that, instead of continuously gliding along the stream of reflection. You get into conceits, as they are called, & all but into puns. By way of a pleasing digression you turn aside to a simile, & you hunt it to death before you resume your proper road.[41]

If "conceits" means, as the reference to Johnson would suggest, the yoking together of heterogeneous ideas or the finding of "occult resemblances in things apparently unlike," Clough's similes are not conceits. Nor are they ever a digression. But they can be ingenious, and they are always, as Clough implies they should be (and as they often are in metaphysical poetry), a definition of thought, or a way

[41]. Dryden lectures (above, n. 27), Lecture II, fol. 7. I have ignored two minor revisions made, I assume, by Charles Eliot Norton (see my "Checklist" [below, n. 51], p. 384) and followed Clough's original text.

of moving forward on a stream of reflection by drawing out fresh aspects of an analogy.

That habit of mind was developing in Clough as early as 1833, when he was telling his sister that absence makes imperfections of character disappear. The dark spots of the moon which are seen through a telescope, he explained, vanish before the naked eye, "blended into soft lovely light"; and thus "the human character beheld through the telescope of familiar intercourse appears clouded with imperfections, when seen at distance, is beautiful and enchanting in the extreme."[42] The boy who made that remark is father to the man who wrote "Qua Cursum Ventus," "Sic Itur," "Epi-Strauss-ium," or "Upon the water, in the boat." These poems illustrate the description of simile given by W. B. Stanford:

> Simile, like prose, is analytic, metaphor, like poetry, is synthetic; simile is extensive, metaphor intensive; simile is logical and judicious, metaphor illogical and dogmatic; simile reasons, metaphor apprehends by intuition . . . simile is to metaphor as prose is to poetry.[43]

This statement has the bias of modern criticism and in any event does not apply to all similes, but it describes Clough's practice and suggests his relationship with Dryden as well as Donne. For Dryden in 1666 had called the supreme gift of the poet the "faculty of imagination . . . which, like a nimble spaniel, beats over and ranges through the field of memory, till it springs the quarry it hunted after"—that is to say, till it finds a simile by which to embody an idea already present in the mind.[44] The metaphorical apprehension of an idea in a flash of intuition may well be, in Aristotle's words, "a greater thing by far," but we need not impugn the rational definition. We might revise Stanford to read, "Simile is to metaphor as discursive poetry is to Romantic or Symbolist poetry," and recognize the connection of Clough's verse, in this respect, with both Donne and Dryden. For though Donne could use the intuitive

---

42. *Correspondence*, *1*, 4; cf. *1*, 279.
43. *Greek Metaphor* (Oxford, 1936), pp. 28–29, quoted in R. A. Foakes, *The Romantic Assertion* (New Haven, 1958), p. 23.
44. *Essays*, ed. W. P. Ker (2 vols. Oxford, 1900), *1*, 14.

metaphor, his characteristic figure is as logical as Dryden's, if more ingenious.[45]

Clough's shorter poems have other qualities that remind us of the Donne tradition. There is the tight dialectic structure of some of the lyrics. "When panting sighs the bosom fill" turns and pivots on the logical connectives: "Or is it but. . . . But what if. . . . Yet when. . . . For if. . . ." Moreover, the focus here, as in most of the love poems, is not on the emotion but on the nature of love. Under the conflicting pressures of Evangelicalism and naturalism, of idealism and realism, Clough was compelled to try to explore and define "that hidden mysterie," with the result that he too, like Donne, might be charged with perplexing "the minds of the fair sex with nice speculations of philosophy, when he should engage their hearts, and entertain them with the softnesses of love."[46] To be sure, he did not imitate Donne's passionate dramatic monologue, as Browning did, but the willingness to use the new word (electrotype, telegraph, oxygen) or the racy word (ologies, belly) in a lyric or an ode, the adoption of conversational rhythm as well as diction, the occasional play of witty paradox, hyperbole, and even puns, resulting in the alliance of levity and seriousness—these characteristics, taken together with the extended simile, are techniques familiar to the earlier seventeenth century, and to the twentieth as well.

When his sister Anne, like most religious people, thought that Strauss's *Leben Jesus* would destroy religious faith, Clough argued against her fears:

> I do not think that doubts respecting the facts related in the Gospels need give us much trouble. Believing that in one way or other the thing is of God, we shall in the end know perhaps in what way and how far it was so. Trust in God's Justice and Love, and belief in his Commands as written in our Conscience

---

45. Cf., for example, the famous compasses in Donne's "A Valediction: forbidding mourning" with the opening lines of Dryden's *Religio Laici*.
46. Dryden, *Essays*, 2, 19.

stand unshaken, though Matthew, Mark, Luke, and John or even St. Paul, were to fall.[47]

In the same year, 1847, he wrote "Epi-Strauss-ium":

> Matthew and Mark and Luke and holy John
> Evanished all and gone!
> Yea, he that erst, his dusky curtains quitting,
> Through Eastern pictured panes his level beams transmitting,
> With gorgeous portraits blent,
> On them his glories intercepted spent,
> Southwestering now, through windows plainly glassed,
> On the inside face his radiance keen hath cast,
> And in the lustre lost, invisible and gone,
> Are, say you, Matthew, Mark and Luke and holy John?
> Lost, is it? lost, to be recovered never?
> However,
> The place of worship the meantime with light
> Is, if less richly, more sincerely bright,
> And in blue skies the Orb is manifest to sight.

The logical evolution pivots on the long "However," rhymed so effectively for the argument with "never." The ingenious simile makes use of two vehicles at once, sun and windows, and brings them together at two points—two times of the day—in order to express both sides of the debate. Moreover, it develops two arguments: that knowledge advances as civilization moves from the more mystical or poetic East to the more rational West, and that although the older Christian myth was lovelier than the plain, bare light of Theism, the latter is closer to the truth and its profession more sincere. The use of Psalm 19, indicated by line 3, adds further meaning:

> The heavens declare the glory of God; and the firmament sheweth his handywork. . . In them hath he set a tabernacle for the sun. Which is as a bridegroom coming out of his cham-

---

47. *Correspondence, 1,* 182.

ber, and rejoiceth as a strong man to run a race. His going forth is from the end of the heavens, and his circuit unto the ends of it.

In Clough's poem, the heavens *do* declare the glory of God better than pictured panes; and once the bridegroom is in our minds, the link with Christ is natural enough, who is now seen, with the help of Strauss, in clearer and truer perspective. At this point we suddenly understand the title. Clough wants us to think of Epi-*thalamium*, too, and to enjoy the buried pun. He means something like, "On Straussism, or a New Conception of Christ and His Bride, the Church."

A larger play of fantasy and wit makes "Natura Naturans" one of Clough's most charming poems, and explains, I think, along with its candid and delicate treatment of a subject so rarely found in Victorian poetry, what Norton meant when he claimed it was "truly individual."[48] This celebration of nature as creative force (*natura naturans*, in Spinoza's terms, as distinct from *natura naturata*, the nature created *by* that force) starts from an incident in a tramcar:

> Beside me,—in the car,—she sat,
>   She spake not, no, nor looked to me:
> From her to me, from me to her,
>   What passed so subtly stealthily?
> As rose to rose that by it blows
>   Its interchanged aroma flings;
> Or wake to sound of one sweet note
>   The virtues of disparted strings.
>
> Beside me, nought but this!—but this,
>   That influent as within me dwelt   10
> Her life, mine too within her breast,
>   Her brain, her every limb she felt.

---

48. Unpublished letter of Mrs. Clough's to Charles Eliot Norton, June 10, 1862, now at Harvard University, in which she agrees it would be a pity to leave out of the 1862 *Poems* "anything that is truly individual." As a matter of fact, she found the poem "abhorrent": see her letter to Norton of April 25, 1862, also at Harvard.

Then, presently, the theme is developed:

> Touched not, nor looked; yet owned we both[49]
>   The Power which e'en in stones and earths
> By blind elections felt, in forms
>   Organic breeds to myriad births;
> By lichen small on granite wall
>   Approved, its faintest feeblest stir
> Slow-spreading, strengthening long, at last
>   Vibrated full in me and her.
>
> In me and her—sensation strange!
>   The lily grew to pendent head,   50
> To vernal airs the mossy bank
>   Its sheeny primrose spangles spread,
> In roof o'er roof of shade sun-proof
>   Did cedar strong itself outclimb,
> And altitude of aloe proud
>   Aspire in floreal crown sublime;
>
> Flashed flickering forth fantastic flies,
>   Big bees their burly bodies swung,
> Rooks roused with civic din the elms,
>   And lark its wild reveillez rung;   60
> In Libyan dell the light gazelle,
>   The leopard lithe in Indian glade,
> And dolphin, brightening tropic seas,
>   In us were living, leapt and played:
>
> Their shells did slow crustacea build,
>   Their gilded skins did snakes renew,
> While mightier spines for loftier kind
>   Their types in amplest limbs outgrew;
> Yea, close comprest in human breast,
>   What moss, and tree, and livelier thing,   70
> What Earth, Sun, Star of force possest,
>   Lay budding, burgeoning forth for Spring.

49. I have chosen Clough's final revision of this line (*Correspondence*, 2, 562).

ROMANTICISM   55

After the stanza beginning "Touched not," the strain of fantasy, slow-spreading, betrays the flicker of a smile in "sheeny primrose spangles" (line 52) and in the competition of cedar and aloe (Shakespeare's Sonnet 99 may come to mind); then expands in a wonderful burst of humorous alliteration and caricature (though firmly grounded on an orderly survey of insects, birds, animals, and fish); is linked in the last line (64) to the dramatic situation by the surprising hyperbole; and concludes, in the complementary stanza on evolution and its dynamic process, with the still more extraordinary hyperbole in which organic and inorganic, stars and lovers, are interpenetrated with the same seminal energy.

From this climax Clough turns, in a quieter and more serious tone, to the idea of consummation, deftly placed in the garden where life began, and the *natura naturans* first flowed with generative heat as innocently as it still should:

> Such sweet preluding sense of old
>   Led on in Eden's sinless place
> The hour when bodies human first
>   Combined the primal prime embrace,
> Such genial heat the blissful seat
>   In man and woman owned unblamed,
> When, naked both, its garden paths
>   They walked unconscious, unashamed.

After this the final stanza draws together the central images, and salutes the "mystical" fusion of desire and love which the incident has validated.

4. Romanticism

Although the reasons for associating his work with neoclassical and metaphysical poetry might justify calling Clough an anti-Romantic, he would not have used the term himself. He disliked the exclusiveness of schools and systems, and he thought breadth and synthesis were necessities of modern thought and modern art. "Shakespeare and Milton should meet together," he told Allingham in 1850, "as Rousseau and Voltaire have in Goethe and in

Beranger."[50] And he might have added, in himself. Or, in terms more directly applicable to his own case, he would have had Wordsworth and Dryden, or Wordsworth and Byron the satirist, meet together in A. H. C. For what he wanted, in the language of nineteenth-century criticism, was to be both a subjective and an objective artist. He wanted to write a poetry of the inner life, whether speculative or psychological (often both at once), and a poetry of realistic and satiric observation. He would combine the opposite aims of Wordsworth's *Prelude* and Dryden's *Absalom* or Byron's *Don Juan*. So far as he formulated it even to himself, that was the ambitious goal which Clough had in mind. Its dual intentions are seen, respectively, in *Dipsychus* and *The Bothie*, or in *Ambarvalia* in poems like "Blank Misgivings..." and "The Latest Decalogue." Or they are found combined in *Amours de Voyage*, where a realistic and satiric study of an Oxford intellectual in Rome is cast into the form of letters that are largely soliloquies.

Before he left Oxford in 1848, Clough's art was predominantly subjective. He had come early under the influence of Wordsworth, and though critical later on of "his excessive ... introspection and self-consideration," he viewed his poetry as expressing, better than Scott's or Byron's, the poet's personal "character," his own "genius and his moral frame." Later, Clough ended his lecture on Wordsworth with the reminder that poetry was a register of inner "phenomena of the most subtle, evanescent, intangible nature; whose chemistry far transcends in strangeness & in dignity all the experiments of all existing retorts & crucibles."[51] This literary influence was reinforced by his Evangelical training, as he all but said himself when he spoke of "those searchings of spirit and delicate self-introspections which are the shibboleth to the tender conscience."[52] But

---

50. *Correspondence*, *1*, 287; and cf. *Dipsychus*, Scene VII, 3–6, *Poems*, pp. 262–63.

51. *Prose*, *1*, 316, 318, 320, or pp. 312, 315, 316. The conclusion is printed in Houghton, "Prose Works of Arthur Hugh Clough; A Checklist and Calendar," *Bulletin of the New York Public Library*, *64* (1960), 386. With that, cf. *Prose*, *1*, 394, or p. 388, where Clough speaks of the writer's laying "the finger on yet unobserved, or undiscovered, phenomena of the inner universe."

52. *Poems and Prose Remains*, *1*, 293. The connection is also suggested in *Mari Magno*, Tale II, 39–42, *Poems*, p. 334.

ROMANTICISM

above all, it was the profound doubts sweeping over him in the forties—doubts not simply of religious faith, but of love, of action, of life itself—that drove him inward and developed a subtlety and complexity of self-consciousness that perhaps only Coleridge equaled among nineteenth-century poets. Like the Adam of his *Adam and Eve,* Clough could have said:

> E'en in my utmost impotence I find
>
> . . .
>
> A wakeful, changeless touchstone in my brain,
> Receiving, noting, testing all the while
> These passing, curious, new phenomena,
> Painful, and yet not painful unto it.
> Though tortured in the crucible I lie,
> Myself my own experiment, yet still
> I, or a something that is I indeed,
> A living, central, and more inmost I
> Within the scales of mere exterior me's. . . .[53]

Except for the record of pain, this highly conscious egoism makes one think of Donne.

But it was not until the age of Victoria that the new philosophy called all in doubt, including, as the passage shows, even the very nature of the speaker. Romantic introspection was focused on the poet's consciousness; Victorian introspection, on his self-consciousness; for under the paralyzing effects of finding no certain value in any line of action or any agreement with any group of people, one lost the relationship to society that defines his identity. He was driven back from "What shall I do?" to "Who am I?"

> O for some winnowing wind, to the empty air
> This chaff of easy sympathies to bear
> Far off, and leave me of myself aware!
> While thus this over-health deludes me still,
> So willing that I know not what I will,

---

53. *Poems,* pp. 414–15.

> O for some friend, or more than friend, austere,
> To make me know myself, and make me fear!⁵⁴

Arnold, too, "sick of asking what I am, and what I ought to be," hears a cry from his heart, saying:

> "Resolve to be thyself; and know that he,
> Who finds himself, loses his misery!"⁵⁵

No doubt, but the search could be baffling; and in sensitive minds the frustration of understanding oneself was, I think, a major source of the ennui that afflicted the age. For a poet it could also lead to a therapy of self-confession. Clough wrote the first "Easter Day" Dipsychus explains,

> To find repose;
> To physic the sick soul; to furnish vent
> To diseased humours in the moral frame.⁵⁶

Once the theme of poetry is "one's own Psyche," the question of form becomes a problem. Clough argued for the invention of a story or situation to embody "your feelings where they are of private personal character" and cited Wordsworth's "Brothers" as a model for the oblique expression of brotherly emotion. But he was half persuaded by John Gell's counterargument that the private feelings of a superior mind, "being more acute, comprehensive and cultivated than those of ordinary mortals," are "well worth knowing, and do a great deal of good to many others," while those of even the second-rate mind provide important materials for the study of psychology.⁵⁷ A few months later, in October 1838, there appeared an article on poetry in the *British Critic* by Frederic Rogers in which the case for subjective art was presented in ways that were bound to be attractive to Clough. For one thing, art of this kind, said Rogers, enables the reader to know himself by forcing him to recognize some of the "numberless minute thoughts

---

54. *Mari Magno*, Tale II, 52–58, *Poems*, p. 334; cf. lines 207–09, pp. 338–39.
55. "Self-Dependence." Also cf. "The Buried Life," "Self-Deception," and Act II of "Empedocles on Etna"; and the discussion below, pp. 197–99. See Wendell Stacy Johnson, "Victorian Self-Consciousness," *Victorian Newsletter, 21* (1962), 4–7.
56. Scene VII, 29–31, *Poems*, p. 264. Cf. *Prose, 1,* 391, or pp. 385–86.
57. *Correspondence, 1,* 73, 76, 77, 78.

and emotions" that pass through the mind without leaving any impression; and this indirect knowledge, so to speak, can sometimes "furnish a picture of or a clue to a whole course of past feeling and action." Furthermore, this very discovery of similarity, if not identity, of experience can help him to mitigate the "sense of insulation [sic] and peculiarity by an intelligent expectation of a wider communion with others." He can discover that others, too, "go through the same alternations of hopes and disappointments, thoughts elevating and degrading, perplexities, struggles, failures, and consolations." Indeed, the poet himself may find his legitimate inspiration in the expectation of such sympathy, and is not to be called egotistical so long as he asks others to feel *with* him instead of *for* him.[58]

A person so exposed as Clough to the loneliness that troubled sensitive minds when conflicting beliefs divided families and friends must have found this argument very telling. He wrote off at once to Gell, urging him to read "a very good article . . . involving a Theory of Poetry, in the last no. of the British Critic." I suspect that this essay, written by the man Clough liked best among the Newmanites and read just before he started writing the poems of 1839–41, comprising much of *Ambarvalia*, confirmed and fixed the influence of Gell, and thus gave most of his subjective poetry a direct expression. Mrs. Clough called the poems in *Ambarvalia* expressions of his inner life.[59]

Once determined upon, the record of personal experience, however embodied—directly or obliquely—and whether focused on ideas or states of mind, required a rhythm and idiom closer to actual speech than could be found from Dryden to Cowper. To some extent, it also required a more connotative and sensory diction in order to capture nuances of shifting feeling and indefinable emotion. But the basic character of Clough's verse remained the same. The plain style and the dialectical pattern were the ground-

---

58. "Poems by Trench and Milnes," *British Critic*, *24* (1838), 274, 276, 281, 282. For the attribution to Rogers, see above, Chap. 1, n. 24.

59. Clough's comment is in *Correspondence*, *1*, 85; Mrs. Clough's in *Prose*, *1*, 40, or p. 41. For a further account of Clough's ideas about subjective vs. objective art, see below, pp. 68–70.

work on which he built a poetry of self-perception beyond the reach, or desire, of John Dryden.

In an untitled poem about degrees of faith, Clough plunges into the middle of an inner debate:

> That there are powers above us I admit;
> It may be true too
> That while we walk the troublous tossing sea,
> That when we see the o'ertopping waves advance,
> And when [we] feel our feet beneath us sink,
> There are who walk beside us; and the cry
> That rises so spontaneous to the lips,
> The "Help us or we perish," is not nought,
> An evanescent spectrum of disease.
> It may be that in deed and not in fancy, 10
> A hand that is not ours upstays our steps,
> A voice that is not ours commands the waves,
> Commands the waves, and whispers in our ear,
> O thou of little faith, why didst thou doubt?
> At any rate— 15
> That there are beings above us, I believe,
> And when we lift up holy hands of prayer,
> I will not say they will not give us aid.

The well-shaped argument gives the poem its logical progression. After the first admission, that there are powers above us, the second, that they may take an active, beneficent role in life, is developed at length, only to be suddenly qualified almost out of existence. But the conclusion is anticipated by the strain of doubt that runs through the previous lines, as the will to believe is checked, now more, now less, by the silent, skeptical mind; for within the outline of logical debate, pro and con, the tension is constantly suggested. To capture this complex ambivalence, far as it is from neoclassical art, Clough has depended primarily on a denotative diction (with the exception of "troublous tossing seas" and "holy hands") and a masterful control of syntactical connectives and the juxtaposition of words.

The initial "admit" is hardly conviction and implies the opposite possibility. It may be true too (in the same way, and, therefore, maybe not) that "there are who walk beside us," and that our cry for help—is answered? No, only the negative, that it may not be a delirious image. Even the more positive, "It may be that in deed and not in fancy" carries a contrary overtone; and all these implications are confirmed by the specific question, "Why didst thou doubt?" Thus we are half prepared for the sudden shift at line 15 as the skeptical mind, worried by the too confident step from supernatural powers to Christ himself, decides that this fine talk is *not* in deed but fancy. Now, however, its high hopes abandoned, the will to believe can take a slightly stronger, because lower, stand. At any rate, I do believe (and not just admit) that there are powers above us—and they *will* aid us? No. They *may* aid us? No. I can only say, "I will not say they will not give us aid." Ten utterly plain words were never more expressive. The effect is that of an absolutely exact, judicial statement in a court of law. But within the context the line is charged with emotion: to that near vanishing point has the belief in supernatural beneficence been driven. This is the Victorian "dialogue of the mind with itself," written as Dryden would have done it.

Stopford Brooke once spoke of Clough's extraordinary power in disclosing "dim, delicate regrets and hopes and fears, . . . in following with soft and subtle tread the fine spun threads of a web of thought, in recording the to and fro questions and answers of our twofold self within." True as that is, a modern reader will not find it so striking as it was in 1908. What *is* striking today in all of Clough's introspective poetry from "Blank Misgivings . . ." to the soliloquies of *Dipsychus* is another characteristic which Brooke also noted: "Few have put remote and involved matters of the soul into such simple words as Clough."[60]

In some of the shorter poems Clough uses a more dramatic speech, in which the tone of voice can shift more quickly, and a language richer in reverberations in order to record the emotional

---

60. *Four Victorian Poets*, pp. 31, 49.

"feel" of what he is thinking. When this happens in a poem like "Uranus," we get a curious and effective combination of neoclassical and romantic styles.

In Plato's *Republic* Socrates had claimed that "astronomy, as now handled by those who embark on philosophy, positively makes the soul look downwards," and argued that it should be studied on a different system, viz: "We must use the fretwork of the sky as patterns, with a view to the study which aims at these higher realities, just as if we chanced to meet with diagrams cunningly drawn and devised by Dedalus or some other craftsman or painter."[61] Using the same passage, Clough made the same charge against modern, scientific philosophy, fearing its downward effect on the soul and pleading for a religious, specifically Platonic, orientation.

Uranus

When on the primal peaceful blank profound,
Which in its still unknowing silence holds
All knowledge, ever by withholding holds—
When on that void (like footfalls in far rooms),
In faint pulsations from the whitening East   5
Articulate voices first were felt to stir,
And the great child, in dreaming grown to man,
Losing his dream to piece it up began;
Then Plato in me said,
"Tis but the figured ceiling overhead,   10
With cunning diagrams bestarred, that shine
In all the three dimensions, are endowed
With motion too by skill mechanical,
That thou in height, and depth, and breadth, and power,
Schooled unto pure Mathesis, might proceed   15
To higher entities, whereof in us
Copies are seen, existent they themselves
In the sole Kingdom of the Mind and God.
Mind not the stars, mind thou thy Mind and God.'
By that supremer Word   20

61. This source was cited in the 1869 edition of the poems: see *Poems* (1951), p. 481.

O'ermastered, deafly heard
Were hauntings dim of old astrologies;
Chaldean mumblings vast, with gossip light
From modern ologistic fancyings mixed,
Of suns and stars, by hypothetic men   25
Of other frame than ours inhabited,
Of lunar seas and lunar craters huge.
And was there atmosphere, or was there not?
And without oxygen could life subsist?
And was the world originally mist?—   30
Talk they as talk they list,
I, in that ampler voice,
Unheeding, did rejoice.

The logical structure, the denotative diction and abstract phrasing, especially in lines 9–19, the paradoxical wit of the child's mind holding all knowledge in its "*un*knowing silence" (not consciously knowing the Platonic truths it possesses a priori) and of holding it by "*with*holding" (by keeping back the conscious awareness of supernatural knowledge, and perhaps also of the mundane knowledge that would displace it, and presently does)—all these qualities have their origins in the seventeenth century. But a phrase like "the primal peaceful blank profound"—so far from neoclassical art in its rich and elusive connotations, derived as much from their syntactical ambiguities as from their individual meanings ("primal" and "profound" both modify "peaceful" as well as "blank")—evokes not only an intense stillness but a mysterious sense of some ultimate source of wisdom older even than creation, something primeval and prenatal. In the beginning was the Word, the Platonic Word. Then the transition to conscious maturity is announced by faint pulsations of sound as well as light (because "like footfalls" inevitably combines with "whitening East") striking the sensitive blank of the child's mind; while the image of dawn throws the protective cover of night back over the opening lines, giving concreteness to the idea of "withholding," and also prepares for the waking from a dream. In the total context, however, "dream" turns out to mean both what is imagined and what is real; they are one and the same. Writing of such verbal subtlety and richness of suggestion is Clough's inheritance from the Romantics. Imagine Dryden talking of "footfalls in far rooms."

After the "Plato in me" (the philosophy literally in him from the beginning, a priori, and the philosopher he now knows by schooling in Mathesis) has spoken the Word, the divine revelation, in an eloquent statement and a final injunction—to mind not the stars but one's own mind and God—Clough turns to what minding the stars has meant in old astrologies and modern astronomy. The meaning is not thought but heard. After the faint sound of Chaldean mumblings that dimly haunt the memory, the gossip of the astronomers is translated suddenly into direct discourse as the idle questions follow each other rapidly, taking up the latest fashionable speculations ("ologistic fancyings") of no great importance to man. In particular, the succession of "of's" and "and's" gives a sense of endless topics endlessly raised and dropped. The very tone of the speech, staccato and a little shrill, creates an immediate contrast with the slow, weighty measure of the Socratic pronouncement that precedes it. The contrast determines the conclusion. I, unheeding the "talk" (a word that gathers together all the mumblings, gossip, and fancyings), I, in his ampler voice (larger in wisdom and more equal to the human need), in his supreme Word, did rejoice.

In this merging of some of the intellectual qualities of seventeenth-century verse with the Romantic capacity to express the a-logical and elusive complexities of personal response, we have philosophical poetry at its best. If the present theme suggests comparisons with Wordsworth and Arnold, I should not claim that "Uranus" was on a scale with the famous "Ode," but it can stand confidently beside "In Utrumque Paratus."

"Easter Day. Naples, 1849" is subjective art of another kind. Here Clough has given his personal feelings a more representative character that prevents them from being personal. Though he speaks of communing with "my secret self," "abstracted and alone," what he communed about was his situation in the bleak universe of modern thought, and specifically about the destructive impact of science and biblical criticism on the Christian myth. He speaks in propria persona, but he is voicing the poignant lament of his contemporaries for the death of Christianity, and perhaps of religion itself:

> Of all the creatures under heaven's wide cope
> We are most hopeless who had once most hope
> We are most wretched that had most believed.
>
> (73–75)

More is involved, however, than merely substituting "we" for "I." By focusing on the account of the Resurrection in the Gospels and questioning its truth, Clough fastens the reader's attention, not on an individual, but on a great event in the history of thought, and the disillusion which it created in a generation that had grown up with confident faith.

For all of that, "Easter Day" is not a philosophical poem. It is an ode, a large piece of formal music in which the same refrain ends every stanza, and other phrases ("ashes to ashes" or "eat, drink, and die") are picked up and rechanted. There is no evolving argument or development of thought. The single idea, that Christ has *not* risen, is present from the start, and the successive stanzas are so many variations on the same theme, drawing out its implications and increasing its emotional impact. But like all good odes, the poem has a firm structure. After the usual prologue (lines 1–8), the first section (lines 9–63) centers on the biblical story of the Resurrection and Christ's subsequent appearances, only to deny their truth. The following section (lines 64–94) deals with the effect of this destructive conclusion on "us" in the nineteenth century. The third section (lines 95–156) is an address, ironic in character, to the women at the tomb and the men of Galilee *then,* to the good men and the ministers of Christ *later on,* and finally to ourselves *now.*

The poignant sense of disillusion is expressed in various ways. There is the increasing impact of the reiterated negatives, starting at once with the "not's" and "no's" of stanza one, and culminating in the final stanza, where "not . . . nor . . . none . . . no . . . nor . . . nor . . . no . . . no . . . no . . ." reaches a climax in the last lines:

> Is He not risen? No—
> But lies and moulders low—
> Christ is not risen.
>
> (154-56)

In the 1860s, when the poem appeared, the final "No—" must often have been read with the emphasis of anguish. That was Clough's reward for transferring his attention from himself to the religious crisis of his time, and then finding a form which expressed it in exactly the way it came home to sensitive minds, as the appalling discovery that the text of the Gospels simply wasn't true.

That discovery is driven home in the second section by the sharp contrasts of *before* (when we believed) and *now* (when we know better), each stressing the loss of something precious.

> What did we dream, what wake we to discover?
>
> (66)

We dreamed of a day of Resurrection when the living Christ would judge the quick and the dead; but

> In darkness and great gloom
> Come ere we thought it is *our* day of doom,
> From the cursed world which is one tomb,
> Christ is not risen!
>
> (68-71)

If this is so, the spiritual life is futile, and we can only

> Eat, drink, and die, for we are men deceived,
> Of all the creatures under heaven's wide cope
> We are most hopeless who had once most hope
> We are most wretched that had most believed.
> Christ is not risen.
>
> (72-76)

Finally, disillusion is expressed by the sardonic irony of recalling religious phrases and then turning them to contrary meanings. With the Burial Service in our minds (". . . ashes to ashes, dust to dust; in sure and certain hope of the Resurrection unto eternal life") and remembering St. Paul's words that "there shall be a resurrection of the dead, both of the just and unjust," we can feel the force of

> He is not risen, no,
> He lies and moulders low;
> Christ is not risen.
>
> Ashes to ashes, dust to dust;
> As of the unjust, also of the just—
> Christ is not risen.
>
> (21–26)

The command in the Sermon on the Mount, "lay not up for yourselves treasures upon earth, where moth and rust doth corrupt . . . but lay up for yourselves treasures in heaven . . ." is the background that gives edge to Clough's injunction:

> Set your affections *not* on things above,
> Which moth and rust corrupt, which quickliest come to end.
>
> (106–07)

And where Christ told Simon and Andrew to come after Him and become fishers of men, Clough warns them to return

> Hence to your huts and boats and inland native shore,
> And catch not men, but fish.
>
> (117–18)

The poem ends with another ironic exhortation:

> Here on our Easter Day
> We rise, we come, and lo! we find Him not;
>
> . . .
>
> No sound, nor in, nor out; no word
> Of where to seek the dead or meet the living Lord;
> There is no glistering of an angel's wings,
> There is no voice of heavenly clear behest:
> Let us go hence, and think upon these things
> In silence, which is best.

But it was a very different set of things which St. Paul had asked the Philippians to think on, things patently disregarded in the secular world described by Clough—truth, justice, purity, and God Himself.[62]

5. Objectivity

While he was still at Rugby, thanks to his reading of the *Biographia Literaria,* Clough was already aware of two kinds of poetry called subjective and objective. Although he related the former to Christianity because it laid primary stress on the individual, he lamented "the great egotism, or subjectivity of our poetical literature of the present day," and praised the poetry of Homer—and of Macaulay's "Battle of Ivry," which he was discussing—because there "we see nothing of the writer's self, and he is but the medium through which we view an object."[63]

Clough's own development, however, took a subjective direction, so much so, in fact, that the revival of his early preference and the emergence of objectivity in his own work may be partly traced to the principle of reaction. As he said himself at a later time, "After long abstraction or too careful self-introspection," men need to recover "their ordinary attitude of life and action"; and he identified the latter specifically with his much admired eighteenth century in a passage that sounds autobiographical: "Pure intellectual action is apt, no doubt, to be for the time so absorbing, as to draw to itself all the agencies of our nature, as to suspend the just and fitting exercise of other, and it may be, nobler functions," namely, the observation of everyday phenomena in "the spirit of Newton and of Locke."[64]

But the recoil to objective art answered something deeper than a desire for balance. It arose from the longing, even the necessity,

---

62. The biblical references are: Acts 24:15; Matthew 6:19–20; Mark 1:16–17; Philippians 4:8.

63. *Rugby Magazine, 1* (1835), 126. Clough is probably indebted here to Coleridge, whose influence on his Rugby essays is clear. For a brief summary of the problem, see Meyer Abrams, *The Mirror and the Lamp* (New York, 1953), pp. 241–44, where Coleridge and Crabb Robinson are quoted.

64. *Prose, 1,* 351, 353, or pp. 348, 350.

to escape, if only momentarily, from the painful world of interminable debates and insoluble questions, of fear and guilt and anxiety, by focusing hard on something external, whether nature, society, or the individual. That, indeed, is the basic reason why so many writers from the 1830s to the 1860s were more and more critical of subjective art. Carlyle's reaction to the letters of Madame Varnhagen von Ense is representative:

> They are *subjective* letters, what the metaphysicians call subjective, not *objective;* the grand material of them is endless depicturing of moods, sensations, miseries, joys and lyrical conditions of the writer; no definite picture drawn, or rarely any, of persons, transactions or events which the writer stood amidst: a wrong material, as it seems to us. To what end, to what end? we always ask. . . . One is wearied of that; the healthy soul avoids that. Thou shalt look outward, not inward. Gazing inward on one's own self,—why, this can drive one mad, like the Monks of Athos, if it last too long! Unprofitable writing this *subjective* sort does seem.[65]

That opinion was supported by the still more potent voice, for Clough, of Matthew Arnold. In explaining the omission of his "Empedocles" from the 1853 *Poems,* Arnold noted that by the fifth century the characteristics of early Greek genius had died out. "The calm, the cheerfulness, the disinterested objectivity have disappeared: the dialogue of the mind with itself has commenced; modern problems have presented themselves; we hear already the doubts, we witness the discouragement, of Hamlet and of Faust." And he proceeded, therefore, to urge the modern poet to deal with "some noble action of a heroic time."[66] A few years before, Clough too had talked of story and drama as preferable to the subjective

---

65. *Critical and Miscellaneous Essays,* ed. H. D. Traill (5 vols. New York, 1899–1900), *4,* 108–09. On the subject of doubt and objective art, see the comment in my *Victorian Frame of Mind,* pp. 334–36.

66. In *Poetical Works,* pp. xvii, xxx. In 1849 (?) he had written his sister Jane, *Unpublished Letters of Matthew Arnold,* ed. Arnold Whitridge (New Haven, 1923), p. 17, "More and more I feel bent against the modern English habit (too much encouraged by Wordsworth) of using poetry as a channel for thinking aloud, instead of making anything."

lyric.[67] But his radical disagreement with Arnold on whether the action should be modern or ancient and the style realistic or "grand" serves to remind us that there are different forms of objective art, depending on the individual and his reaction to factors other than his own subjectivity.

Though Clough's mind at Oxford was dominated by religious speculation and introspective analysis, the buried stream of his nature, his strong impulse toward social observation, in moods of bright detachment or angry denunciation, was flowing on steadily and breaking through to occasional expression. Beneath the reserve and shyness lay a good deal of his father's fondness for "society and amusement," and this was nourished by the Oxford scene. His high-spirited and often brilliant conversation was as charming to his companions as it could be exciting to himself. "I can talk tremendous," he once confessed with pardonable pride. In 1839, at the age of twenty, he was inviting a friend to come to commencement in these words:

> You will also have the opportunity of seeing Conybeare Pater issuing fulminatory condemnations of the Fathers at the heads of astonished Newmanists from St. Mary's pulpit: himself in shape, conformation and gestures most like one of his own icthyosauri and his voice evidently proceeding from lungs of a fossil character. Again you will see Chevalier Bunsen, Poet Wordsworth, and Astronomer Herschel metamorphosed into Doctors of Civil Law, a sight worthy, especially in the second case, of all contemplation. Furthermore there will be boat races with much shouting and beer-drinking, a psychological study of great interest.

That mood of social comedy had to wait until 1848 for its expression in art, that is to say, until Clough escaped from the burden of religious and professional decision, and could relax in an "after-boyhood."[68]

---

67. *Prose, 1,* 316, or p. 312; *Correspondence, 1,* 287.
68. For his father, see *Prose, 1,* 9, or p. 9; for his talk, see Arnold, *Letters to Clough,* p. 22, and above, Chap. 1, p. 24. The commencement passage is in *Correspondence, 1,* 91–92, and his "after-boyhood" in *Mari Magno,* Tale II, 29, *Poems,* p. 333.

In the meanwhile, however, he reintroduced "into English poetry some of that sense of direct social reality which the satiric tradition, running through the eighteenth century down to Crabbe, and perhaps Byron, had possessed—but which Romanticism, concentrating upon inward states of experience, had tended to destroy." That general account of the matter by John Heath-Stubbs[69] may be sharpened and extended by recognizing the combined influence first of the moralists, Thomas Arnold and Thomas Carlyle, and then of the satirists, Juvenal and Persius. For Clough's indignation at the complacent luxuries and intellectual affectations of Oxford, and at the selfishness and greed of the middle class with its glorification of competition, both of which his "earnest" masters had inveighed against, broke out at almost the same moment that he first read Roman satire. In an undergraduate essay, significantly called "The Moral Effect of Works of Satire," he found this genre to be "engendered of love for truth & right," and he placed its high point in "Rome under the Imperial tyranny." Citing Juvenal and Persius as supreme masters, he went on to say:

> In an age of great & overpowering ambition the first movement towards amendment, or the last feeling of regret for the past is often shown in a development of Satirical Poetry.
> Being then as in its highest form it is, the means whereby a love of Virtue and Excellence in circumstances of general depravity has best found a vent, we cannot doubt its efficiency as a moral engine in the service of this feeling.

Though he thought it stood too close to "the jarring & discordant elements of . . . Life" to attract the philosophical poet, nevertheless "Satire in many ways [was] genuine Poetry."[70] Thus it was that religion and literature combined to make Clough a satirist, the finest satirist in verse, I think, between Byron and Eliot.

By 1840–41, contemporary society in both Oxford and London

---

69. *The Darkling Plain* (London, 1950), p. 108.
70. This is item 15, vii, in my "Checklist," (above, n. 51), p. 381. A few months earlier in 1839 he had attacked the commercial spirit in another essay: see item 15, iii, p. 380; and also cf. items 21, 22, 24, 28, 29. For his criticism of intellectual affectations, see the references above in n. 12.

was under attack in "Look you, my simple friend," "Duty—that's to say complying," and "To the Great Metropolis"; to be followed later, as Clough felt the impact of Christian Socialism, by "In the Great Metropolis" and "The Latest Decalogue." In the last two poems, he relies on the oblique method of irony he used so brilliantly in *Amours de Voyage* and *Dipsychus*—the speaker unwittingly exposes himself. The Prophet of Competition in "The Latest Decalogue" (he could be called the Aaron of Clough's poem on Mt. Sinai) addresses his disciples:

> Thou shalt have one God only; who
> Would be at the expense of two?
> No graven images may be
> Worshipped, except the currency:
> Swear not at all; for for thy curse
> Thine enemy is none the worse:
> At church on Sunday to attend
> Will serve to keep the world thy friend:
> Honour thy parents; that is, all
> From whom advancement may befall:
> Thou shalt not kill; but needst not strive
> Officiously to keep alive:
> Do not adultery commit;
> Advantage rarely comes of it:
> Thou shalt not steal; an empty feat,
> When it's so lucrative to cheat:
> Bear not false witness; let the lie
> Have time on its own wings to fly:
> Thou shalt not covet; but tradition
> Approves all forms of competition.[71]

71. Here and elsewhere Clough uses "competition" to mean a selfish, cutthroat spirit which he condemns on moral rather than economic grounds: see, for example, *Correspondence*, *1*, 126–27; and cf. Carlyle, *Past and Present* (1843; London, 1897), Book III, chap. 2, p. 146, and any of the Christian Socialists. The first idea for the poem seems to be in Clough's letter to the *Balance* (Feb. 6, 1846), p. 42. "The very Decalogue itself—the definitive 'Thou shalt not do murder,' and 'Thou shalt not steal,' may pass into a very dubious 'Thou shalt not do murder, *without great provocation*,' and 'Thou shalt not steal, *except now and then.*' "

> The sum of all is, thou shalt love,
> If any body, God above:
> At any rate shall never labour
> *More* than thyself to love thy neighbour.

It is the shocking candor of this speech, with its cynical disregard of the slightest moral concern, that gives the tone its special acerbity.

The observation of society was complemented by the observation of individuals. In the very year Clough was recommending the Oxford commencement as "a psychological study of great interest," he was finding the children of Bonamy Price "perfect psychological studies"; and staring at them, no doubt, exactly as he stared years later at Mrs. Brookfield: As he "sat at the foot of my sofa," she wrote to Thackeray, with his "keen expression of investigation," his "eyes cut one through and through."[72] The full fruit of this exploration lies in the long poems, but it also appears in some dramatic pieces, usually dialogues or monologues, written partly under the influence of Browning. Though Clough did not have Browning's sense of theater or his eye for individual personality, and could not, therefore, achieve his lifelike immediacy, the notation of psychological complexities in a poem like "Jacob" is every bit as sharp.

The dying patriarch, speaking to his sons, looks back on his life with shame rather than guilt, that is, with a sense of having failed to live up to an ideal image of himself.[73] From Abraham and Isaac he had received a "dower of innocence and perfectness of life," an "antique pure simplicity" which he had failed to preserve—indeed, had despoiled. But it was not his fault; it was the fault of new conditions of life.

> ... I have had to force mine eyes away,
> To lose, almost to shun, the thoughts I loved,
> . . .
>   (19–20)

---

72. Unpublished letter to John P. Gell, April 18, 1839, in the Bodleian Library; Mrs. Brookfield is quoted from Goldie Levy, *Arthur Hugh Clough, 1819–1861* (London, 1938), p. 119.

73. Cf. Helen Merrell Lynd, *On Shame and the Search for Identity* (New York, 1958), pp. 22–26.

> To buffet and to battle with hard men,
> With men of selfishness and violence;
> To watch by day and calculate by night,
> To plot and think of plots, and through a land
> Ambushed with guile, and with strong foes beset,
> To win with art safe wisdom's peaceful way.
>
> (23–28)

The wisdom he has won has been that of the serpent, and the feeling of shame has made his way anything but peaceful:

> Ah me! this eager rivalry of life,
> This cruel conflict for pre-eminence,
> This keen supplanting of the dearest kin,
> Quick seizure and fast unrelaxing hold
> Of vantage-place; the stony-hard resolve,
> The chase, the competition, and the craft
> Which seems to be the poison of our life
> And yet is the condition of our life!
> To have done things on which the eye with shame
> Looks back, the closed hand clutching still the prize!
>
> (81–90)

But the buried reference in line 83 ("Jacob" meant "supplanter") reminds us that the stealing of Esau's birthright occurred long before he had entered any "land ambushed with guile" and makes it impossible for us to find the "condition" of his life entirely to blame. Indeed, the half-conscious confession of his own responsibility, both for the kind of life he has lived and for the sins he has committed in its service, runs through the poem and finds expression in ambiguities that reveal a suppressed sense of guilt below the shame. Or, to put this more exactly, Jacob hovers between presenting himself as the pathetic victim of circumstance, shamed by failure he could not prevent, and the culpable agent of his own undoing. Immediately before insisting he has had to force his eyes away from what he loved, he calls his days "evil and few" leaving the question of responsibility undefined; and immediately after saying he has had to battle with hard and selfish men, he remarks that the chosen race will never again be of a "blameless" kind. The account of the stolen birthright is a beautiful piece of rhetoric—or of rationalization:

> Think ye, my sons, in this extreme old age
> And in this failing breath, that I forget
> How on the day when from my father's door,
> In bitterness and ruefulness of heart,
> I from my parents set my face and felt
> I never more again should look on theirs,—
> How on that day I seemed unto myself
> Another Adam from his home cast out,
> And driven abroad into a barren land,
> Cursed for his sake, and mocking still with thorns
> And briars that labour and that sweat of brow
> He still must spend to live?
>
> (41–52)

The analogy with Adam is applied only to the pathetic exile, but the other analogy, with the sinner who deserved casting out, comes immediately to mind and provides an ironic revelation of the guilt that Jacob would conceal from his sons and perhaps from himself. Indeed, he speaks below of his life's being troubled with "sins in the field," but that apparent confession is countermanded—though not entirely—by the reference that follows to the sins of his children that have "ploughed deep" upon his back (another image of pathos).

The obvious comparison of the dying Jacob to the dying Bishop of St. Praxed's, both speaking to their sons, shows that Clough has all of Browning's insight into the recesses of consciousness but none of his power to create a living scene. The visual setting of "The Bishop Orders His Tomb," the personal idiom, the realization of the audience and its influence upon the speaker are qualities almost wholly lacking in "Jacob." We may compare the opening lines of each:

> Vanity, saith the preacher, vanity!
> Draw round my bed: is Anselm keeping back?

> Nephews—sons mine . . . ah God, I know not! Well—
> She, men would have to be your mother once,
> Old Gandolf envied me, so fair she was!
> What's done is done, and she is dead beside,
> Dead long ago, and I am Bishop since,
> And as she died so must we die ourselves,
> And thence ye may perceive the world's a dream.
>
> (1–9)
>
> My sons, and ye the children of my sons,
> Jacob your father goes upon his way,
> His pilgrimage is being accomplished.
> Come near, and hear him ere his words are o'er.
> Not as my father's or his father's days,
> As Isaac's days or Abraham's, have been mine;
> Not as the days of those that in the field
> Walked at the eventide to meditate,
> And haply to the tent returning found
> Angels at nightfall waiting at their door.
>
> (1–10)

The striking difference, however, is not necessarily to Clough's disadvantage, for the comparison suggests that he is not writing a dramatic speech in the realistic sense of the word, but something halfway between that and an elegiac ode. Another poem which begins in a similar way—

> Hearken to me, ye mothers of my tent;
> Ye wives of Lamech, listen to my speech—

is called "The Song of Lamech." In the present case, like Tennyson in "Oenone" (whose refrain, "O mother, hear me yet before I die" may be echoed in line 4), Clough is using verbal repetition, internal rhyme, alliteration, and musical rhythms to express a mood of remembered joy. After the lines on battling one's way through a land beset by foes, the note of nostalgia for an earlier world of innocence and peace reappears:

> Alas! I know, and from the outset knew,
> The first-born faith, the singleness of soul,

OBJECTIVITY 77

> The antique pure simplicity with which
> God and good angels communed undispleased,
> Is not; it shall not any more be said
> That of a blameless and a holy kind
> The chosen race, the seed of promise, comes.
> The royal high prerogatives, the dower
> Of innocence and perfectness of life,
> Pass not unto my children from their sire
> As unto me they came of mine.
>
> (29-39)

In those phrases and rhythms no one could hear the voice of a dying man addressing his children. He hears a poetic lament for a lost Eden.

Although Clough seems to have had his father in mind, and was certainly thinking of Victorian "competition" and imagining an earlier age of "antique pure simplicity" before the Industrial Revolution,[74] the sense of shame (with the rationalization of guilt that often accompanies it) and the craving for an earlier state of purity was central in his own experience. Earlier, at Oxford, he had been swept by feelings of moral failure and of nostalgia for the garden of Rugby; and he gave them subjective expression in "So I went wrong," "Enough, small room," and "Blank Misgivings..." Now, in the late forties, striving to objectify his art, and grown

---

74. Anne Jemima Clough, in her manuscript life of her brother, now in the Honnold Library at Pomona College, Claremont, wrote: "That one on Jacob is to me especially pathetic. I could believe it to be written as a sort of remembrance of his Father—& the struggles and trials of mercantile life—the hard battle that a real gentleman and a Christian man with an affectionate honourable too yielding character had had with Life.... He was not successful & made mistakes that brought much trouble—especially in his latter years." Cf. Clough's undergraduate essay in my "Checklist," item 15, iii, p. 380: "The toil of body & mind, the watchfulness & the anxiety which are involved in the earlier stages of mercantile life are fully sufficient to make a man love overmuch the money he wins so hardly. Eager Competition but too certainly renders him selfish.... What wonder if we lose at once those nobler feelings of simple times which bid us labour indeed for our daily food yet forbid us to raise such an object above its secondary & subordinate station. No wonder if the maxim of men's conduct should now become Seek money first & Virtue after: and if they themselves should be ready to sacrifice self-respect and affection, kindly feelings and noble impulses of all kinds in obedience to this new Principle."

aware of the ugly character of commercial life, no doubt partly from observing his father, he must have found the account of Jacob in Genesis made to order, or at least ready to be shaped into a form that would transmute his personal feelings into an impersonal story. In this he succeeded so well that, as he said in his Rugby essay, "we see nothing of the writer's self, and he is but the medium through which we view an object."[75]

Nevertheless, the form is not a complete success because Clough tried to combine two quite different types of art: the subtleties of self-analysis in a dramatic speech and the pathos of nostalgia in a lyrical elegy. In earlier Old Testament poems—"The Song of Lamech," "Genesis XXIV," "Repose in Egypt," and "Jacob's Wives"—he did not make this mistake. There he concentrated on expressing "ordinary feelings, the obvious rather than the rare facts of human nature,"[76] in a form as far from realism as Arnold could have wished—a pastoral setting and a style of poetic simplicity and quiet beauty. In this way he captured the antique purity of the patriarchal world in poems that have the very "singleness of soul" he is celebrating. Their quality—and their difference from "Jacob"—can be felt at once in the opening lines of "Jacob's Wives":

> These are the words of Jacob's wives; the words
> Which Leah spake and Rachel to his ears,
> When in the shade at eventide he sat
> By the tent-door, a palm tree overhead,
> A spring beside him, and the sheep around.
>
> And Rachel spake and said, The nightfall comes;
> Night, which all day I wait for, and for thee.
>
> And Leah also spake, The day is done;
> My lord with toil is weary and would rest.

These Old Testament poems of 1849–50 reflect Clough's struggle to give his poetry a more objective form, but he was dissatisfied

75. *Rugby Magazine, 1* (1835), 126.
76. *Prose, 1,* 360–61, or p. 357.

with this particular pattern, and they mark a direction he did not pursue. They point toward the pictures of biblical or classical subjects in Pre-Raphaelite poetry and painting, where broad emotions are treated with the same conscious simplicity and remoteness, touched with pathos or nostalgia. And they point back to the first appearance of this style in 1848. In that important year of Clough's development, he wrote a poetic drama—his first long poem—with something of the same patriarchal atmosphere, but there with a primary concern for religious and ethical ideas.

3

ADAM AND EVE

IT HAS BEEN GENERALLY SUPPOSED that Clough made no defense of his resignation from Oriel. According to Mrs. Clough "his utterance to the world on quitting Oxford" in 1848 was not the "serious vindication of his conduct" that was expected, probably in a theological pamphlet, but what she called "his first long poem, the 'Bothie of Tober-na-Vuolich.' "[1] The fact is, however, that Clough did write an *apologia pro abdicatione sua*. It was not a pamphlet but a poem, written before *The Bothie*, in the spring of 1848, *Adam and Eve*.[2] But for various reasons—the dismay of friends like Shairp, Prichard, and Arnold, I suppose, and perhaps a feeling that the poem needed to be filled out with the new scenes he wrote for it in 1849 and 1850—it was withheld, and by a curious accident the amusing *Bothie* was published instead.[3] And though it appeared in 1869 and is one of Clough's major poems, being the fullest expression he ever made of his religio-ethical philosophy, and recording in living form the ideas he later embodied, less completely, in his review of F. W. Newman's "The Soul" and his "Notes on the Religious Tradition," it has remained almost unnoticed, even by his critics.[4]

1. *Prose, 1*, 37–38, or p. 39. He resigned his tutorship at Easter and his fellowship in October. *The Bothie* was written in the fall of 1848.
2. See Arnold, *Letters to Clough*, pp. 86, 87, where the poem is referred to as though complete in July 1848. By overlooking these letters, the editors of *Poems* (1951), p. 577, give the impression that *Adam and Eve* dates from 1849, and therefore turn the reader's attention away from the biographical context of 1848.
3. For Shairp and Prichard, see Clough's *Correspondence, 1*, 217–19, 238–40; for Arnold, the previous note. Perhaps all that was written by July 1848, was Scenes I, II, VI, VII, XII, XIV: see *Poems*, p. 577.
4. I know of only three brief discussions: Sidgwick's in his *Miscellaneous Essays*, pp. 74–75; G. P. Johari's in "Arthur Hugh Clough at Oriel and at University Hall,"

Clough gave the manuscript no title. When first published in the 1869 *Poems*, it was called, probably on Symonds' suggestion, "Fragments of the Mystery of the Fall," and in the 1951 edition simply "The Mystery of the Fall." But Arnold and Mrs. Clough both refer to it as his "Adam and Eve"; and Clough himself called the notebooks in which he wrote the first drafts, "Adam and Eve Notebook I" and "Adam and Eve Notebook II."[5] The matter is important because the customary title fixes attention on the Fall of Man (on the mystery surrounding its meaning and, in a secondary sense, on the play about it), whereas the correct title, as I think, points to the central conflict between Adam and Eve, between his liberal ethical philosophy and her Christian orthodoxy (between, one might almost say, with their long epistolary debate in mind, Clough and Edward Hawkins, Provost of Oriel and symbol of traditional Oxford). Moreover, the focus is as much on their contrasting views of Cain as of the Fall.

It is quite true that Clough left Oxford partly for reasons unconnected with religion,[6] but his letters of 1847–48, to his personal friends as well as to the Provost, show that subscription to the Thirty-Nine Articles and, back of that, belief in the historical truth of the Old and New Testament stories, as well as in the great dogmas of the faith, were under skeptical review. By the summer of 1848, Christianity itself was no longer his "actuating religion." By the following March, he was closing the debate with Hawkins by asking:

> Is Xtianity really so much better than Mohometanism, Buddhism (a more extensive faith) or the old heathen philosophy? Are those virtues and graces, which are our religious and moral tradition, really altogether Christian? is there not a good deal of Homer and Virgil in them? Nay, if the loftiest of

---

PMLA, 66 (1951), 417–20 (where the early date is brought out); and Lady Chorley, *Clough*, pp. 202–03. The poem is not even mentioned, I believe, in the books on Clough by Waddington and Osborne, or in the essays by Bagehot, Hutton, and Symonds.

5. Arnold (above, n. 2); Mrs. Clough in *Poems* (1951), p. 576; Clough, ibid., p. 577.
6. See Mulhauser's introduction to the *Correspondence, I*, xix–xx.

them belong to Christianity, are they exclusively Christian in matter of fact, or necessarily Christian in matter of philosophy?

I don't think young men are at all inclined to part with Christianity, absolutely: but they have no Christian ideal, which they feel sure is really Christian, except the Roman Catholic.

It is hardly surprising that a month earlier Prichard was warning Clough that it was unsafe "to throw off submission to Xn law and belief," and explaining that those who felt the ingrained evil of their hearts most deeply would object to "your 'moral philosophy.'"[7] Clearly, *Adam and Eve* is the final result, in artistic terms, of the long religious debate that culminated in 1848, when Christianity was replaced by an ethical-religious philosophy that came from many sources, but especially from Thomas Arnold and Wolfgang von Goethe.

For the form of the poem, Clough was directly indebted, of course, to Byron's *Cain,* a poetic drama written by another of his heroes, and one not only exploring the theme of Christian revolt but also pleading for the moral sense as a substitute for ritual and dogma. The parallels are so close that one can no more forget *Cain* in reading *Adam and Eve* than *Faust* in reading *Dipsychus.* Clough liked to pour his own wine into old bottles; it gave him confidence and at the same time the pride of re-creation. In this case, as in that of his dramatic monologues when compared with Browning's, Clough is less vivid and dramatic than Byron, and more philosophical.

Perhaps one should add, more didactic. Through Clough's critical essays and lectures, from Rugby and Balliol to University College and America, there runs a strain of moral intention; and though in practice he was more often concerned with philosophic observation or psychological probing, his work is marked—though seldom marred—by the hand of the Victorian prophet. Of the longer poems this is true of *The Bothie, Mari Magno,* and, above all, *Adam and Eve.* In 1851 Clough remarked that even if Wordsworth failed to "sweep away with him the exulting hearts of youth"

---

7. *Correspondence, 1,* 218, 249, 239.

as Byron had, nevertheless, he strove "to lay slowly the ponderous foundations of pillars to sustain man's moral fabric, to fix a centre around which the chaotic elements of human impulse and desire might . . . move in their ordered ellipses, to originate a spiritual vitality." Nothing could be a better statement of Clough's general purpose in *Adam and Eve,* or explain more clearly why the poem was so different from its Byronic model. More specifically, when he asked in 1853, "Cannot the Divine Song . . . inform us, and prove to us, that though we are what we are, we may yet, in some way, even in our abasement, even by and through our daily work, be related to the purer existence," he must have remembered the salvation of his own Cain.[8]

1. *Christian Guilt and the Moral Conscience: The Fall of Man*

The portrayal of Adam is more subtle and complex than we should suppose, and of Eve, too, in lesser degree. Her opening cry "Oh, guilt, guilt, guilt!" is answered by his rational vindication:

> Be comforted; muddle not your soul with doubt.
> 'Tis done; it was to be done; if indeed
> Other way than this there was, I cannot say:
> This was one way, and a way was needs to be found.
> That which we were, we could no more remain
> Than in the moist provocative vernal mould
> A seed its suckers close, and rest a seed.
>
> . . .
>
> Come, my wife;
> We were to grow, and grow I think we may,
> And yet bear goodly fruit.
>
> (I, 9–15, 19–21)

When this provokes the same desperate outburst, Adam speaks more bluntly:

---

[8]. *Prose, 1,* 322, or p. 318; *1,* 361, or p. 357. Clough's moral aesthetic is well described, and perhaps overemphasized, by Michael Timko, "The Poetic Theory of Arthur Hugh Clough," *English Studies, 43* (1962), 240–47.

> You weary me with your "Oh, guilt, oh, guilt!"
> Peace to the senseless iteration. What!
> Because I plucked an apple from a twig
> Be damned to death eterne! parted from Good,
> Enchained to Ill! No, by the God of gods,
> No, by the living will within my breast,
> It cannot be and shall not; and if this,
> This guilt of your distracted fantasy,
> Be our experiment's sum, thank God for guilt,
> Which makes me free!—
>
> (I, 23–31)

And he proceeds to explain the whole myth of the serpent, the apple, and the curse as a fantastic dream of Eve's. On what authority? On that of the living *moral* will within his breast. That is the supreme word against which biblical tradition and human action are to be judged. This is clear from a soliloquy in Scene II:

> E'en in my utmost impotence I find
> A fount of strange persistence in my soul;
>
> . . .
>
> I, or a something that is I indeed,
> A living, central, and more inmost I
> Within the scales of mere exterior me's,
> I—seem eternal, O thou God, as Thou;
> Have knowledge of the Evil and the Good,
> Superior in a higher Good to both.
>
> (II, 31–45)

Even in his utmost weakness, struggling with the problem of the Fall, in the very "straits of anguish and of doubt" (III, 54), this inmost self has a sense of eternity and a knowledge of good and evil. In a perceptive passage describing the skepticism that swept over Arnold and Clough at Oxford, Stopford Brooke concluded: "They . . . at last fell back on their own souls alone, on the unchallengeable sense of right they felt therein, on the imperative of duty and on resolution to obey it. Nothing else was left."[9] For

---

9. *Four Victorian Poets,* p. 67.

Adam, at any rate, however little truth there was in the Christian myth, the imperative was divine—though it might be hard to distinguish between different imperatives:

> God's Voice is of the heart: I do not say
> All voices, therefore, of the heart are God's;
> And to discern the Voice amidst the voices
> Is that hard task, my love, that we are born to.
>
> (IV, 63–66)

Adam means to include himself in the "we," for by moments the voice he hears and thinks is God's is that of Eve crying guilt and disobedience. In Scene I, he had confessed he could almost believe "*your* dream *my* dream too, and the dream of both no dream but dread reality" (lines 98–99); and Scene II opens with his own conflicting voices, speaking alternately. Once this "dipsychian" nature of the hero is realized, we understand the initial lines of the poem, which otherwise would seem to belong to Eve:

> *Adam.* Since that last evening we have fallen indeed!
> Yes, we have fallen, my Eve! O yes!—
> One, two, and three, and four;—the appetite,
> The enjoyment, the aftervoid, the thinking of it—
> Specially the latter two, most specially the last.
> There, in synopsis, see, you have it all:
> Come, let us go and work!
>   Is it not enough?
> What, is there three, four, five?
> *Eve.*   Oh, guilt, guilt, guilt!
>
> (I, 1–8)

To this Adam answers with his "Be comforted," since what is done is done and not a sin. And yet we hear in his opening lines the unmistakable note of guilt.

I do not mean that Adam is a dual personality. He is primarily a rationalist seeking a religious philosophy that will satisfy both his intelligence and his moral sense.[10] But since he is also a human being, he can be swept momentarily by old patterns of thought.

---

10. Cf. Johari (above, n. 4), p. 407.

The voice that tells him to curse himself and die, or to think Eve's dream is dread reality, is followed by another "oftener far and stronger . . . more searching," bidding him:

> "On! on! it is the folly of the child
> To choose his path and straightway think it wrong,
> And turn right back, or lie on the ground to weep.
> Forward! go, conquer! work and live!" Withal
> A Word comes, half-command, half-prophecy,
> "Forgetting things behind thee, onward press
> Unto the mark of your high calling." Yea,
> And voices, too, in woods and flowery fields
> Speak confidence from budding banks and boughs,
> And tell me, "Live and grow," and say, "Look still
> Upward, spread outward. Trust, be patient, live."
>
> (I, 108–18)

This is the Goethean message of the poem;[11] it is the word of Adam, the essential Adam. For he continues:

> Therefore, if weakness bid me curse and die,
> I answer, No! I will nor curse myself
> Nor aught beside; I shall not die, but live.
>
> (I, 119–21)

The weakness is largely the force of tradition and habit, but it is partly uxoriousness. If Adam can sincerely feel the guilt he blames in Eve, he can also deny or minimize the disturbing truth he holds in order to ease his wife's anxiety. After saying that Cain "is born of us, and therefore is not pure" (III, 51), he is ready, upon seeing her distress, to ask:

> Did I say that? I know not what I said;
> It was a foolish humour;
>
> . . .
>
> Not pure, indeed!—And if it is not pure,
> What is? Ah well! but most I look to the days

---

11. I have been unable to trace these quotations—if they are quotations. The ideas are common in Goethe, notably in *Faust*, Part II, 4684–4688.

> When these small arms, with pliant thews filled out,
> Shall at my side break up the fruitful glebe,
> And aid the cheery labours of the year—
> Aid, or, in feebler wearier years, replace,
> And leave me longer hours for home and Eve.[12]
>
> (III, 81–82, 86–92)

The interesting thing is that Eve, too, for all her conventional piety and genuine fear of Adam's radicalism, is as capable of being drawn to his ideas as he to hers:

> Oh, but you let strange words at times fall from you.
> They are to me like thunderbolts from heaven;
> I watch terrified and sick at heart,
> Then haste and pick them up and treasure them.
> What was it that you said when Cain was born?
> "He's born of us and therefore is not pure."
> O, you corrected well, my husband, then
> My foolish, fond exuberance of delight.
>
> (IV, 85–92)

Is she attracted by him or by his intelligence? By both, I suppose. But he yields to her at once as he replies:

> My child, believe me, truly I was the fool;
>
> . . .
>
> And I beseech you treasure up no words.
> You know me: I am loose of tongue and light.
>
> . . .
>
> Put not, when days come on, your own strange whim
> And misconstruction of my idle words
> Into the tender brains of our poor young ones.
>
> (IV, 93, 96–97, 100–02)

In these Scenes (I–IV), Clough is experimenting with the dichotomies, and even trichotomies, of character which he so brilliantly explored in *Dipsychus*.

---

12. Besides the lines preceding these, also see Scene II, 61–66, and Scene IV, 93–102, partly quoted just below.

2. Christian Atonement and the Moral Conscience: The Murder of Abel

The analogue of the Fall is the Murder of Abel. Here again an act of disobedience—this one unequivocally evil—is the object of different reactions, not only in Adam and Eve, but now in Cain as well. After Scene V, where a highly dramatic situation is handled too briefly and suddenly to be effective, we have the characterization of Abel as the son of Eve (and a second Johannes Agricola) in Scene VI. Cain is then introduced as the enemy of both, and the admirer of his father. But he is not his father's son because for him the will is not moral but passionate. After Abel is killed, he coolly remarks:

> Dead is it then? O wonderful! O strange!
>
> . . .
>
> If we are plagued and pestered with a fool
> That will not let us be, nor leave us room
> To do our will and shape our path in peace,
> We can be rid of him. There—he is gone;
> Victory! victory! victory!
>
> (IX, 5, 8–12)

A moment later he becomes openly sadistic as he regrets that Abel was so passive—much more fun if he had been forced to yield, with Cain's fingers digging slowly deeper into his throat. In this mood he disposes of the incriminatory question with a scornful "Was I his keeper? . . . Each for himself," and concludes that henceforth he shall know his will and do it by his might. We remember Clough's charge that Byron, for all his genius, was "whirled away by the force of mere arbitrary will, whose only law was its own wilfulness, to follow passion for passion's sake, and be capricious for the love of one's own caprice."[13]

But this is not quite true of Cain (or of Byron either, for that matter). If he followed his passions, it was not for their own sake, not basically. His earlier self-analysis gives the clue to his action:

---

13. *Prose, I*, 321, or p. 317.

CHRISTIAN ATONEMENT AND MORAL CONSCIENCE

> My father, he is cheerful and content,
> And leads me frankly forward. Yet, indeed,
> His leading—or (more truly) to be led
> At all, by any one, and not myself—
> Is mere dissatisfaction: evermore
> Something I must do, individual,
> To vindicate my nature, to give proof
> I also am, as Adam is, a man.
>
> (VII, 17–24)

The struggle to free himself from his father and assert his own ego is thus the real, and not unnatural, motive of the murder. But the motive is unchecked by any moral consideration. Once he views the killing of Abel as something strikingly individual because never attempted before, and at the same time an act of emancipation, Cain lets his passions loose.

It follows, by the logic of art, that the function of the murder (as in Byron's play, too) is the discovery of the conscience. Even as Cain is boasting that

> Henceforth I shall walk freely upon earth,
> And know my will, and do it by my might,
>
> (IX, 39–40)

he is suddenly swept with horror and guilt:

> My God!—it will not be at peace—my God!
> It flames, it bursts to fury in my soul.
> What is it I have done?
>
> . . .
>
> I see it, I behold it as it is,
> As it will be in all the times to come:
> Slaughter on slaughter, blood for blood, and death,
> For ever, ever, ever, evermore!
> And all for what?
>   O Abel, brother mine,
> Where'er thou art, more happy far than me!
>
> (IX, 41–43, 45–50)

Presently Cain is telling Adam of the voice he heard asking "Where is thy brother?" and calling the heart within him that answered "Am I my brother's keeper?" an evil heart. And when the voice spoke again in his soul, the heart ceased to speak.[14]

This leads to a new problem: given his agony of guilt, what should Cain do? Eve urges "rites and holy means of grace" ordained to save the sinner and begs him above all to "seek atonement from a gracious God." But Cain will have none of it. All he asks is "one thing—never to forget." And when Eve makes a new plea that he prostrate his soul in penitential prayers to God to change and melt his heart, he answers emphatically, "Atonement —no: not that, but punishment"—the punishment of his conscience.[15]

This passage is a reflection of Clough's own doubts. In 1847 he had asked his sister Anne what was "the meaning of 'Atonement by a crucified Saviour'?" It might have a meaning "consistent with God's Justice—that is, with the voice of our Conscience," and might even be "the one true expression of our relations to God"; but do the Anglo-Catholics know what that meaning is? the Evangelicals? the Papists?[16] Clough's objection must have been Cain's: that no one else can pay your debt; you must pay it yourself. That is why Cain begs for Adam's curse: "Your curse will make me not forget."[17] But if Adam shares this view—"how can I say refuse the revelations of the soul?"—he adds, nevertheless, and again with the voice of Goethe:

> Yet be not over scrupulous, my son,
> And be not over proud to put aside
> The due consolements of the circling years.
> What comes, receive; be not too wise for God.
> The past is something, but the present more—
>
> (XIII, 67–71)

the present in which one is to go forward, work, and live.[18] And

14. Scene XII, 19–26.
15. Scene XI, 9–13, 15, 32–46, 54.
16. *Correspondence, I,* 182.
17. Scene XIII, 8–9.
18. I refer back to Scene I, 108–18. The two ideas go naturally together. Goethe's most famous expression of them is in *Faust,* Part II, Act v.

for the future? There is the healing comfort of time, and there is "the certainty of things." Somehow, somewhere, the truth will be known. In that faith one may fortify his soul.[19]

The closing scene, which is a kind of epilogue, is elegiac in tone rather than dramatic. Adam begins in the manner of Jacob:

> O Cain, the words of Adam shall be said;
> Come near and hear your father's words, my son.
> (XIV, 1–2)

As in "The Song of Lamech," his words describe the reunion of Cain and Abel, with Abel saying,

> "Forgive me, Cain.
> Ah me! my brother, sad has been thy life,
> For my sake, all through me—how foolishly;
> Because we knew not both of us were right."
> (XIV, 9–12)

—right, I take it, to serve God each in his own way. To mitigate the Puritan ethic of guilt and expiation adopted by Cain, Adam extols the Goethean virtues of forgiveness and self-tolerance.

But the poem does not end on this softer note. At the close, the dark background of life, from which Clough never looked away for long, is seen on the horizon, behind the final exaltation of the moral will. Adam is speaking:

> In spite of doubt, despondency, and death,
> Though lacking knowledge alway, lacking faith
> Sometimes, and hope; with no sure trust in ought
> Except a kind of impetus within,
> Whose sole credentials were that trust itself;
> Yet, in despite of much, in lack of more,
> Life has been beautiful to me, my son,
> And if they call me, I will come again.
> But sleep is sweet, and I would sleep, my son.
> Behold, the words of Adam have an end.
> (XIV, 41–50)

---

19. Scene XIII, 76–92; cf. "It fortifies my soul to know," *Poems*, p. 75.

4

THE BOTHIE OF TOBER-NA-VUOLICH

WHEN CLOUGH PUBLISHED *The Bothie of Tober-na-Vuolich* in November 1848, his friends were astonished, partly because they expected a defense of his resignation (whether a theological pamphlet or an *Adam and Eve*), but mainly, I think, because they could not identify the author with the work. The prize pupil of Dr. Arnold had written a poem that was called "indecent and profane, immoral and Communistic."[1] The reticent man who had been struggling with religious doubts and composing intellectual lyrics for *Ambarvalia* had produced a comedy of Oxford undergraduates. Emerson's reaction was hardly unique:

> It delights and surprises me from beginning to end. I can hardly forgive you for keeping your secret from me so well. I knew you was good and wise, stout of heart and truly kind, learned in Greek, and of excellent sense,—but how could I know or guess that you had all this wealth of expression, this wealth of imagery, this joyful heart of youth, this temperate continuity, that belongs only to high masters. . . . Tennyson must look to his laurels. . . . I am recalling every passage of speech and action of my staid and reticent friend, to find the hints and parallels of what I read.[2]

The hints and parallels were there, of course, even if not generally known. After the intellectualism of Oxford and the long indecision ("Shall I resign?" involving "What shall I do?" involving "Who am I?") and after the confession of faith he had made in *Adam*

---

1. For their expectation, see Mrs. Clough, *Prose*, *1*, 37–38, or p. 39; for their view of the poem, Clough's *Correspondence*, *1*, 240.
2. Ibid., p. 232.

and *Eve,* Clough could now respond unequivocally to the objective tendencies of his nature, and release the buoyant, even boyish, spirits so long suppressed. Furthermore, waiting to be turned from theory to realization, there lay in his mind the idea of a large modern poem capturing the spirit of the age, wrestling with its problems, reflecting its complex experience, and speaking its idiom.

1. The Modern Poem

That idea, in one form or another, had emerged in England by the 1820s. In *Don Juan,* Byron was publishing what he called a great satire on European society, and perhaps more justly, "an epic as much in the spirit of our day as the Iliad was in Homer's."[3] In 1824 Carlyle's translation of *Wilhelm Meister,* a book widely read by the Victorians, established the pattern of carrying a modern youth through a series of incidents in search of a philosophy and even in search of his own identity—a pattern soon imitated in *Sartor Resartus* (written in 1830–31), Sterling's *Arthur Coningsby* (1833), and Maurice's *Eustace Conway* (1834). In the essay prefixed to his translation, Carlyle had said:

> In reading Goethe's poetry, it perpetually strikes us that we are reading the poetry of our own day and generation. No demands are made on our credulity; the light, the science, the scepticism of the age, are not hid from us. He does not deal in antiquated mythologies, or ring changes on traditional poetic forms; there are no supernal, no infernal influences, for *Faust* is an apparent rather than a real exception: but there is the barren prose of the nineteenth century, the vulgar life which we are all leading; and it starts into strange beauty in his hands; and we pause in delighted wonder to behold the flower of Poesy blooming in that parched and rugged soil.

Carlyle also insisted that the modern poet should "address us on interests that *are,* not that *were,* ours; and in a dialect which finds

---

3. Letter to John Murray, Oct. 25, 1822, *The Letters of Lord Byron,* ed. R. G. Howarth (London and New York, 1936), pp. 336–37; Thomas Medwin, *Conversations of Lord Byron* (London, 1824), pp. 247–48.

a response, and not a contradiction, within our bosoms." If he also, like Goethe, embodied in his work a wide range of experience ("a world of Earnestness and Sport, of solemn cliff and gay plain"), he might build "some such temple for the Spirit of our age, as the Shakspeares and Spensers have raised for the Spirit of theirs."[4]

On these lines, John Sterling, admirer of Goethe and friend of Carlyle, developed the classic statement of the "new poem" in his review of Tennyson for the *Quarterly* in 1842. There he began with a description of the "busy, vigorous, various existence" of the modern world which is the very matter of a great poem. But if "Chaucer exhibits to us all that lay around him," and Shakespeare *his age* "with its far deeper wants and more abundant forces," whom have *we* had to express "the secret of our modern England, and to roll all out before him the immense reality of things?" Scott turned to the past and Byron to the faraway and exotic—except in "one of his works, only one, which is a splendid attempt at a creative survey of modern life" drawn from "a wide range and keenness of observation," the *Don Juan*. But "the weakness as to all deeper thought, and the incomplete groundplan" keep it short of ideal. Perhaps the person who "most nearly succeeded in this quest after the poetic *Sangreal*" was George Crabbe, for no one has shown greater knowledge of all classes or brought together such "diverse elements of circumstance and character." But Crabbe lacked poetic sweetness and fire.

When Tennyson is brought to the bar of this standard, he cannot expect to avoid criticism. However charming the fanciful pieces in which "we too are wandering, led by nymphs, among the thousand isles of old mythology," it is a far higher task "to bewitch us with our own daily realities, and not with their unreal opposites." In "Ulysses" there is the wisdom and the "epic tone" we want, but the hero is ancient when he might have been a modern voyager like Columbus or Drake. Tennyson's best poems, Sterling thinks, are the idylls, defined as representations of some situation in private life, expressed in a flow of lyrical feeling (a soliloquy or mono-

---

4. *Wilhelm Meister* (2 vols. New York, 1901), *1*, 28–30; cf. Carlyle's "State of German Literature" (1827), *Essays, 1*, 65–66, where he says that in Goethe "the Nineteenth Century stands before us."

logue, I take it), or expanding into "a narrative or description of ... persons, events, or objects." Of these, "Locksley Hall," in its thought, passion, and imagery, is "the direct outbirth and reflection of our own age."[5]

Two years later when Elizabeth Barrett was meditating "a poem comprehending the aspect and manners of modern life, and flinching at nothing of the conventional," she, too, thought of "Locksley Hall," but decided that for all its "grand general adjuration to the 'Mother-age,'" there was "no story, no *manners.*" It was only a situation. What was needed was a "poetical novel."[6] In 1847 "The Princess" approached that goal, but its modern problem was treated in a form and style that were far from modern. What Mrs. Browning had in mind was *Aurora Leigh, Maud,* or Alexander Smith's *A Life Drama,* and other works of the Spasmodic School. But none of them was written until the fifties. It was Clough, the admirer of Byron, Goethe, and Carlyle, and the reader of Tennyson, who first translated this aesthetic theory into a poem—or rather into poems, for it is the germinating idea of *Amours de Voyage* and *Dipsychus* as much as of *The Bothie.* In an epilogue to the first Clough wrote:

> *Go, little book!*
>
> . . . . .
>
> *. . . and if curious friends ask of thy rearing and age,*
> *Say, "I am flitting about many years from brain unto brain of*
> *Feeble and restless youths born to inglorious days."*

With some adjustment, this could be said of the other two poems as well, for they also capture the spirit of the age as young men were feeling it in the 1840s, and embody it in a new way.

Indeed, the novelty of *The Bothie* was recognized at the time. Emerson, hailing Clough as a "new poet," spoke of "the truly modern question and modern treatment" as a striking feature of the poem, while W. M. Rossetti called attention to "a peculiar modernness, a reference distinctly to the means and habits of society in

---

5. "Poems by Alfred Tennyson," *Essays and Tales* (2 vols. London, 1848), *1,* 431–36, 438, 442, 452–53, 458. The essay first appeared in the *Quarterly Review,* 70 (1842), 385–416.

6. *Letters,* ed. F. G. Kenyon (2 vols. New York and London, 1897), *1,* 204, letter dated Oct. 8, 1844.

these days, a recognition of every-day fact, and a willingness to believe it as capable of poetry as that which, but for having once been fact, would not now be tradition." Even in the early sixties, it was still referred to as "a new, a bold, and somewhat grotesque experiment."[7]

Needless to say, Arnold was well aware of Clough's place in the literary scene and he did not like it. Given the principles of his preface to Poems (1853), he was certain to be critical, and probably caustic, for there he condemned modern subjects embodied in "modern language, familiar manners, and contemporary allusions," and demanded "some noble action of a heroic time" written in the grand style. Shortly after *The Bothie* was published, he wrote to Clough:

> I have been at Oxford the last two days and hearing Sellar and the rest of that clique who know neither life nor themselves rave about your poem gave me a strong almost bitter feeling with respect to them, the age, the poem, even you. Yes I said to myself something tells me I can, if need be, at last dispense with them all, even with him: better that, than be sucked for an hour even into the Time Stream in which they and he plunge and bellow. I became calm in spirit, but uncompromising, almost stern. More English than European, I said finally, more American than English: and took up Obermann, and refuged myself with him in his forest against your Zeit Geist.

This view was broadened out in a letter of 1855, where Arnold said, apropos of "Maud," that Tennyson "seems in his old age to be coming to your manner in the Bothie and the Roman poem. That manner, as you know, I do not like."[8]

---

7. *Journals of Ralph Waldo Emerson*, ed. E. W. Emerson and W. E. Forbes (10 vols. Boston and New York, 1909–14), 7, 560, and 8, 16; *Germ*, no. 1 (1850), 44; W. Y. Sellar, *North British Review*, 37 (1862), 338 (for the attribution, see above, chap. 1, n. 28). Cf. the reviewer of the *Poems and Prose Remains*, probably Mortimer Collins, in the *British Quarterly Review*, 50 (1869), 575–76: "Well do we recollect the first appearance of this thin volume . . . and how delighted men were with what looked like the first fasciculus of a new style of English poetry—the poetry of young Oxford."

8. The 1853 preface is quoted from Arnold's *Poetical Works*, pp. xx, xxx; *Letters to Clough*, pp. 95, 147. On the "Roman poem," see also p. 132, and on Alexander Smith, p. 136.

Clough saw his own poems, and criticized Arnold's, from the same perspective. The opening pages of his "Recent English Poetry," a review in which *A Life Drama* was favorably compared with Arnold's first two volumes, *The Strayed Reveller* and *Empedocles on Etna*, defined the poetics of his own masterpieces, and must therefore be quoted at length. After remarking that in some ways Alexander Smith was the disciple of Keats (mainly in an excessive use of imagery), Clough continued:

> Poems after classical models, poems from Oriental sources, and the like, have undoubtedly a great literary value. Yet there is no question, it is plain and patent enough, that people much prefer "Vanity Fair" and "Bleak House." Why so? . . . Is it, that to be widely popular, to gain the ear of multitudes, to shake the hearts of men, poetry should deal more than at present it usually does, with general wants, ordinary feelings, the obvious rather than the rare facts of human nature? Could it not attempt to convert into beauty and thankfulness, or at least into some form and shape, some feeling, at any rate, of content—the actual, palpable things with which our every-day life is concerned. . . . Might it not divinely condescend to all infirmities; be in all points tempted as we are; exclude nothing, least of all guilt and distress, from its wide fraternization; not content itself merely with talking of what may be better elsewhere, but seek also to deal with what *is* here?
>
> The modern novel is preferred to the modern poem, because we do here feel an attempt to include these indispensable latest addenda—these phenomena which, if we forget on Sunday, we must remember on Monday—these positive matters of fact, which people, who are not verse-writers, are obliged to have to do with. . . . The novelist does try to build us a real house to be lived in; and this common builder, with no notion of the orders, is more to our purpose than the student of ancient art who proposes to lodge us under an Ionic portico.[9] We are, unhappily, not gods, nor even marble statues. While the poets, like the architects, are—a good thing

---

9. This is perhaps pointed at Arnold's "The Strayed Reveller."

enough in its way—studying ancient art, comparing, thinking, theorising, the common novelist tells a plain tale. . . .

We do not at all mean to prepare the reader for finding the great poetic desideratum in this present Life-Drama. But . . . these poems were not written among books and busts, nor yet

> By shallow rivers, to whose falls
> Melodious birds sing madrigals.

They have something substantive and lifelike, immediate and first-hand, about them. There is a charm, for example, in finding, as we do, continual images drawn from the busy seats of industry; it seems to satisfy a want that we have long been conscious of, when we see the black streams that welter out of factories, the dreary lengths of urban and suburban dustiness,

> the squares and streets,
> And the faces that one meets,

irradiated with a gleam of divine purity. There are moods when one is prone to believe that, in these last days, no longer by "clear spring or shady grove," no more upon any Pindus or Parnassus, or by the side of any Castaly, are the true and lawful haunts of the poetic powers: but, we could believe it, if anywhere, in the blank and desolate streets, and upon the solitary bridges of the midnight city, where Guilt is, and wild Temptation, and the dire Compulsion of what has once been done—there, with these tragic sisters around him, and with Pity also, and pure Compassion, and pale Hope, that looks like Despair, and Faith in the garb of Doubt, there walks the discrowned Apollo, with unstrung lyre; nay, and could he sound it, those mournful Muses would scarcely be able as of old, to respond and "sing in turn with their beautiful voices."[10]

History and biography have united—as they often do, but seldom so clearly—to determine a theory of art. For this is the aesthetics of the "modern poem," from Byron, Carlyle, and Goethe (his *Herman*

---

10. *North American Review*, 77 (1853), 2–5, reprinted in *Prose*, *1*, 360–63, or pp. 356–59.

and Dorothea in particular) to Sterling and the Brownings, given its clearest formulation; and in the back of his mind, as Clough indicates, is the influence of the novel of modern life as he knew it in Jane Austen, Thackeray, Balzac, and George Sand (especially her *Jeanne*).[11] But it is also the personal statement of Clough the realist with his love of facts (all the facts, nothing excluded), the Evangelical fearing the insincerities of artifice, the subjective poet so weary of "comparing, thinking, theorising" that he wants to tell a plain tale of ordinary feelings, and the victim of Arnold's criticism eager to strike back.[12]

The Bothie is no longer modern. It has lost the contemporary appeal of its realism and its radical ideas—radical in the 1840s—on social equality, the duty of work, and the role of woman, whether peasant or fine lady. (Chartism, Christian Socialism, and Tennyson's *Princess,* published in the previous year, are in the immediate background.) No one today will find the hexameters a point of angry attack or eloquent defense. And though there are signs of its revival, the narrative poem is not in vogue. What keeps *The Bothie* fresh and alive is its masterly fusion of plot, character, setting, and ideas; its suggestion, because of the range of feeling and variety of tone, of a broad picture of life, at any rate youthful life;

---

11. On the influence of *Herman and Dorothea* note Clough's admiration for the poem, *Correspondence, 1,* 93; William Whewell, *North British Review, 19* (1853), 140–41 (attribution in Isaac Todhunter, *William Whewell* [2 vols. London, 1876], *1,* 294–95); R. H. Hutton, "Arthur Hugh Clough," *Literary Essays* (London and New York, 1892), pp. 290–92. Clough read *Jeanne* with such enthusiasm in 1845 he thought of translating it, believing it "would take" because "the hero is an Englishman, and by no means a common but a very veritable kind of hero." He is Sir Arthur Harley, who falls in love with the peasant girl Jeanne, and despite his friends' arguments against it, proposes to her.

12. On Clough's realism, cf. his admiration for eighteenth-century philosophy, above, pp. 44–45, and his advice to Allingham, *Correspondence, 1,* 287, to "follow Chaucer and facts." It is hardly surprising that Clough disliked Arnold's 1853 preface (*Correspondence, 2,* 470); indeed, the preface, which was written later in the year, was probably in part a reply to Clough's essay. Cf. an undated letter of Clough's to Longfellow at Harvard University [bMS Am 1340.2 (1205)]. "Did you read Matt Arnold's Sohrab & Rustum? I should like to know what you think of it. I myself have rather a feeling of the pseudo-antique about it—& do not concur properly in the Pre-Shakespearian theory." *Sohrab* is also criticized in *Correspondence, 2,* 470, 477.

and most of all, its sheer charm, or whatever it is that makes it one of the most delightful poems in English literature.

2. *Narrative Synthesis*

In itself the action is handled with quiet suspense and forward thrust. Clough never forgets he is telling a story, at least not until Canto IX when the story is over. The characterization, though not so subtle as it is in *Amours de Voyage,* is remarkably deft, hitting off temperament, speech, and dress with graphic economy, and sharpening the sketch of individuals by the clash or comparison of personalities: Hewson vs. Lindsay, Hewson and Adam, Lindsay and Arthur, Kitty vs. Elspie. Moreover, the reading party as a whole is vividly created. Though the subject has often been attempted, undergraduates have perhaps never been caught with better success—swimming, reading, dancing, and endlessly talking (about politics and women and love and philosophies of life), arguing, debating, telling stories, in the latest slang and the typical wit (a mixture of sexual jokes and academic puns)—the whole shot through with a spirit of gaiety and friendship that is suddenly touched, here and there, by a note of irritation or dislike.[13]

Philip Hewson, the hero, is a Chartist with social ideals of equality and the duty of work, but he has the "eager, impetuous" temperament of the reformer, which can sometimes make him "wild and flighty."[14] This blending of wisdom with exaggeration is nicely recorded in his fiery speech of Canto II. For after satirizing the artificialities of courtship ("evening parties, shooting with bows . . . turning the leaves on the dreary piano, offering unneeded arms") and pleading for women to be helpmates instead of dolls, he rushes on to demand that ladies abandon ballroom, carriage, and satins for "washing, cooking, and scouring, or . . . uprooting

---

13. For the biographical background of reading parties in 1846, 1847, and 1848, and some identifications of the characters, see *Prose, 1,* 28–30, 107–08, 114–15, or pp. 29–31, 110–11, 117–18; *Correspondence, 1,* 229–30, and *2,* 621; A. H. A. Hamilton, *Academy, 23* (Jan. 6, 1883), 11; an unpublished letter by Thomas Arnold, Jr., to Mrs. Clough, July 16, 1897, in the Bodleian Library; and William Tuckwell, *Reminiscences of Oxford* (London, 1900), Appendix F, p. 263.

14. Cantos IX, 46, and VIII, 145. Cf. Canto I, 125–28.

potatoes," and dress in "plain linsey-woolsey"; for what is useful, he claims, is graceful, and "labour alone, can add to the beauty of women." But Philip's ideas are not just those of a Chartist with what the Piper calls his "confounded *égalité*." They are also those of a young man whose experience counts as heavily as his thinking. "One day," he says, when I was

>   strolling, ungainly in hobbadiboyhood,
> Chanced it my eye fell aside on a capless, bonnetless maiden,
> Bending with three-pronged fork in a garden uprooting
>   potatoes.
> Was it the air? who can say? or herself, or the charm of the
>   labour?
> But a new thing was in me; and longing delicious
>   possessed me,
> Longing to take her and lift her, and put her away
>   from her slaving.
> Was it embracing or aiding was most in my mind?
>   hard question!
> But a new thing was in me; I, too, was a youth among
>   maidens:
> Was it the air? who can say? but in part 'twas the charm
>   of the labour.
>   (II, 42–50)

Hewson's theories are beautifully connected with his passions, and both are interwoven in his prediction of what household work and homespun clothes can accomplish:

> So, feel women, not dolls; so feel the sap of existence
> Circulate up through their roots from the far-away centre
>   of all things,
> Circulate up from the depths to the bud on the twig that
>   is topmost!
> Yes, we should see them delighted, delighted ourselves in
>   the seeing,
> Bending with blue cotton gown skirted-up over striped
>   linsey-woolsey,

> Milking the kine in the field, like Rachel, watering cattle,
> Rachel, when at the well the predestined beheld and
>   kissed her,
> Or, with pail upon head, like Dora beloved of Alexis,
> Comely, with well-poised pail over neck arching soft to the
>   shoulders,
> Comely in gracefullest act, one arm uplifted to stay it,
> Home from the river or pump moving stately and
>   calm to the laundry.
>
>   (II, 92–102)

The beauty of labor is wonderfully fused with the beauty of feminine posture.[15]

After an outburst of Lindsay's, and Hobbes' amusing description of Hewson as "a Pugin of women" (having the same scorn of the purely ornamental and the same belief in the union of "use and grace"), Adam the tutor, who sees the truth in Philip's view, disliking luxurious living himself and believing on moral grounds in the duty of work, also sees its excesses, which he calls "distortions." One should seek only the good, he says, and not the attractive, and since inequality is a fact of creation, one should remain in his station. To which Hewson replies, acidly:

>   Alas! the noted phrase of the prayer-book,
> *Doing our duty in that state of life to which God has
>   called us,*
> Seems to me always to mean, when the little rich boys say it,
> Standing in velvet frock by mama's brocaded flounces,
> Eying her gold-fastened book and the watch and chain at
>   her bosom,
> Seems to me always to mean, Eat, drink, and never mind
>   others.
>
>   (II, 202–07)

The education of Philip Hewson that follows through the next cantos is the education of both the young radical and the young

---

15. A full account of the background can be read in John Killham, *Tennyson and "The Princess"* (London, 1958), chaps. 5 and 6 on the feminist controversy, with references to *The Bothie* on pp. 118, 142.

man, for doctrine and experience continue to interact in a living character. In Canto III the incipient affair with Katie, the farmer's daughter at Rannoch, is the meeting point of advanced theory and masculine susceptibility:

> But tell me, said Hobbes, interposing,
> Did you not say she was seen every day . . .
>   washing, cooking, scouring?
> How could he help but love her? nor lacked there perhaps
>   the attraction
> That, in a blue cotton print tucked up over striped
>   linsey-woolsey,
> Barefoot, barelegged, he beheld her, with arms bare
>   up to the elbows,
> Bending with fork in her hand in a garden uprooting
>   potatoes?
>   (III, 228–34)

The following Canto is not entirely successful. In Philip's moral struggle to resist temptation, the admonitory vision of the ruined girl turned prostitute is a Victorian convention now outmoded. Adam's lecture on the weakness of women and the difference between gaining wisdom by intuition and by experience—though entirely in character—seems too long, or it seems too much like a lecture from Clough. But Adam seizes effectively on the opportunity to drive home his earlier advice ("seek only the good," and seek it "in your station"); and the saving glance of Elspie, with its elaborate meaning (lines 135–44), is a skilful projection of Philip's conscience. What is more, his passionate longing to return to Katie has the specificity of mixed emotions and oblique sexuality:

> Spirits escaped from the body can enter and be with
>   the living;
> Entering unseen, and retiring unquestioned, they bring,
>   —do they feel too?—
> Joy, pure joy, as they mingle and mix inner essence
>   with essence;

> Would I were dead, I keep saying, that so I could go
> and uphold her!
>
> . . .
>
> Is it impossible, say you, these passionate, fervent
> impulsions,
> These projections of spirit to spirit, these inward embraces,
> Should in strange ways, in her dreams, should visit her,
> strengthen her, shield her?
> Is it possible, rather, that these great floods of feeling
> Setting-in daily from me towards her should, impotent
> wholly,
> Bring neither sound nor motion to that sweet shore they
> heave to?
> Efflux here, and there no stir nor pulse of influx!
> Would I were dead, I keep saying, that so I could go
> and uphold her!
>
> (IV, 40–43, 48–55)

Thus, if Philip chooses the good in Canto IV, he is far from ignoring the attractive; indeed, he is the more exposed, after this frustration, to the attraction of someone of his own class. Furthermore, to the extent that his radical ideas are exaggerated, they are the more easily abandoned under contrary pressure. It is only momentarily, therefore (but long enough for the impact to arrest attention), that we are surprised by the rightabout-face in Canto V. Philip is still dancing but "dancing in Balloch . . . in the castle with Lady Maria." And being Philip, he proceeds at once to erect a new theory—or is it a rationalization? Because his distaste of idle luxury and his sympathy for the poor are entirely genuine, he reveals his skepticism in the very act of profession:

> What of the poor and the weary? their labour and pain is
> needed.
> Perish the poor and the weary! what can they better
> than perish,
> Perish in labour for her, who is worth the destruction of
> empires?
>
> . . .

> Dig in thy deep dark prison, O miner! and finding be
>   thankful;
> Though unpolished by thee, unto thee unseen in perfection,
> While thou art eating black bread in the poisonous air of thy
>   cavern,
> Far away glitters the gem on the peerless neck of a Princess,
> Dig, and starve, and be thankful.
> (V, 51–53, 64–68)

The extravagant phrasing betrays an act of the will! Indeed, that is all but implied by the opening line: "Often I find myself saying, and know not myself as I say it." His praise of Lady Marias has the same ambiguity:

> Suffer that service be done you, permit of the page and
>   the valet,
> Vex not your souls with annoyance of charity schools or of
>   districts,
> Cast not to swine of the sty the pearls that should gleam
>   in your foreheads.
> Live, be lovely, forget them, be beautiful even to proudness,
> Even for their poor sakes whose happiness is to behold you;
> Live, be uncaring, be joyous, be sumptuous; only be lovely.
> (V, 72–77)

That could hardly be spoken straight by Philip Hewson the Chartist unless he were madly in love. Otherwise it would be half ironic. The opening line gives the answer: "Often I find myself saying, in irony is it, or earnest?" But under the circumstances, it *is* half earnest too, and he gives the last command a qualification that makes it his own:

> Live, be uncaring, be joyous, be sumptuous; only be lovely,—
> Sumptuous not for display, and joyous, not for enjoyment;
> Not for enjoyment truly; for Beauty and God's great glory!
> (V, 77–79)

In similar fashion the next paragraph, in which he comes round to Adam's philosophy and wonders if God has not, after all, disposed his works "in a wonderful order" and made "man, as the beasts, to live the one on the other," begins with the warning: "It seems inspiration—of Good or of Evil!" Plainly, a new Katie with more character will have no trouble displacing Lady Maria, especially in a man and a thinker who, in both roles, is "the eager, impetuous Philip."

Clough drew his hero with a sure hand, but he was anxious about his heroine and the speech of the lovers, never an easy thing for a young writer to handle, and here complicated by distinctions of class.[16] His success in this area is now difficult to judge, because literary fashions and actual mores, too, can change so much that what is natural for one generation may seem stilted to another. Allowance must be made for some Victorian sentimentality: Philip's tears are especially trying. Elspie must be read within the context of Romantic primitivism and the need of the Victorian intellectual to find in woman an incarnation of the simplicity and force of elemental nature. After describing a city at dawn as "resumed to Primal Nature and Beauty," Philip adds, "Such—in me, and to me, and on me the love of Elspie!" That explains her commanding presence in Cantos VII–VIII and her complete domination of her social and intellectual superior, not noted for his timidity or shyness.[17] But her speech is, and was, a problem. Many will agree with Froude that she has "too great command of language and metaphor, and that very few women and no young girls ever did talk in finished simile, however clever they were."[18] One might answer that not many Roman soldiers talked of Antony and Cleopatra in the brilliant metaphors of Enobarbus. If the artist may not put the right words into mouths that otherwise would be dumb or fumbling, a good deal of literature must be devalued. But "right" must mean not only expressive but also in keeping, that is, blended into the texture. In this story, Elspie's speech, side by side with the other voices, had to be realistic. It could show great com-

---

16. See Canto VI, 97–104.
17. The quotation is in Canto IX, 107–08. For the background see *Victorian Frame of Mind*, pp. 385–87. Hewson's reaction from intellectualism to love is made explicit in Canto VIII, 111–19; cf. "July's Farewell," *Poems*, p. 75.
18. Clough, *Correspondence*, *1*, 235.

mand of language and metaphor, but the particular idiom had to be one which, like Enobarbus's, we could imagine her using. No one was ever as witty as Millamant, but her wit becomes her so well we suspend our disbelief; whereas Elspie's elaborate similes, thrown off in conversation, seem incongruous and, therefore, unbelievable. Only their form, however, not their content, is out of keeping. As she considers her possible union with Philip, Elspie thinks of the new bridge over the burn:

> I have been building myself, up, up, and toilfully raising,
> Just like as if the bridge were to do it itself without masons,
> Painfully getting myself upraised one stone on another,
> All one side I mean; and now I see on the other
> Just such another fabric uprising, better and stronger,
> Close to me, coming to join me: and then I sometimes
>   fancy,—
> Sometimes I find myself dreaming at nights about arches
>   and bridges,—
> Sometimes I dream of a great invisible hand coming down, and
> Dropping the great key-stone in the middle: there in my
>   dreaming,
> There I feel the great key-stone coming in, and through it
> Feel the other part—all the other stones of the archway,
> Joined into mine with a strange happy sense of completeness.
>   (VII, 61–72)

The phrasing of the final lines makes it plain that the keystone is a phallic image, and the dream is "Freudian." The next day she explores the relationship with Philip in another simile equally revealing:

> You are too strong, you see, Mr. Philip! just like the sea
>   there,
> Which *will* come, through the straits and all between the
>   mountains,
> Forcing its great strong tide into every nook and inlet,
> Getting far in, up the quiet stream of sweet inland water,
> Sucking it up, and stopping it, turning it, driving it
>   backward,

> Quite preventing its own quiet running: and then, soon after,
> Back it goes off, leaving weeds on the shore, and wrack and
>   uncleanness:
> And the poor burn in the glen tries again its peaceful
>   running,
> But it is brackish and tainted, and all its banks in disorder.
> That was what I dreamt all last night. I was the burnie,
> Trying to get along through the tyrannous brine, and
>   could not;
> I was confined and squeezed in the coils of the great salt
>   tide, that
> Would mix-in itself with me, and change me.
>   (VII, 120–32)

And then she concludes,

>   And I struggled, and screamed, I believe, in my dream.
>   It was dreadful.
>   You are too strong, Mr. Philip! I am . . .
>   .   .   .
>   quite afraid and unwilling.
>   (VII, 133–34, 136)

This is clearly a sexual nightmare in which the manifest content is so thin it could only pass unanalyzed in a modest and "pure minded" young woman living in 1848. By an extraordinary piece of daring, Clough has put the most suggestive language into the mouth of a person who could not possibly be suggestive, and by so doing has not only underlined her simplicity but revealed the unconscious mode in which sexual fears find verbal expression.

But when Philip meekly promises to depart tomorrow, Elspie at once forgets her dread, and boldly taking his hand kisses the cold fingers. This reversal of feeling is brilliantly expressed in the same imagery, with the masculine tide now ebbing and the feminine burn rushing after it:

> That great power withdrawn, receding here and passive,
> Felt she in myriad springs, her sources, far in the
>   mountains,

> Stirring, collecting, rising, upheaving, forth-outflowing,
> Taking and joining, right welcome, that delicate rill in
>   the valley,
> Filling it, making it strong, and still descending, seeking,
>
>   . . .
>
> With a delicious forefeeling, the great still sea before it.
>   (VII, 157–161, 163)

In Canto VIII, however, a new revulsion comes over "the spirit of Elspie" as she feels a new terror, that of "deserting her station." The ensuing argument, recalling an earlier pattern of ideas, stresses equality, now of husband and wife (contra Tennyson's *Princess*), and the democratic distaste for "the old solemn gentility stageplay." Elspie refuses to become a "lady" waited upon by footmen, not because she cannot fill the role, but because she wants to abide by her training and continue to work; to which Philip answers, "God forbid you should ever be aught but yourself."

It is characteristic of Clough's success in blending character and theme that Canto IX opens, a few lines later, with Philip erecting this remark into an abstract principle and connecting it with his equalitarian theory of labor. Regardless of class or of sex, let each of us "do the thing we are meant for":[19] Lady Marias *perhaps* to be lovely and idle; other women (again, contra Tennyson) to have careers in teaching and nursing. And true to his temperament, Philip pushes his latest idea to extremes:

> If you were meant to plough, Lord Marquis, out with you,
>   and do it;
> If you were meant to be idle, O beggar, behold, I will
>   feed you.
> If you were born for a groom, and you seem, by your
>   dress, to believe so,
> Do it like a man, Sir George, for pay, in a livery stable;
>
>   . . .

---

19. This idea, which is the moral of the poem, had appeared in Canto VI, 72, and is reiterated in Canto IX, 17, 39, 67, 70; see p. 511 for drafts where Clough used the Aristotelian "ergon." See also *Poems and Prose Remains, 1*, 304, for a formal statement a year or so later.

> Hast thou for cooking a turn, little Lady Clarissa? in with
> them,
> In with your fingers! their beauty it spoils, but your own it
> enhances;
> For it is beautiful only to do the thing we are meant for.
>
> (IX, 18–21, 37–39)

This is too much for Adam the grave man with his caution and his common sense. He reiterates the social theory he had expounded in Canto II:

> When the armies are set in array, and the battle beginning,
> Is it well that the soldier whose post is far to the leftward
> Say, I will go to the right, it is there I shall do best service?
> There is a great Field-Marshal, my friend, who arrays our
> battalions;
> Let us to Providence trust, and abide and work in our
> stations.
>
> (IX, 41–45)

Philip's retort to that, with its sharp question pointed at the weak sides of conservatism, renews the earlier debate. How, he asks, can we distinguish between the circumstance we should take arms against and the circumstance we should accept as an act of Providence?[20] Specifically, in the Victorian battle of ideas, which Arnold, too, was picturing at the same time in the same imagery,

> What are we to resist, and what are we to be friends with?
> If there is battle, 'tis battle by night: I stand in the darkness,
> Here in the mêlée of men, Ionian and Dorian on both sides,
> Signal and password known; which is friend and which is
> foeman?

---

20. Cf. *Correspondence*, 2, 433, and his letter in the *Balance*, Jan. 23, 1846, p. 26: "One may be told, indeed, and the admonition is not without force, that one must trust to Providence; that, in all positions, grace 'is sufficient for us'; no single human being is tempted above his power; the duty must be simply and trustfully met; we must do our work in that state of life to which we are called. But the question is, are we called to it? is it a providentially ordered duty?"

NARRATIVE SYNTHESIS

> Is it a friend? I doubt, though he speak with the voice of a
>   brother.[21]
>
> (IX, 50–54)

Indeed, the situation is even worse.

> O that the armies indeed were arrayed! O joy of the onset!
> Sound, thou Trumpet of God, come forth, Great Cause, to
>   array us,
> King and leader appear, thy soldiers sorrowing seek thee.
>
> . . .
>
> Neither battle I see, nor arraying, nor King in Israel,
> Only infinite jumble and mess and dislocation,
> Backed by a solemn appeal, 'For God's sake do not
>   stir, there!'
>
> (IX, 59–61, 63–65)

But Philip is no longer the Philip of Canto II. He is able now, now that he has looked with pleasure into the castle at Balloch, to accept a philosophy of order—at any rate in theory. In the middle of this radical passage he says:

> Still you are right, I suppose; you always are, and will be;
> Though I mistrust the Field-Marshal, I bow to the duty of order.
>
> (IX, 55–56)

But the phrasing is dubious, and his concluding words seem to reiterate his own position:

> Yet you are right, I suppose; if you don't attack my
>   conclusion,
> Let us get on as we can, and do the thing we are fit for;
> Every one for himself, and the common success for us all,
>   and
> Thankful, if not for our own, why then for the triumph of
>   others,

---

21. For the relation of the night battle to Arnold's "Dover Beach," written a year later, and a passage in Thucydides much admired by Thomas Arnold, see Clough, *Correspondence, 1*, 218; Tinker and Lowry (above, Chap. 1, n. 10), pp. 175–76; Buckner B. Trawick, "The Sea of Faith and the Battle by Night in *Dover Beach*," *PMLA, 65* (1950), 1282–83.

Get along, each as we can, and do the thing we are meant for.
That isn't likely to be by sitting still, eating and drinking.

(IX, 66–71)

The last line reveals a continuing distaste for aristocratic life; and in the next letter his "soul of souls" is filled with "the old democratic fervour" for an equalitarian society where no one should sit still and everyone should work—preferably, he seems to feel, with his hands. Certainly, he himself, after taking a first class degree at Oxford, married a farmer's daughter and in New Zealand "hewed, and dug; subdued the earth and his spirit." Still, he was not insincere in telling Adam he supposed he was right. He thought he was—the Oxonian in him thought he was—and yet he lived by another creed, being committed deeply to the anti-aristocratic radicalism of the 1840s.[22]

3. Range and Variety

A modern poem that would capture the spirit of the age had to aim at a synthesis of elements hitherto kept apart for reasons of simplicity or decorum. It had to have range of experience and diversity of tone, and perhaps a mixture of genres. For the age had not only felt the romantic delight in plenitude, it was itself, as Clough noticed, crowded with "new books and new events." The self-consciousness that accompanied the decay of established ideas and turned the individual back upon himself had opened up new areas of feeling and observation. Life was more complex, and one was more aware of the complexity. Less than a year before *The Bothie* was written, Arnold was saying to Clough that had Shakespeare and Milton been writing now, they would have had "the

22. Cantos I, 125–28; II, 19–21, 53–67, 202–07, 210–12; V, 50–87; VIII, 146–51; and IX, 14–39, 71, 80–81, all show his strong anti-aristocratic bias. Clough's own point of view was very similar: see in particular a canceled passage, now in the Bodleian Library, of "ὁ θεὸς μετὰ σοῦ," where a Scotch lassie is being addressed:

Thrice blessed, oh, the life wherewith, new blood of strength & health,
Thy pure & democratic lips endue the child of wealth
O blessed hundredfold, to hold enfranchised by thy kiss
The charter, & the freeman's fee of unfactitious bliss:
Of the lies of breeding, birth, & rank confession made, the grace
Of absolution plenary to gain in thy embrace . . .

multitude of new thoughts and feelings to deal with a modern has"; while Clough himself a little later was telling Allingham that one should write not "short things" but narrative poems because "a large experience . . . is necessary to attract the modern world to poetry. Shakespeare and Milton should meet together as Rousseau and Voltaire have in Goethe and in Beranger."[23]

Compared with "The Rape of the Lock" or "Michael" or "Marmion," Clough's *Bothie* has far greater breadth: gentlemen and peasants at work and play, the beauties of autumn scenery, the sentiment and the passion of love, a large pattern of social and political ideas, and a mass of literary allusion and learned puns. What gives this range of material a special quality was noticed by Kingsley in his perceptive review. Calling attention to "the strange jumble" of "marquises and gillies, shooters and tourists—the luxuries and fopperies of modern London amid the wildest scenery and a primitive people—Aristotle over Scotch whiskey—embroidered satin waistcoats dancing with bare-legged hizzies—Chartist poets pledging kilted clansmen," he praised Clough for picturing "the sublime and the ridiculous hand-in-hand, as they usually are," and daring "to set down honestly just what he saw."[24]

In what may be called tone or mood, there is a similar range with similar incongruities. The modern poetry of Goethe had blended "Earnestness and Sport," and the modern poems of Byron had been "droll or pathetic, descriptive or sentimental, tender or satirical, as the humour strikes me,"—all qualities of Clough's temperament that had already been expressed separately. The tradition of the "new poem" united them. Also, as Kingsley observed, the "playful, mock-heroic key gave scope for all sorts of variations into the bucolic, sentimental, broad-farce, pathetic, Hebrew-prophetic, what not."[25]

23. Clough, *Prose, 1,* 332, or p. 328; Arnold, *Letters to Clough,* p. 65 (cf. "The Function of Criticism," *Essays in Criticism,* p. 7); Clough, *Correspondence, 1,* 287.

24. *Fraser's Magazine, 39* (1849), 105.

25. On Goethe, see above, p. 94; Byron was adopting a remark by William Beattie, *Childe Harold,* preface to Cantos I and II; Kingsley (above, n. 24), p. 105. Cf. J. J. Garth Wilkinson's letter to Clough, Dec. 29, 1848, in the Bodleian Library: "You will be called comic, serious, descriptive, metaphysical, or human-natural, just as the reader himself runs; but the Poem is all these at once."

For that scope the hexameters were particularly useful. More than one critic has praised their effective expression of both the familiar realities of daily life or political discussion, and at the same time subjects like autumn landscape and the sentiment of love that require "poetical grace and ideal elevation."[26] Something of this flexibility can be seen in the opening lines of Canto II:

> Morn, in yellow and white, came broadening out from the mountains,
> Long ere music and reel were hushed in the barn of the dancers.
> Duly in *matutine* bathed before eight some two of the party,
> Where in the morning was custom, where over a ledge of granite
> Into a granite bason the amber torrent descended.
> There two plunges each took Philip and Arthur together,
> Duly in *matutine* bathed, and read, and waited for breakfast:
> Breakfast, commencing at nine, lingered lazily on to noon-day.

A moment later the same metric is carrying the eloquent speech —tirade, Lindsay would have called it—of "Hewson the Chartist, the poet." One might argue that blank verse would have been as malleable; but the endless objections to Clough's hexameters because they are not proper hexameters, that is, classical hexameters (as Clough, of course, was well aware), seem silly. The ancient metric is no longer in our ears, and in any event we are prepared to judge the form of a poem, however irregular, by its effectiveness. As Kingsley put it, if Clough has not written hexameters, he *has* written *"Bothiaics,"* and very good ones too.[27]

---

26. William Whewell, *North British Review*, *19* (1853), 146 (for attribution, see above, n. 11).

27. *Fraser's Magazine* (above, n. 24), p. 107. He goes on to denounce "the pedantry of metre-mongers . . . letting the spirit of verse starve while they haggle for the letter," and speaks categorically of Clough's complete mastery of the meter. For one "metre-monger," see above, Chap. 1, n. 33. For Clough on the poem's metric, see *Poems*, p. 496, and an undated letter to his mother in the Bodleian Library, probably written shortly after *The Bothie* appeared in early Nov. 1848, in which he explains: "Dactylics of six feet: but the dactyls replaceable by trochees; and sundry irregularities allowed:— e.g. sometimes a syllable dropped, sometimes added;—and sometimes a trochee re-

The meter was primarily an imitation of Homer,[28] but if we try to classify *The Bothie,* we think not only of the epic—and of Dryden and Pope in their mock-heroic vein—but also of Wordsworth and Tennyson. For the poem is a mixed genre: it is a modern idyll written in the epic manner, partly "straight," partly comic. Its muse was not Calliope nor the Thalia of pastoral poetry. She was, as she should have been, a hybrid. "Muse of the Epos and Idyll," Clough calls her, "Muse of great Epos, and Idyll the playful and tender."[29]

The repeated epithets and the elaborate similes, along with the hexameters, are the obvious Homeric elements. But more important are the two things that for Arnold made *The Bothie* more like the *Iliad* than any other English poem: "the rapidity of its movement, and the plainness and directness of its style." As a result, it "produces a sense in the reader which Homer's composition also produces . . . the sense of having, within short limits of time, a large portion of human life presented to him, instead of a small portion."[30] In this respect, the form supports the range of material and variety of tone in giving the impression of breadth.

Though the term idyll still meant a country story, usually about love, in a setting of field and stream, it had come to mean something more realistic than the classical work of Theocritus or Virgil. Generalizing from Tennyson's "Dora" and "The Gardener's Daughter," with Wordsworth's "Michael" and Goethe's *Herman and Dorothea* undoubtedly in mind, Sterling had spoken of a

---

placed by an iambus." The second "Letter of Parepidemus," *Prose, 1,* 395–402, or pp. 389–96, and reprinted in *Poems,* pp. 582–86, is a general discussion of hexameters. The editors of *Poems,* pp. x–xiii, give a careful analysis. But the ordinary sensitive reader, keeping the meaning well in mind, will have no difficulty whatever. In the same way, one can read Hopkins without knowing anything about sprung rhythm—though that may be heresy.

28. Clough wrote to Emerson, *Correspondence, 1,* 240–41: "Will you convey to Mr. Longfellow the fact that it was a reading of his Evangeline aloud to my Mother and sister which, coming after a reperusal of the Iliad, occasioned this outbreak of hexameters."

29. Canto IX, 139, 142.

30. *On Translating Homer,* pp. 213–14. For the Homeric strain in the poem, also see Hutton, *Literary Essays,* pp. 292–94.

"faithful eye for visible nature" and a "lively painting . . . drawn from the heart of our actual English life" as central characteristics. But, as the examples suggest, the idyll continued to be bathed in something of an ideal light, never quite seen on land or sea—or Scotch Highland.[31]

Both criteria are suggested, respectively, by the title (a bothie is a farmer's hut or cottage) and the subtitle, "A Long-Vacation Pastoral." Interpenetrating the realism is a fine strain of Arcadian unreality. The character of Elspie, the somewhat "dreamy" ending in which the Oxford gentleman marries the peasant girl and lives happily ever after—in faraway places—and even the wit and gaiety of the reading party are not to be scrutinized too closely by "fact and common sense." Nor should they be. "To glorify the life he yet faithfully represents" is a legitimate purpose for a poet, and entirely true to our imaginative experience.[32] And it was also true to Clough's experience at the time. He was writing from Liverpool in the autumn of 1848, the first autumn in twenty years that he had not been at school or university. He was on vacation, no doubt of it, and enjoying at long last "a sort of after-boyhood."[33] In this mood, Oxford undergraduates and Highland lassies could not be treated with the severity of Crabbe.

4. Charm

This delicate heightening of reality is part of the charm of the poem. Because the sense of actual life is so firmly created, the touch of idealism is made to seem real, and this is far more winning than outright fantasy. Then there is the portrayal of youth, which can be enormously attractive if it is free from sentimentality. Newman described the age in a famous sermon:

> How beautiful is the human heart, when it puts forth its first leaves, and opens and rejoices in its spring-tide. Fair as may

---

31. Sterling (above, n. 5), p. 456. Goethe's *Herman and Dorothea*, which probably had some influence on Clough's poem (see above, n. 11) is another union of epic and idyll, as G. H. Lewes noted in his *Life and Works of Goethe* (first ed. 1855; London, 1908), Book VI, chap. 4, pp. 430–31.
32. *Saturday Review, 14* (July 26, 1862), 109.
33. "The Clergyman's First Tale" in *Mari Magno,* line 29.

be the bodily form, fairer far, in its green foliage and bright blossoms, is natural virtue. . . . Generosity and lightness of heart and amiableness, the confiding spirit, the gentle temper, the elastic cheerfulness, the open hand, the pure affection, the noble aspiration, the heroic resolve, the romantic pursuit, the love in which self has no part,—are not these beautiful?[34]

Much of that spirit is found in *The Bothie,* but not all of it. For there the temper of the young is a little less ardent, a little more earthy. And it has a further quality overlooked by Newman, a quality which runs through the whole poem and is, I think, its most charming feature: a wonderful freshness and vivacity. Clough spoke of the Oxonians reading, talking, roaming, "All in the joy of their life, and glory of shooting-jackets"; or, more compactly, of "the joy of eventful living."[35] The description of swimming in the mountain pool catches this quality in symbolic action. When exploring the upper reaches of a stream, the Reading Party had seen

> on a sudden before them
> Slabs of rock, and a tiny beach, and perfection of water,
> Picture-like beauty, seclusion sublime, and the goddess of
> bathing.
> There they bathed, of course, and Arthur, the Glory of
> headers,
> Leapt from the ledges with Hope, he twenty feet, he thirty;
> There, overbold, great Hobbes from a ten-foot height
> descended,
> Prone, as a quadruped, prone with hands and feet protending;
> There in the sparkling champagne, ecstatic, they shrieked
> and shouted.
>
> (III, 55–62)

Champagne indeed! The same kind of joyful energy pervades their conversation; and Hobbes is equally bold and amusing, though

---

34. "The Second Spring," reprinted in *Sermons and Discourses (1839–57),* ed. C. F. Harrold (2 vols. New York and London, 1949), 2, 347.

35. Cantos III, 248; and V, 7, 36, 126. Cf. Emerson's phrase, quoted above, p. 92, "this joyful heart of youth."

far more skilful, as he descends on Philip with the witty analogy between his theory of women and Pugin's theory of Gothic.[36]

These various qualities are brought together in a letter written to Clough by Garth Wilkinson: "Full to brimming, as it is, of youthhood and external nature, I yet feel that my greatest gratitude to it arises from the manner in which it takes one's tenderest experiences back into their native air. . . . It is 'long vacation' all over, alike for soul and sense." That comes as close as one could expect to defining the complex charm of *The Bothie of Tober-na-Vuolich*.[37]

36. Cantos II, 131–54; V, 91–100; and IX, 152. Arnold, *On Translating Homer*, p. 300, spoke of the poem's "out-of-doors freshness, life, naturalness, buoyant rapidity."

37. Letter cited in n. 25.

5
AMOURS DE VOYAGE

IN CLOUGH'S NEW POEM, written nine months later, the charm of *The Bothie* has vanished, but its place is taken by a study of modern life which is more subtle and penetrating. The focus is now on contemporary attitudes rather than ideas, and on the exploration of ambivalent feelings about art, heroism, and love, and about oneself. For in contrast to Philip, the young radical of the forties who was concerned with only two things, democracy and love, Claude is the young intellectual of the time who has all the complexities of awareness, inner and outer, that come of extreme sensitivity. Moreover, the primary method of analysis is now oblique. Where Philip had been criticized directly by his companions and the turn of events, Claude is under ironic contemplation: by what he says of himself he becomes, in part, an unwitting object of comedy. In less than a year, Clough's art has gained the sophistication of the great novelists. *Amours de Voyage* is a minor masterpiece.[1]

1. The Oxonian at Rome

By calling Claude an intellectual, I mean to deny that he is a dilettante but not that he possesses certain characteristics of the breed which some people find unattractive. He is introverted and egocentric, awkward and fumbling in social situations, given to endless analyses of everything from abstractions to personal relations, unwilling or unable to commit himself wholeheartedly to any positive action, and capable by moments of a self-contempt

---

1. J. D. Jump, "Clough's *Amours de Voyage*," *English*, 9 (1952–53), 176. This article, on pp. 176–78, is brief but suggestive.

that almost amounts to masochism. More than that, he has the vanities and affectations that no one likes, and which are especially conspicuous in the *young* intellectual. There is the ready criticism of everything hallowed by authority, the mock modesty, the impeccable taste—that is to say, the most fashionable taste (avant garde) —the offhand use of French or Italian, the paraphrase of famous quotations, and everywhere the cleverness that calls attention to itself:

> What do I find in the Forum? An archway
>   and two or three pillars.
> Well, but St. Peter's? Alas, Bernini has
>   filled it with sculpture!
> No one can cavil, I grant, at the size of
>   the great Coliseum.
> Doubtless the notion of grand and capacious
>   and massive amusement,
> This the old Romans had; but tell me, is this
>   an idea?
> Yet of solidity much, but of splendour little
>   is extant:
> "Brickwork I found thee, and marble I left
>   thee!" their Emperor vaunted;
> "Marble I thought thee, and brickwork I find
>   thee!" the Tourist may answer.
>   (I, 43–50)

To the provincial Georgiana this sort of thing is "very stupid," but Vernon, who is also an Oxonian, recognizes it at once for what it is, *"very* clever" (I, 64), with the "very" deliberately italicized. By the nicest exaggeration Clough is exposing the young tourist to the amused smile of the comic spirit. We can almost see the creative process in action by comparing one of his own letters with one of Claude's. In April 1849, two days after reaching Rome, Clough wrote to his mother:

> St. Peters disappoints me: the stone of which it is made is a poor plastery material. And indeed Rome in general might

be called a *rubbishy* place; the Roman antiquities *in general* seem to me only interesting as antiquities—not for any beauty. The Arch of Titus ... is I could almost say the only one really beautiful relic, that I have yet seen. ... I have seen two beautiful views since I came, one from San Pietro in Montorio, the other from the Lateran Church over the Campagna—the weather has not been very brilliant.[2]

In Claude's first letter to Eustace, he reports:

Rome disappoints me much,—St. Peter's, perhaps, in especial;
Only the Arch of Titus and view from the Lateran please me:
This, however, perhaps, is the weather, which truly is horrid.

. . .

Rome disappoints me much; I hardly as yet understand, but
Rubbishy seems the word that most exactly would suit it.
All the foolish destructions, and all the sillier savings,
All the incongruous things of past incompatible ages,
Seem to be treasured up here to make fools of present
    and future.
Would to Heaven the old Goths had made a cleaner sweep of it!
                         (I, 13–15, 19–24)

What Clough had said with simple directness, Claude gets off with the jaunty air of the bright young man saying the "shocking" thing in the smart way. There is the addition of *much,* the St. Peter's *in especial,* the self-importance of there being only two views that *please him,* the *horrid* weather, the pausing to call attention to the bold originality of *rubbishy,* the omission of any general praise (Clough himself had found the antiquities "interesting as antiquities"), the neat anthitheses (foolish destructions and sillier savings, incongruous things from incompatible ages), and the "amusing" hyperbole of wishing the Goths had made a clean sweep of it. All this rephrasing of his own letter comes ultimately from Clough's suspicion of something ostentatious in himself, and immediately from creating, on that foundation, a fictional character whose affectation will be underlined.

2. *Correspondence, 1,* 252.

But to imagine that Claude is simply an object of ridicule, or that all his talk is raillery and "blasé disgust at men and things," would be as great a mistake as to miss the irony.[3] Claude has the virtues as well as the vanities of the intellectual: the sharp mind, the range of knowledge and interest that includes philosophy and politics as well as art, the sensitive awareness of his own attitudes, and by moments, sufficient detachment to criticize himself. Indeed, the fusion of affectation with intelligence—and with prejudice too —is one of the poem's most brilliant achievements.

> Luther, they say, was unwise; like a half-
>   taught German, he could not
> See that old follies were passing most tran-
>   quilly out of remembrance;
> Leo the Tenth was employing all efforts to
>   clear out abuses;
> Jupiter, Juno, and Venus, Fine Arts, and Fine
>   Letters, the Poets,
> Scholars, and Sculptors, and Painters, were
>   quietly clearing away the
> Martyrs, and Virgins, and Saints, or at any
>   rate Thomas Aquinas:
> He must forsooth make a fuss and distend his
>   huge Wittenberg lungs, and
> Bring back Theology once yet again in a flood
>   upon Europe:
> Lo you, for forty days from the windows of
>   heaven it fell; the
> Waters prevail on the earth yet more for a
>   hundred and fifty;
> Are they abating at last?
>
>   (I, 87–97)

It is impossible not to be amused by the sweeping dismissal of medieval Catholicism and the bland assumption of ecclesiastical wisdom (if *only* Claude had been in charge of the Reformation),

---

3. The quoted phrase is J. C. Shairp's: see Clough, *Correspondence*, *1*, 275.

but it is equally impossible not to recognize the historical insight of viewing Protestantism, not as the awakening of the modern spirit, as it was usually interpreted by the Victorians, but as the substitution of one scholasticism for another. Only the most advanced liberals were saying that Luther—and Calvin, too—gave the man-made subtleties of theology a new life that was only now at long last, in the mid-nineteenth century, yielding to the force of reason. And yet this poised Oxonian with his liberal intelligence is young enough, or English enough, to talk like the most bigotted Protestant. A moment later he refers to the followers of Saint Ignatius as those "vile, tyrannous Spaniards" who arrived with the Reformation and are still here,

> Here, with emasculate pupils and gimcrack churches of Gesu,
> Pseudo-learning and lies, confessional-boxes and postures,—
> Here, with metallic beliefs and regimental devotions,—
> Here, overcrusting with slime, perverting, defacing, debasing,
> Michael Angelo's dome, that had hung the Pantheon in heaven,
> Raphael's Joys and Graces, and thy clear stars, Galileo!
> (I, 109–14)

Claude may have his point, but such an emotional outburst, at the very least, is in bad taste; and its attempted justification in the last lines is entirely sophistical.

The Oxford intellectual is also an Oxford gent, "highly connected" (I, 257) and socially conscious. No doubt his criticism of the middle-class Trevellyns has its validity,[4] but the tone is snobbish. After calling them "neither man's aristocracy . . . nor God's," he apologizes in the most patronizing manner:

> Ah, what a shame, indeed, to abuse these most worthy
> people!
> Ah, what a sin to have sneered at their innocent
> rustic pretensions!
> Is it not laudable really, this reverent worship of
> station?

4. Canto I, 125–34, 205–12.

> Is it not fitting that wealth should tender this homage
> to culture?
>
> (I, 135–38)

What an insufferable puppy! But suddenly, to our astonishment, he stands off and views himself with wry detachment:

> Dear, dear, what do I say? but, alas, just now,
> like Iago,
> I can be nothing at all, if it is not critical
> wholly;
> So in fantastic height, in coxcomb exaltation,
> Here in the Garden I walk, can freely concede
> to the Maker
> That the works of his hand are all very good:
> his creatures,
> Beast of the field and fowl, he brings them
> before me; I name them;
> That which I name them, they are,—the bird
> the beast, and the cattle.
>
> (I, 143–49)

What an insufferable puppy I am! The critic, we see, can criticize himself with fine candor. Self-mockery is Claude's most modern characteristic and the principal link with his later counterpart, Eliot's Prufrock. Presently it is interwoven with the snobbishness in a passage that suddenly reveals a simple honesty of feeling that makes Claude both more attractive and more human. Is his enjoyment of the Trevellyns, he asks himself, "the horrible pleasure of pleasing inferior people?" In any event, for the first time in his life, he confesses, he is socially at ease:

> I, who have always failed,—I, trust me, can
> suit the Trevellyns;
> I, believe me,—great conquest,—am liked by
> the country bankers.
> And I am glad to be liked, and like in return
> very kindly.
>
> (I, 218–20)

Claude has even a touch of humility.

2. The Ennuyé

The intellectual of the forties was disillusioned and depressed. In the contemporary idiom he was ennuyé. After the Romantic vogue of Werther and René, of Manfred and Childe Harold, he had to be. But fashions begin in realities and sometimes exist side by side with realities: one can half affect what he half feels. The ennuyé was born of the breakdown in traditional ideas and values which followed the industrial, political revolution of the eighteenth century and the development of the critical mind. He was living, in Mill's phrase, in an age of "criticism and negation," unable to follow the old patterns of life without question, and baffled by the choice between a score of new, or new-old, philosophies of religion, politics, or ethics. Certain of nothing, driven inward on an endless search for beliefs, he was frustrated of action and enormously self-conscious.[5] Under Clough's title two of the epigraphs are:

> *Oh, you are sick of self-love, Malvolio,*
> *And taste with a distempered appetite!*
> —Shakspeare

> *Il doutait de tout, même de l'amour.*
> —French Novel

He doubted (Claude doubted) not only ideas but also the great ideals of life—Beauty, Friendship, Heroism, even Love.

As the poem begins, the ennuyé is plainly revealed in the lines that follow the criticism of antiquities:

> However, one can live in Rome as also in London,
> Rome is better than London, because it is other than
>   London.
> It is a blessing, no doubt, to be rid, at least for a time, of
> All one's friends and relations,—yourself (forgive me!)
>   included,—

---

5. Mill's phrase is in his *Autobiography* (above, Chap. 1, n. 16), chap. 5, p. 139. On the general subject, see *Victorian Frame of Mind*, chap. 3, sec. 5, called "Ennui and Doubt." Self-consciousness is also discussed above, pp. 57–58.

All the *assujettisement* of having been what one has been,
What one thinks one is, or thinks that others suppose one.

(I, 26–31)

In this fatigued, self-conscious mood, one is unlikely to believe in anything, and to act is almost impossible. Small wonder Claude was called (like his creator, too, on one occasion) the Hamlet of the age.[6]

But the mood of ennui was unstable. One is not always thinking or always doubting, and enthusiasms are hard to eradicate, especially in a period not only influenced by Romanticism but frightened of doubt. When men were "destitute of belief, yet terrified at Scepticism" (Carlyle's phrase), the union of a critical mind with a still-believing heart—at any rate, of one still yearning to believe, whether in ideas or in ideals—was a natural phenomenon. But in many cases the union was conflict, and that in turn aggravated the pain of doubt and deepened the mood of ennui. Indeed, when J. A. Symonds defined "the *maladie du siècle*," he called it "the nondescript cachexy, in which aspiration mingles with disenchantment, satire and scepticism with a childlike desire for the tranquility of reverence and belief."[7]

This, I think, is what Clough had in mind, at least primarily, when he said that *Amours de Voyage* had been "flitting about many years" in the brains of "feeble and restless youths" (V, 221–22). For in the poem and in the age, the critical spirit strikes at most of the romantic capitals—at God and Heroes, at Beauty and Art and Liberty, as well as at Love—paralyzing the will to act, and yet the

---

6. W. Y. Sellar in 1862 (above, Chap. 1, n. 28), p. 341; W. H. Hudson in 1896, *Studies in Interpretation*, pp. 130–31, where a parallel is drawn by quoting Hamlet saying that his resolution "is sicklied o'er with the pale cast of thought," and that great enterprises may therefore "lose the name of action" (I, i); Morchard Bishop, "Thyrsis.... A Study of Arthur Hugh Clough," *The Pleasure Ground*, ed. M. Elwin (London, 1947), p. 71, where Claude is called "Hamlet in modern dress"; Jump (above, n. 1), p. 176. It is worth noticing that Claude quotes or paraphrases Hamlet in Cantos III, 67, 279, and V, 165. Clough himself reminded J. R. Mozley of Hamlet (above, Chap. 1, n. 33), pp. 349–50.

7. Carlyle's phrase is in his essay on Scott, *Essays*, *4*, 56; Symonds' definition is in *Last and First*, p. 100. Cf. *Victorian Frame of Mind*, chap. 4, "The Critical Spirit—and the Will to Believe," especially sec. 2.

great assertions are hardly injured. They keep on being repeated with something of the old ardor by the very men who have struck them down with fact and reason; and this rekindles the desire for action. In short, the historical situation set up a back-and-forth, yes-and-no oscillation of feeling, and forced the skeptic and the idealist to live together, in comic or pathetic discord.

This is the guiding clue to *Amours de Voyage*. Though there are overlappings, as there would be in actual life, the skeptical-enthusiastic tension pivots in Canto I on Roman Art and Beauty; in Canto II, on Patriotism and the Hero; in the remaining cantos, on Love and Marriage.

The initial prologue at once fixes the general pattern, with the idealist speaking first:

> *Over the great windy waters, and over the*
> *clear-crested summits,*
> *Unto the sun and the sky, and unto the*
> *perfecter earth,*
> *Come, let us go,—to a land wherein gods of*
> *the old time wandered,*
> *Where every breath even now changes to*
> *ether divine.*
> *Come, let us go; though withal a voice whisper,*
> *"The world that we live in,*
> *Whithersoever we turn, still is the same*
> *narrow crib;*
> *"Tis but to prove limitation, and measure a*
> *cord, that we travel;*
> *Let who would 'scape and be free go to his*
> *chamber and think;*
> *"Tis but to change idle fancies for memories*
> *wilfully falser;*
> *"Tis but to go and have been."—Come, little*
> *bark! let us go.*
>
> (I, 1–10)

In the concluding lines we hear the voice of the opening letters with its bored or clever disparagement of Roman antiquities, now seen in the larger context of ennui. But presently Claude is admiring the "great Chapel of Sixtus," praising the Vatican marbles, finding St. Peter's, which had been ticked off as especially disappointing, rather impressive, and calling the statues of the Horse Tamers the

> ... marvellous Twain, that erect on the
> Monte Cavallo
> Stand by your rearing steeds in the grace of
> your motionless movement,
> Stand with your upstretched arms and tranquil
> regardant faces,
> Stand as instinct with life in the might of
> immutable manhood.
>
> (I, 186–89)

The canto concludes with an epilogue on Rome which reads like a dialogue of the believing heart with the critical head, each rephrasing the other's question:

> *Is it religion? I ask me; or is it a vain superstition?*
> *Slavery abject and gross? service, too feeble, of truth?*
> *Is it an idol I bow to, or is it a god that I worship?*
> *Do I sink back on the old, or do I soar from the mean?*
> *So through the city I wander and question, unsatisfied ever,*
> *Reverent so I accept, doubtful because I revere.*
>
> (I, 279–84)

The final words are unexpected and precise. He is not only doubtful of revering what may not be true, but doubtful *because* he reveres—that is, because he finds himself adopting a "believing" attitude which both Oxford mores and modern intelligence have taught him to suspect.

3. *The Anti-Hero*

In Canto II the background of the Roman republic fighting for survival against the reactionary forces of France serves a double function. By turning Rome into a besieged city, Clough is able to play off art against war in a series of picturesque contrasts: the

THE ANTI-HERO

aesthete and the soldier, sight-seeing and cannonading, love-making and death. But his main purpose is to explore the same ambivalent psychology, with a significant difference. In this case the critical spirit is not amusing, or rather, it was not amusing in 1849; it was shocking. The hero of a Victorian poem remarks, in the most supercilious way, that although it may be sweet and decorous to die for one's country, nevertheless, he regrets to say he must decline the honor. After all, "individual culture is also something"; and in any event to protect oneself is "fulfilling the purpose Nature intended." Now supposing, he continues, referring apparently to the British Embassy,

> the French or the Neapolitan soldier
> Should by some evil chance come exploring the Maison Serny
> (Where the family English are all to assemble for safety),
> Am I prepared to lay down my life for the British female?
> (II, 65–68)

To question the validity of dying for the women of England is bad enough. To refer to them as "females" is to betray the whole code of the chivalric hero. This *was* shocking.

But it was characteristic of the ennuyé. His critical mind and his skeptical temper made him suspicious of heroism. Were there any heroes in the past—or the present? Were there any causes worthy of heroic self-sacrifice? To question the existence of heroes had not been uncommon a century before when men like Hume, Voltaire, and Gibbon had talked of heroism as a mask for selfish ambition or a patent form of madness and delusion. In the Romantic reaction, with its enthusiasm for great men, especially the heroes of old, only Byron suggested that perhaps the knights of Charlemagne and Arthur were as "unknightly" as his own Childe Harold, and that Burke need not have regretted that the Age of Chivalry was dead: it had never existed.[8] Among the Victorians Clough was the earliest, I think, except for Thackeray, to speak out loud and bold:

---

8. Addition to the preface, *Childe Harold*, Cantos I and II. Cf. Arnold, "Rugby Chapel," lines 145–61, saying that but for his father, "the noble and great who are gone" would have "seem'd but a dream of the heart."

> To think that men of former days
> In naked truth deserved the praise
> Which, fain to have in flesh and blood
> An image of the imagined good,
> Poets have sung and men received,
> And all too glad to be deceived,
> Most plastic and most inexact,
> Posterity has told for fact;—
> To say what was, was not as we,
> This also is a vanity.
>
> . . .
>
> The commonplace, whom daily we
> In our dull streets and houses see,
> To think of other mould than these
> Were Solon, Cato, Socrates,
> Or Mahomet or Confutzee,
> This also is a vanity.[9]

The other prerequisite for heroism was becoming even harder for the skeptical eye to discover. When all the institutions of the past were being subjected to rational scrutiny, and old and new ideas in every area of knowledge were being debated in articles, books, and conversation, it was not easy to find a cause that seemed true enough, or important enough, to fight for. Clough had said as much in *The Bothie:*

> What are we to resist, and what are we to be friends with?
>
> . . .
>
> Yet is my feeling rather to ask, where *is* the battle?
>
> . . .
>
> O that the armies indeed were arrayed! O joy of the onset!
> Sound, thou Trumpet of God, come forth, Great Cause, to array us,
> King and leader appear, thy soldiers sorrowing seek thee.
>   (IX, 50, 57, 59–61)

9. *Poems*, pp. 395–96.

Even "my country" and the spirit of patriotism that we associate with nineteenth-century nationalism, and which we imagine was unquestioned before World War II, was already failing to maintain its traditional freedom from criticism. In an age of political revolution, then as now, the individual could be attracted to the creed of the enemy or cry a plague on both nations; and the victory of one's own country might not seem victory at all. In the famous opening of *Childe Harold,* Canto III, published only a year after Waterloo, Byron was asking if that bloody field had, in fact, left earth more free? Or had it only substituted one thraldom for another? Brave men had died bravely, but what had been achieved?

Rider and horse,—friend,—foe,—in one red burial blent!

In the reactionary period that followed the war, a champion of democracy could easily find himself questioning the wisdom of patriotism. Maybe it was simply an emotion being exploited by the Tories. On his return from a fortnight in Paris in 1833, a young Englishman nicknamed Yankee Clough, a disciple of "the radical Dr. Arnold," wrote a letter in which he said:

> Everyone commonly likes his own native land the best, but truth is so concealed by the blarney of false patriotism that it is very hard to discover what are the real merits and demerits of England. . . . False patriotism is but selfishness on a large scale and nothing can be false patriotism unless it be a desire to conceal the faults of our country rather than acknowledge and amend them.

Through the forties such sentiments were deepened by Clough's sympathy with Chartism and the 1848 revolutions throughout Europe, for the working-class movement was international in outlook and suspicious of national governments in the hands of the bourgeoisie. Only a month or so before *Amours de Voyage* was begun, William Allingham wrote to Clough: "But to you perhaps, as to me certainly, 'Patriotism' and 'Our Country' seem generally very unmeaning watchwords."[10]

---

10. Clough, *Correspondence, 1,* 5; Allingham's letter, Mar. 17, 1849, is in the Clough collection at the Bodleian Library. When Clough noticed in his "Jonathan Swift" [Harvard bMS. Eng. 1036 (7), fol. 27] that Robert Walpole called "professions of

The combined effect upon the literary tradition of a critical-skeptical view of high motives and great causes was what we might expect. The writer who could not believe in the traditional hero might portray the supreme individual in revolt against society, call him the Egotistical Hero (Byron's Manfred is the archetype in England); or, with conscious intention to criticize the tradition, he might create the "Anti-Hero" (represented by Don Juan or Childe Roland); or he could turn away from heroism altogether and substitute the introspective intellectual afflicted with ennui, the Unheroic Hero (see the protagonists of "Maud" and "Locksley Hall," Arnold's Empedocles and Obermann, Clough's Dipsychus). It was possible, however, to combine the last two by creating an unheroic hero who was critical of heroism. This is Claude. His story is that of "feeble and restless youths born to *inglorious* days," and ready to say so.[11]

But that is only half the story. So far as Claude is the Anti-Hero, he is not the pure breed. He has a disgraceful—or redeeming—habit of being swept, momentarily, by enthusiasms; besides, "Il doutait de *tout*," which includes doubting his own doubt of heroic action. He begins blandly enough:

Dulce it is, and *decorum,* no doubt, for the country to fall,—to
Offer one's blood an oblation to Freedom, and die for the Cause.

(II, 32–33)

But the language in which he proceeds to defend his own refusal is ambiguous. He might have said: Though it is sweet and decorous to be a hero,

Still, individual culture is also something, and no one
Lives who is bound to feel that he of all others is called on,
Or would be justified, even, in abandoning the work
He is doing for mankind.

---

honesty & patriotism" nothing but "school-boy flights," and told a youthful member of Parliament he would soon leave off thinking of himself as a Roman patriot and be wiser, Clough remarked: "The master quality of his mind was common sense. He estimated things very much at their real value."

11. Canto V, 222. The italics are mine. In Canto II, 294–95, Claude calls himself "the timid, the sensitive soul" in contrast to "the audacious, the wilful, the vehement hero."

THE ANTI-HERO

That is the argument "straight." But Claude puts it this way:

> Still individual culture is also something, and no man
> Finds quite distinct the assurance that he of all others is called on,
> Or would be justified, even, in taking away from the world that
> Precious creature, himself.
>
> (II, 34–37)

The sarcasm shows him detached and self-critical. A few lines later, when he argues that playing it safe is fulfilling the purpose of Nature, he adds, "a wise one, of course, and a noble, we doubt not." This kind of sophisticated irony, in which a person expresses an attitude he sincerely adopts and yet at the same time mocks himself for holding it, is very modern and very un-Victorian. But suddenly the ridicule is transformed into heroic assertion. War and fighting, Claude is saying in the same tone, half sincere, half ironic, are "vain and ephemeral folly, of course, compared with pictures, statues, and antique gems," when he suddenly shifts attitude, awkwardly but surely:

> Indeed: and yet indeed too,
> Yet, methought, in broad day did I dream,—tell it not in
> St. James's,
> Whisper it not in thy courts, O Christ Church!—yet did I, waking,
> Dream of a cadence that sings, *Si tombent nos jeunes héros, la Terre en produit de nouveaux contre vous tous prêts à se battre;*
> Dreamt of great indignations and angers transcendental,
> Dreamt of a sword at my side and a battle-horse underneath me.
>
> (II, 57–64)

No, don't tell a soul in the fashionable circles of London and Oxford that their friend Claude could quote the "Marseillaise" and dream of committing himself to any cause, least of all that of the people—and to the point of fighting for it! Anyway, as he keeps repeating in self-defense, and to prevent Eustace from taking him seriously enough to tell the tale, it *was* only a dream—he never intended to carry it out. And a moment later, recovering his critical poise, he asks: "Am I prepared to lay down my life for the British female?" Why of course not. If he *must* fight and die,

> Sooner far should it be for this vapour of Italy's freedom,
> Sooner far by the side of the d—d and dirty plebeians.
> Ah, for a child in the street I could strike; for the
>   full-blown lady—
> Somehow, Eustace, alas! I have not felt the vocation.
>
> (II, 75–78)

Historically, as we have seen, those radical sympathies and the rejection of patriotism went together. But, as the epithets imply, Claude is no more ready to die for plebeians than ladies. And he has little faith in military triumphs, even Republican ones:

> Victory! Victory! Victory!—Ah, but it is, believe me,
> Easier, easier far, to intone the chant of the martyr
> Than to indite any pæan of any victory. Death may
> Sometimes be noble; but life, at the best, will appear an
>   illusion.
> While the great pain is upon us, it is great; when it is over,
> Why, it is over. The smoke of the sacrifice rises to heaven,
> Of a sweet savour, no doubt, to Somebody; but on the altar,
> Lo, there is nothing remaining but ashes and dirt and ill
>   odour.
>
> (II, 150–57)

In that mood the "labial muscles" that yesterday swelled with a Marseillaise cadence "lapse and languidly mumble," while people and papers are screaming Victory. But suddenly Claude adds, as if under his breath:

> Well, but
> I am thankful they fought, and glad that the Frenchmen
>   were beaten.
>
> (II, 162–63)

The next day he cries out, "All honour to thee, thou noble Mazzini!" Indeed, lo and behold, it turns out that Mary "was wrong about Mr. Claude *being selfish,*" and that he did turn up "on the terrible thirtieth of April" at the British Embassy, ready to lay down his life, after all, "for the British female"—though surely with a wry smile.[12]

4. *The Intellectual in Love*

With the persistent bad luck that has dogged Clough's poetry, most of his critics have found little to be said for Claude, and still less for his role as lover. What has become the standard reading first appeared in Walter Bagehot's essay of 1862:

> The moving force, as in most novels of verse or prose, is the love of the hero for the heroine; but this love assuredly is not of a very impetuous and overpowering character. The interest of this story is precisely that it is not overpowering. The over-intellectual hero, over-anxious to be composed, will not submit himself to his love; over-fearful of what is voluntary and factitious, he will not make an effort and cast in his lot with it.[13]

In a sense this is true, but its implications are wrong because it disregards the complexity of the poem. If Claude was overintellectual, he may have had the virtues of his defect; and to be over-fearful of the factitious is at least a good fault. Perhaps he thought love and marriage worth sacrificing for something that might be more valuable. Perhaps, despite his resolution, he *did* fall in love, genuinely if not passionately, and was thwarted in the end largely by accident. To put the objection briefly, Bagehot does not find anything admirable in Clough's hero—an opinion which was not shared by Clough himself. When his old friend Shairp cried out against this "Werterish" figure in whom "there is no hope, nor strength, nor belief in these," Clough said: "But do you not, in the conception, find any final Strength of Mind in the unfortunate

---

12. Canto II, 228–29. On the combination of hero and anti-hero, also see Canto V, 113–28.
13. *Literary Studies,* 2, 271–72.

fool of a hero?"[14] Such a statement, published in 1865, made it a critical duty to look for some redeeming force in Claude's character and a more sympathetic view of his reluctance to fall in love. Nevertheless, J. A. Symonds was soon agreeing that it was "very stupid" of Claude to give up his pursuit of Mary so soon, and adding: "He is *meant,* however, to be a poor creature, distracted by his own waywardness of speculation, and confused in his impulses." This assumption, despite the corrective interpretations of Henry Sidgwick and R. H. Hutton, still remains the orthodox view of protagonist and poem.[15]

It is quite true that Claude's timidities and his endless hesitations, and all the finespun thinkings and rethinkings, make us want to shake him, and they would be more intolerable still but for his self-criticism: "Pitiful fool that I was, to stand fiddle-faddling in that way!" (IV, 38). Clough himself was well aware of the liabilities of analysis, and, by contrast, of the attractions of love, especially to the Victorian intellectual. When he heard with envy of Tom Arnold's engagement in 1850, he reported that "foolish Shairp will hang on till he is quite bald, I think:—putting the pro's and con's, and philosophizing about sentiment, till he become loathsome to womankind and a burden to himself."[16] For Shairp, read "Clough" and see the early letters to Blanche Smith. Or better, read "Claude," for with more and more emphasis on his vacillation, he continues in the later cantos to be a subject for comic observation.

Yet primarily he remains the intellectual who can be swept at times by enthusiasm. His response to Mary, therefore, is ambivalent. There is the desire to follow his natural emotions, and also to look at love romantically, that is, idealistically. These desires urge him to go forward. On the other hand, the critical, skeptical

---

14. *Correspondence, 1,* 275, 278. Clough's statement first appeared in *Letters and Remains* (1865), p. 218.

15. Symonds, *Last and First,* p. 106, from his 1868 essay. The italics are mine. For Hutton, see below, n. 23; for Sidgwick, above, Chap. 1, n. 5.

16. For Clough's weariness of speculation, see *Prose, 1,* 377–78, 379, and 390–91, or pp. 372, 374, and 384–85; *Poems,* no. 34, p. 90. Shairp is criticized in *Correspondence, 1,* 286. On the intellectuals and love, see *Victorian Frame of Mind,* pp. 385–93, and the references to Clough, p. 386, n. 122.

mind is opposed to any amorous attachment because of the danger of insincerity and the cost involved.

The problem of sincerity arose partly from Evangelical training, instilling a fear of acting from concealed motivation, and partly from the collapse of traditional patterns of action, forcing the individual to question whether what he did, or planned to do, was suited to his nature (was it for him a true line or a false line?).[17] The resulting difficulty of decision, under either influence, demanded hesitation. One had to resist "the ruinous force of the will" (III, 155) that would rush him into action, and wait for some inner assurance he could trust:

> I do not like being moved: for the will is excited;
>   and action
> Is a most dangerous thing; I tremble for something
>   factitious,
> Some malpractice of heart and illegitimate process;
> We are so prone to these things with our terrible
>   notions of duty.
>
>   (II, 272–75)

And, therefore, Claude continues in the next letter:

> Ah, let me look, let me watch, let me wait, unhurried,
>   unprompted!
> Bid me not venture on aught that could alter or end
>   what is present!
> Say not, Time flies, and Occasion, that never returns,
>   is departing!
> Drive me not out, ye ill angels with fiery swords,
>   from my Eden,
> Waiting, and watching, and looking! Let love be its
>   own inspiration!
> Shall not a voice, if a voice there must be, from the
>   airs that environ,
> Yea, from the conscious heavens, without our knowledge
>   or effort,

17. Cf. above, p. 34, and below, p. 197.

> Break into audible words? And love be its own inspiration?
> (II, 276–83)

He had used a variation of the same argument in refusing to fight. He would not, he had said, determine now to do "what may, perhaps, be the virtuous action" (which means either the dutiful action or the right action for him); for

> Am I not free to attend for the ripe and indubious instinct?
> Am I forbidden to wait for the clear and lawful perception?
> (II, 86–87)

It is true, as Claude is quick to realize, that this may be "a weak and ignoble refining" (II, 95), a mere rationalization for inaction. But it is also true that the fear of the factitious is the mark of a fine moral nature. Indeed, we come to recognize that Claude's greatest virtue, perhaps, is his capacity to be honest with himself. He will not indulge in comforting illusions; he will not pretend to be in love or to be a hero if he is not. He sees himself as clearly, as sincerely, as a human being can hope to.

More important for understanding his resistance to falling in love is his recognition of the cost involved—especially for the intellectual—in becoming immersed in emotional ardors and marital commitments. In the initial letter dealing with love (Canto I, letter ix), Claude speaks at first with enthusiasm of the feminine presence being a necessity for "poor soft souls" like himself,

>   filling with sweetness,
> Thrilling with melody sweet, with harmonies strange overwhelming,
> All the long-silent strings of an awkward, meaningless fabric.
> (I, 172–74)

But after that romantic affirmation he suddenly turns right about and adds:

> Yet as for that, I could live, I believe, with children;
>   to have those
> Pure and delicate forms encompassing, moving about you,

THE INTELLECTUAL IN LOVE 139

> This were enough, I could think; and truly with glad
>   resignation
> Could *from the dream of romance, from the fever of flushed
>   adolescence,*
> Look to escape and subside into peaceful avuncular functions.
>   (I, 175–79; my italics)

As the last line might suggest, Claude's fear of being in love is not unconnected with a fear of sex,[18] but it comes mainly from a deep distaste for the unreal and distorted vision of life that love creates. In this respect Claude's intellectualism is his allegiance to clear-eyed intelligence, feet on the ground. What Clough was to say of Goethe is almost true of his own protagonist: "He was too far-seeing, too transcendentally intelligent, to be blindly in love. The imagination was enchanted, the soul was agitated, the heart also suffered; but the Mind, which was the man, revolved upon its centre."[19]

In letter xii, the basic character of this intellectualism is defined. Claude is tying ties, he says, which "will, and must, woe is me, be one day painfully broken." He is landing on the magical island of Circe but he has the moly of Hermes to protect him; he is descending into the enchanting cavern, but with a rope on his loins to upbear him again. For in the end, he says, in lines crucial to the full meaning of the poem, I

> shall plant firm foot on the broad lofty spaces I quit,
>   shall
> Feel underneath me again the great massy strengths of
>   abstraction,
> Look yet abroad from the height o'er the sea whose salt wave
>   I have tasted.
>   (I, 250–52)

And so he does, but only by chance and with a waste of spirit he cannot now conceive of. "Abstraction," of course, stands for the life of the mind, from which, as from a height, one looks down

---

18. See Canto III, 173–81.
19. "Poems and Ballads of Goethe," *Fraser's Magazine*, 59 (1859), 714.

calmly and clearly on the sea of natural existence with all its flux of emotion, in which for a moment—this moment in Italy—Claude is being immersed. A few years later Clough was to write his fiancée: "I am, my dear Blanche I know and confess, sometimes carried away into a world of abstraction when I write or study and so forth. But surely I am not likely to be *able*, did I wish it, to stay there long. I believe my ambition, also, such as I have . . . tends in that direction. Yet I am always so glad to come away from it."[20]

The implied tension between the life of the poet and thinker and the life of husband and parent had long been in his mind. In 1846 he was saying that the question of reconciling his work with marriage was for him a problem of considerable difficulty. Since he had no money of his own, it would force him into a more lucrative career in order to support a Victorian wife in the style to which she was accustomed; and he must have thought that the distractions and responsibilities of a home would interfere with the life he desired. In 1852 he told Blanche: "What I looked forward to originally . . . was unmarried poverty and literary work."[21] Later, in the essay on Goethe, he went on to quote a poem of Coleridge's, but with what he called "a slight variation," intending the original to be recalled:

> All thoughts, all passions, all delights,
> Whatever stirs this mortal frame,
> All are but ministers of—divine intelligence,
> And feed that sacred flame.

The slight variation was the substitution of "divine intelligence" for Coleridge's "love."[22]

---

20. *Correspondence*, 2, 375–76. Cf. Mrs. Clough's remark, *Prose*, *1*, 48, or p. 50, that he was "capable of looking at outward things from a truly philosophic height."
21. *Correspondence*, *1*, 170; *Prose*, *1*, 172, or p. 178. Cf. H. M. Margoliouth on Wordsworth's inner debate whether or not to marry, *Wordsworth and Coleridge 1795–1834* (London, 1953), p. 103: "Wordsworth was self-dedicated to poetry, it was his profession, his vocation, his justification for living. . . . He was a poet of actual and potential achievement. . . . He had no other responsibilities, cares or duties: he was nature's celibate priest. Could he, conscientious and prudent as he was, become responsible for a wife and family and yet remain wholly dedicated to his high calling?"
22. *Fraser's Magazine* (above, n. 19), p. 714.

The intelligence to which Claude is dedicated (the "abstraction" of letter xii) includes, of course, the realistic vision of letter ix. Sidgwick linked the two in his description of what he called the "philosophic" mood of the poem:

> It consists in devotion to knowledge, abstract knowledge, absolute truth, not as a means for living happily, but as offering in its apprehension the highest kind of life. It aspires to a central point of view in which there is no distortion, a state of contemplation, in which, by "the lumen siccum of the mind," everything is seen precisely as it is.
>
> This is the first phase of the mood as it appears in Canto I., xii.: in conflict with a germinating passion which is felt to draw away from centrality, to shed a coloured radiance which is not lumen siccum, to involve, in fact, a sort of magic, enchantment, deceit.[23]

Though far from common, this point of view was not unique. In Tractarian Oxford a celibate life devoted to religious writing was widely acclaimed, and sometimes followed by choice. Carlyle, Huxley, and others, as well as Clough himself, were scornful of "woman-worship" and the high doctrine that "Love is everything."[24] Arnold, steeped in Lucretius, talked of love as a "fool passion [that] gulls men potently," or spoke of his heart never having quitted without shame its

remote and spheréd course
To haunt the place where passions reign.[25]

---

23. In Arthur and Eleanor Sidgwick, *Henry Sidgwick: A Memoir* (London and New York, 1904), pp. 193–94. Cf. R. H. Hutton, "Amiel and Clough," *Criticisms on Contemporary Thought and Thinkers* (2 vols. London and New York, 1900), *1*, 205: "The whole drift of his *Amours de Voyage* was to show that fidelity to the intellectual vision is inconsistent with the class of connections into which the sentiments of a tender heart bring men." I do not agree, however, that this is "the *whole* drift" of the poem, or even the whole scope of the treatment of love.

24. For Clough, see *Correspondence*, *1*, 300 (where he uses the quoted phrase), 301; also above, p. 45.

25. Arnold's "Tristram and Iseult," III, 134, and "Switzerland," Poem 4, 14–17. A. T. Lyttelton, "The Poetry of Doubt: Arnold and Clough," *Living Age*, *137* (1878), 413, remarked that "Switzerland" was "the record of the struggle between the fascination of love and the soul which shrinks from love because it would be self-contained,"

The imagery of descending from a "starry height" to the life of emotion reappears in his most ambitious discussion of the subject, "The New Sirens." Here the poet, speaking for artists and thinkers, addresses the sirens of a new, *romantic* love:

> From the dragon-warder'd fountains
> Where the springs of knowledge are,
> From the watchers on the mountains,
> And the bright and morning star;
> We are exiles, we are falling,
> We have lost them at your call—
> O ye false ones, at your calling
> Seeking ceiled chambers and a palace-hall!
>
> (33–40)

But their call, if false, is beautifully calculated to appeal to the weary intellectual, sick of doubt and longing for "life":

> "Come," you say, "opinion trembles,
> Judgment shifts, convictions go;
> Life dries up, the heart dissembles—
> Only, what we feel, we know.
> Hath your wisdom felt emotions?
> Will it weep our burning tears?
> Hath it drunk of our love-potions
> Crowning moments with the wealth of years?"
>
> (81–88)

Clough read "The New Sirens" in March 1849. A few weeks later he was at Rome, starting to write a poem centering on the same theme but in another form.[26]

---

and he saw in "Switzerland" and "Faded Leaves" the effort "to preserve to the soul its calmness and self-possession." Arnold was certainly influenced by Lucretius, *De rerum naturae,* Book IV, and probably Clough was too.

26. Clough also read Arnold's explanation of the poem (Arnold, *Letters to Clough,* pp. 105–07), where a key passage addressing the sirens (lines 139–54) was paraphrased: "Do your thoughts revert to that life of the spirit to which, like me, you were once attracted, but which, finding it hard and solitary, you soon abandoned for the vehement emotional life of passion as 'the new Sirens'?"

THE INTELLECTUAL IN LOVE 143

The difference between a philosophical allegory and a piece of psychological realism meant a crucial difference in treatment. Where Arnold presented the polarities in broad terms and static relationship, and argued the case for wisdom, Clough wanted to follow the changing complexities of a developing situation. He had, therefore, to emphasize the wavering balance between the attractions of love and the resistance of the rational mind; he had to suggest, as we have seen, that the intellectual life itself was not ideal and that love was something if not everything (he had, that is, to be skeptical also of the dedication to knowledge); and, at the same time, he had to carry forward the other aspects of character and setting. His achieved success in so hard an assignment is a measure of his great gift for synthesis.

In Canto II, the major focus is on war and heroism, or anti-heroism; but near the end, when Claude shifts his attention to Mary, we see that his attachment has strengthened because she possesses two characteristics essential for its growth:

> Oh, rare gift,
> Rare felicity, this! she can talk in a rational way, can
> Speak upon subjects that really are matters of mind and of
>   thinking,
> Yet in perfection retain her simplicity; never, one moment,
> Never, however you urge it, however you tempt her,
>   consents to
> Step from ideas and fancies and loving sensations to those
>   vain
> Conscious understandings that vex the minds of man-kind.
>   (II, 255–61)

Her refusal to insist on any personal, intimate "understanding" is enormously reassuring to Claude.[27] And after admitting that every moment in her "exquisite presence" is "bliss," his reaffirmation of intellectual values, in a context of imagining she dislikes him, sounds superior and defensive:

---

27. This reading is confirmed in Canto III, 203–06.

> It is an easier matter for us contemplative creatures,
> Us, upon whom the pressure of action is laid so lightly;
> We, discontented indeed with things in particular, idle,
> Sickly, complaining, by faith in the vision of things in general
> Manage to hold on our way without, like others around us,
> Seizing the nearest arm to comfort, help, and support us.
>
> (II, 309–14)

But for all that, he seizes the chance to escort the Trevellyns to Florence in order "not to lose her" (II, 291); and his answer to Eustace's question about his being in love is measured and precise: "I do not think so, exactly" (II, 265). One step more and he *will* think so, barely.

That step is taken in Canto III, where the major theme emerges to dominate the action, and the long debate culminates, after a series of advances and retreats, in the decision to propose. The dialogue of the mind with itself begins with Claude's asking whether the grain would sprout in the furrow

> Could it compare, and reflect, and examine one thing with another?
> Would it endure to accomplish the round of its natural functions,
> Were it endowed with a sense of the general scheme of existence?
>
> (III, 44–46)

But the implied negative is immediately questioned, as he remembers his passage from Marseilles to Civita Vecchia—and also his previous use of the sea as symbol:

> Standing, uplifted, alone on the heaving poop of the vessel,
> Looking around on the waste of the rushing incurious billows,
> "This is Nature," I said: "we are born as it were from her waters,
> Over her billows that buffet and beat us, her offspring uncared-for,
> Casting one single regard of a painful victorious knowledge,

> Into her billows that buffet and beat us we sink and are
>   swallowed."
> This was the sense in my soul, as I swayed with the poop
>   of the steamer;
> And as unthinking I sat in the hall of the famed Ariadne,
> Lo, it looked at me there from the face of a Triton in marble.
>
> (III, 49–57)

The Triton was a sea-deity with the body of a man above the waist (with the mind of a man) and of a dolphin below the waist (with the instincts of an animal). Though the note of triumph is there, common sense—and desire?—draw a different conclusion. "Let us not talk of growth," Claude decides; "we are still in our Aqueous Ages," still, that is to say, natural beings living for the most part in the water from which we came, and out of which we have emerged ("grown") only slightly, painfully, into a higher realm of rational thought and perspective. It is much too soon for man to think of abandoning the natural life. That is "the simpler thought," he concludes, referring to the previous paragraph with its opposite lesson, "and I can believe it the truer." But the "can" reduces the conviction well short of, "and I believe it the truer."

Letter iv is a variation on the same theme. The blossom of knowledge at the top of the Tree of Life in the Garden is forever flowering, flowering alone and decaying, "needless, unfruitful"; and so,

> Ye that extrude from the ocean your helpless faces,
> Ye over stormy seas leading long and dreary processions,
> Ye, too, brood of the wind, whose coming is whence we discern
>   not,
> Making your nest on the wave, and your bed on the crested
>   billow,
> Skimming rough waters, and crowding wet sands that the tide
>   shall return to,
> Cormorants, ducks, and gulls, fill ye my imagination!
> Let us not talk of growth; we are still in our Aqueous Ages.
>
> (III, 91–97)

But the adjectives ("helpless," "stormy," "long and dreary") betray a want of enthusiasm. This may be capitulation; it is hardly conversion. And it is immediately challenged from another quarter. The unromantic skeptic starts to talk about amative selection, picking up an earlier question (asked in Canto I, 225-26):

> Juxtaposition, in fine; and what is juxtaposition?
> Look you, we travel along in the railway-carriage, or steamer,
> And *pour passer le temps,* till the tedious journey be ended,
> Lay aside paper or book, to talk with the girl that is next one;
> And, *pour passer le temps,* with the terminus all but in
>   prospect,
> Talk of eternal ties and marriages made in heaven.
>   Ah, did we really accept with a perfect heart the illusion!
> Ah, did we really believe that the Present indeed is the
>   Only!
> Or through all transmutation, all shock and convulsion of
>   passion,
> Feel we could carry undimmed, unextinguished, the light
>   of our knowledge!
>
>   (III, 107-16)

Both alternatives being impossible, only rather specious reasons can be found to justify commitments: that one can look forward, at least, to escaping at death and living in another type of ocean, a divine ocean; that as limited beings we can scarcely hope "to attain upon earth to an Actual Abstract," and should leave contemplation to God, "to His hands knowledge confiding," sure that He intends us to eat "the victual that He has provided." But this admission is suddenly met with sarcasm, as Claude remembers his initial question and thinks of quite a different god, a pagan idol of love and marriage:

> Allah is great, no doubt, and Juxtaposition his prophet.[28]

---

28. Cf. Clough's letter to Blanche Smith, Dec. 31, 1851, now at the Bodleian Library: "Here in this dim deceitful misty moonshiny night-time of existence we grope about & run up against each other; & peer blindly but enquiringly into strange faces, and sooner or later (for comfort's sake for the night is cold, you see, & dreary) clasp hands & make vows & choose, & keep together—& withdraw again sometimes & wrench away hands, & seize others & do we know not what."

THE INTELLECTUAL IN LOVE 147

In the next letters the antiromanticism is more pronounced, and its ultimate source is perhaps revealed. Claude turns from juxtaposition to affinities, but only to those which the empathy of imagination can provide. In this way he "can be and become" anything he meets with, ox or ass, dog or kitten. Then he can feel "a common, though latent vitality" even in rocks and trees; and so, "to escape from our strivings, mistakings, misgrowths, and perversions" (the anti-intellectual connotation is evoked by recalling the previous letters on growth), he

> Fain could demand to return to that perfect and
> primitive silence,
> Fain be enfolded and fixed, as of old, in their
> rigid embraces.
> (III, 171–72)

In that clasp of Nature he would be safe. But what of less rigid and warmer embraces? Those, too, he can contemplate with pleasure— almost:

> And as I walk on my way, I behold them consorting
> and coupling;
> Faithful it seemeth, and fond, very fond, very
> probably faithful;
> All as I go on my way, with a pleasure sincere and
> unmingled.
> Life is beautiful, Eustace, entrancing, enchanting to look at;
> As are the streets of a city we pace while the carriage
> is changing,
> As is a chamber filled-in with harmonious, exquisite pictures,
> Even so beautiful Earth; and could we eliminate only
> This vile hungering impulse, this demon within us of craving,
> Life were beatitude, living a perfect divine satisfaction.
> (III, 173–81)

No wonder Claude thinks immediately of *"Mild monastic faces in quiet collegiate cloisters,"* which he calls, significantly, a "celibatarian phrase" (the cloisters of Oxford were still all male in 1849);

and a moment later he thinks also of "the calm and composure and gentle abstraction that reign" there.

So oriented, he is naturally alarmed when Eustace mentions that "terrible word, Obligation." No, Mary has bound him to nothing. No, he protests, with a touch of guilt,

> when I came, with mean fears in my soul, with a semi-performance
> At the first step breaking down in its pitiful rôle of evasion,
> When to shuffle I came, to compromise, not meet, engagements,
> Lo, with her calm eyes there she met me and knew nothing of it,—
> Stood unexpecting, unconscious. *She* spoke not of obligations, Knew not of debt;
>
> (III, 201–06)

at which point, her attractions reviving, he cries out in a new reversal of feeling (letter x), "*Hang* this thinking, at last! what good is it? oh, and what evil!" Would that he might lie down, contented and mute, "with the beasts of the field, my brothers" (brothers not now by force of empathy but of natural instinct, brothers too of "cormorants, ducks, and gulls") and, he adds with a smile, "eat grass, like Nebuchadnezzar." But the smile does not undercut the seriousness. The long debate is over, replaced in the next letter (xi) by a lovely description of Tibur and the Sabine Valley. In the last letter (xiii) Claude has given up even the beauties of nature in order to see "something better" at Florence (III, 290).

In Canto IV, the search begins on a note of almost frantic eagerness which shows that now at long last Claude is in love, not passionately (that would be impossible) but genuinely. "*Weariness welcome*," he cries out,

> and labour, wherever it be, if at last it
> Bring me in mountain or plain into the sight of my love.
>
> (IV, 9–10)

Reaching Florence and finding her gone, he rushes on,

> sick of the statues and pictures!—

THE INTELLECTUAL IN LOVE 149

> No, to Bologna, Parma, Piacenza, Lodi, and Milan,
> Off go we to-night,—and the Venus go to the Devil!
>
> (IV, 16–18)

—in favor of a real one. This is downright impetuous for "Mr. Claude"; and a moment later, for the first time in the poem, he celebrates the joys of being, not a "childless and bachelor uncle," but a bridegroom and husband and father—and in the water imagery that symbolizes the natural life of emotion:

> There is a tide, at least, in the *love* affairs of mortals,
> Which, when taken at flood, leads on to the happiest fortune,—
> Leads to the marriage-morn and the orange-flowers and the altar,
> And the long lawful line of crowned joys to crowned joys
>   succeeding.—
> Ah, it has ebbed with me! Ye gods, and when it was flowing,
> Pitiful fool that I was, to stand fiddle-faddling in that way!
>
> (IV, 33–38)

The reference to "ebbing" is a little ominous, but when he misses the trail at Bellaggio, he hurries back to Florence to get fresh directions, certain that Mary is calling him to join her—"Ah, could I hear her call! could I catch the glimpse of her raiment!" (IV, 50).

This, indeed, is but one in a series of mischances, beginning with Georgiana's attempt to help things along by persuading Vernon to ask Claude about his intentions. Claude thought the question came from Mary, was astounded and horrified, and excused himself at once from joining the party for the trip to Florence. By the time he learned the truth, through Mary's friend Miss Roper, and got hold of horses (after twice failing to do so because a war happened to be going on), he reached Florence after the Trevellyns had gone. He missed them at Milan because they "left in a hurry"; missed them at Como because the *cameriere* lost the letter Mary had left for him; missed them at Bellaggio because after they left the hotel, "on the very way to the steamer," they changed their plans.[29] Bating a single one of these misses and Claude would have gone on

---

29. Cantos III, 271–82, 291, and IV, 1, 2 and 65, 20, 60–61. Two more mischances are at IV, 52–53, and V, 26; V, 30, 173–75.

to "the marriage-morn and the orange-flowers and the altar." It was that close, and to suppose him incapable of love and frightened of action is to ignore Canto IV and much of V. He was, literally, in the perceptive epithet of his creator, an "unfortunate" hero.[30] But it is also true that if Claude had not been Claude, he would have seized his Roman opportunity or refused to abandon the search.

In the last canto a highly difficult subject is handled with great skill. Clough had not only to forego the advantages of a happy ending but also to court certain criticism for flouting a Victorian imperative. Even his friend Emerson could not forgive him "for the baulking end or no end," and asked: "How can you waste such power on a broken dream? Why lead us up to the tower to tumble us down?" It was true, he confessed, that a few persons liked "this veracity of much preparation to no result," but as for him (and surely for most of Clough's readers), "I hold tis bad enough in life, and inadmissible in poetry." Clough's answer was simply that he "always meant it to be so and began it with the full intention of its ending so";[31] and no one today would question it. Given the combination of character and accident, the outcome is inevitable.

But when Clough laid claim to "some merit" in the conclusion,[32] he meant more than this. He meant, I should think, that even under such adverse circumstances he had succeeded in maintaining the reader's sympathy for Claude. He had exposed his "fool of a hero," piling up a series of rationalizations, most of them ridiculous, to explain away his quitting the search, but he had also brought out the poignant sense of loss for both lovers, and Claude's rededication to the search for knowledge, partly in desperation, though partly with courage and conviction.

The rationalizations begin with the old fear of factitious motivation: *"Action will furnish belief"* he agrees when Eustace argues the pragmatism adopted by Victorian doubters, but he adds at once, "Will that belief be the true one?" In any case, he is "weary of

30. *Correspondence, 1,* 278.
31. Ibid., 2, 548, 551.
32. Ibid., 2, 546.

making inquiries," and "ashamed . . . of asking people about it" (ashamed to have people see a "philosopher" led around by the nose). How ridiculous to sit moping, and trying over and over again to fix her image in his memory. So, let him bear to forget her. "I will not cling to her falsely: Nothing factitious or forced shall impair the old happy relation."[33] And, besides, if I "aspire evermore to the Absolute only," she, too, will somehow be doing the same thing, and therefore

> I shall be thine, O my child, some way, *though I know not in what way.*
> Let me submit to forget her; I must; I already forget her.[34]
> (V, 61–62; my italics)

Indeed, if we meet again, "all might be changed. . . . Or perhaps there was nothing to be changed." Surely fate was against us, and

> Great is Fate, and is best. I believe in Providence *partly.*
> What is ordained is right, and all that happens is ordered.
> *Ah, no, that isn't it.* But yet I retain my conclusion.
> I will go where I am led, and will not dictate to the chances.
> (V, 176–79; my italics)

The phrases I have italicized betray, to say the least, some dissatisfaction with the outcome; and this breaks through to passionate regret and a complete reversal of values. No sooner has he decided to aspire to the Absolute and "submit to forget her" than he cries out:

> Utterly vain is, alas! this attempt at the Absolute,—wholly!
> I, who believed not in her, because I would fain believe
>   nothing,
> Have to believe as I may, with a wilful, unmeaning acceptance.
> I, who refused to enfasten the roots of my floating existence
> In the rich earth, cling now to the hard, naked rock that
>   is left me.—

---

33. Lines 20, 28, 31, 51.
34. Cf. Clough's letter to Blanche Smith written later, in May 1852, *Correspondence*, I, 313, where he says that even though they should now be sundered, they have achieved "an union in some sense lasting, I must believe it, though I know not how."

Ah! she was worthy, Eustace,—and that, indeed,
   is my comfort,—
Worthy a nobler heart than a fool such as I could have given.
                                                    (V, 63–69)

The transformation of imagery is significant: the indifferent soil of the grain in Canto III has now become rich fertile earth, and the broad lofty height of speculation, once so eagerly sought, nothing but a hard, naked rock one must cling to or perish.[35] In that mood, Claude sees himself as a coward slinking from the field: "Courage in me could be only factitious" (V, 84–85). The hope he had once cherished "lies like a sword" in his soul (V, 142–44). If he thinks of immortality, he asks:

Shall we come out of it all, some day, as one does from a tunnel?
Will it be all at once, without our doing or asking,
We shall behold clear day, the trees and meadows about us,
And the faces of friends, and the eyes we loved looking at us?
Who knows? Who can say?
                                                    (V, 181–85)

But once, we remember, he looked forward to immortality as an escape from love into the absolute world of abstraction.[36] The Claude of Canto V is a new and warmer human being.

But he is still dedicated to the life of reason. Finding himself reduced almost to tears by the sound of a barrel organ playing a hymn tune, he wonders if perhaps he was touched in this way by a great truth. He cannot believe it. Any religious assurance based on pure emotion he is certain would be factitious. No, he says,

I will look straight out, see things, not try to evade them;
Fact shall be fact for me, and the Truth the Truth as ever,
Flexible, changeable, vague, and multiform, and doubtful.—
Off, and depart to the void, thou subtle, fanatical tempter!
                                                    (V, 100–04)

Such a vigorous affirmation of principle and such a refusal to pur-

---

35. Cantos III, 40–42, and I, 250–52.
36. Canto III, 117–29.

THE INTELLECTUAL IN LOVE

chase comfort at the cost of intellectual honesty command our respect.

A few moments later, however, as he hears of the fall of Rome and the Republic, counterpointing the collapse of his love affair, Claude is swept again with ennui, this time to the lowest point of weakness and dejection. The gallant Medici has been taken, noble Manara slain, and I—"sit moping and mourning" for Mary and "myself much smaller."

> So plumb I the deeps of depression,
> Daily in deeper, and find no support, no will, no purpose.
> All my old strengths are gone. And yet I shall have to
> do something.
> Ah, the key of our life, that passes all wards, opens
> all locks,
> Is not *I will,* but *I must.* I must,—I must,—and I do it.
> (V, 151–55)

So he goes to Rome, only to find that now "the priests and soldiers possess it," and there is no Mary Trevellyn, and he has no heart for marbles and frescoes. But suddenly the will to live—to think, at any rate—revives. Haply, he says to himself, "I may . . . resume some day my studies"; and with that inner assurance, untouched by any fear of *its* being factitious, he rededicates himself to the intellectual life:

> Not as the Scripture says, is, I think, the fact. Ere our death-day,
> Faith, I think, does pass, and Love; but Knowledge abideth.
> Let us seek Knowledge;—the rest may come and go as it
> happens.
> Knowledge is hard to seek, and harder yet to adhere to.
> Knowledge is painful often; and yet when we know, we are
> happy.
> Seek it, and leave mere Faith and Love to come with the
> chances.
> (V, 197–202)

With irritable blindness Shairp accused the poem of having "no hope, nor strength." Claude had both, and Clough insisted that far from going off "into mere prostration and defeat," his "unfortunate fool of a hero" achieved a "final Strength of Mind."[37]

Nevertheless, the poem hardly closes on a note of victory; and there is nothing sentimental about a reader who regrets the outcome even as he praises its artistic rightness. Clough himself called *Amours de Voyage* a "tragi-comedy or comi-tragedy," meaning that something of supreme importance to Claude, and to Mary too, was denied them both by a combination of circumstances.[38] Claude's profound doubt, even of love, his fear of the factitious, his feeling of shame about sex, the long chain of mischances that prevented him from finding Mary, and his dedication to the intellectual life, all unite to thwart the full growth of his nature, and therefore of hers. In the outcome we feel a deep sense of waste. Two lives that might have been enriched are left poorer and narrower. It must often be so, however rarely recorded in art. In Mary's final letter to Miss Roper we catch the aching awareness of a crucial opportunity irrevocably lost:

> You have heard nothing; of course, I know you can have
> heard nothing.
> Ah, well, more than once I have broken my purpose, and
> sometimes,
> Only too often, have looked for the little lake-steamer
> to bring him.
> But it is only fancy,—I do not really expect it.
> Oh, and you see I know so exactly how he would take it:
> Finding the chances prevail against meeting again, he
> would banish
> Forthwith every thought of the poor little possible hope,
> which
> I myself could not help, perhaps, thinking only too much of;
> He would resign himself, and go. I see it exactly.

---

37. *Correspondence, 1,* 275, 278. Claude's description of knowledge in lines 200–01 is itself sufficient to dispose of the charge that he was a dilettante.
38. Ibid., 2, 546.

So I also submit, although in a different manner.
Can you not really come? We go very shortly to England.

(V, 206–16)

"So I also submit." The submission to a fate that might have been avoided and yet never is, is Clough's deepest insight into human experience. It is the central theme of *Dipsychus*.

6

DIPSYCHUS

WHEN *Dipsychus* WAS FIRST PUBLISHED in the *Letters and Remains* of 1865, an able critic in *Macmillan's Magazine* made a confident prediction. In the past, he said, Clough had been spoken of as the author of *The Bothie,* but "henceforth, he will be known as the author of 'Dipsychus,' and of some lyrics of unsurpassable beauty, where deep reflection meets with a pathetic and musical utterance."[1] It *should* have been so (though one would want the *Amours de Voyage* to be included in any list of his major work), but it has *not* been so. *Dipsychus* is Clough's masterpiece, but it remains unread and its achievement unrecognized.

This neglect is partly explained by its form. In unwelcome contrast with the other narratives, it has almost no plot; and many of the scenes—even sections within scenes—are so discrete that at first it seems impossible to bring them together into a coherent whole. Like J. A. Symonds, one cannot make out whether *Dipsychus* "is very shallow or very profound, whether it means almost nothing or is the cream of everything."[2] But the modern reader, expecting to study a difficult poem and accustomed to unexplained relationships, will accept the initial hazard. In another sense of the term, the form may put one off by its very severity. From start to finish *Dipsychus* is simply a series of dialogues between only two characters in which nothing happens except a swim at the Lido and a ride in a gondola. By comparison, the varied play of action and character in the two previous narratives, and in Goethe's *Faust,* which Clough was "imitating," makes them more immedi-

---

1. *Macmillan's Magazine, 15* (1866), 89. The critic was William Henry Smith (above, Chap. 2, n. 22).
2. *Letters and Papers,* ed. H. F. Brown (New York, 1923), p. 18.

ately appealing, though the stringent focus on the struggle between the protagonists has its own impact.

Furthermore, the text of the poem, because it was never shaped into final form, has two conspicuous flaws. After the reader finishes the play, he is suddenly faced with six pages called "Dipsychus Continued," written at a later time when Clough had lost hold of the original creative mood. Symonds' comment is definitive:

> One is surprised at the commonplace and rather vulgar *dénouement* which the poet seems to have designed. It contrasts so strangely with the elevated and subtle tone of the first part, and forms so distinct a bathos or anti-climax, that we are disposed to abandon any attempt at its interpretation, believing that in its present mutilated state it cannot be fairly criticised, and to confine our attention to the first part.[3]

This perceptive statement is marred, however, by the implication, which Symonds had earlier made explicit, that the continuation was "the *second part* of 'Dipsychus.' " Mrs. Clough not only gave it the title of "Dipsychus Continued: *A Fragment*" and called it "a sketch for a continuation of 'Dipsychus,' written much later," but specifically said that it was *"in no sense a second part."*[4] Nevertheless, Sidgwick and other critics have repeated Symonds' opinion, and the placing of the continuation right after the last scene (even by the 1951 editors) is still persuading innocent readers to consider it an integral part of the poem, and thus to let it influence their final impression.

The second flaw is more serious because it cannot be handled, like the first, by an appeal to contrary evidence. In printing the poem from the various drafts and revisions which Clough had made, the editors of both the editions (1865 and 1951) had to determine the text. For the most part the final wording was clear, but they could not discover the intended order of Scenes IV–VII. No matter what the arrangement, the interconnections are loose, so

---

3. *Last and First*, pp. 113–14.
4. *Letters and Remains*, pp. 146, 206. The italics are mine. Lady Chorley, *Clough*, pp. 264–65, has shown that it was very probably written in America, and therefore between Dec. 1852 and June 1853. The poem was largely composed at Venice in 1850.

that the development of the action between Scenes III and VIII is less rigorous than it should be. This is not a serious disability, but it means that as *Dipsychus* stands, lacking Clough's final revision, the poem must be judged inferior to *The Bothie* or *Amours de Voyage* as a formal work of art.[5]

In range and relevance of perception, *Dipsychus* surpasses them both, and its central theme is more original and profound. The somewhat remote or special character of experience in the earlier narratives is gone, and Dipsychus—or rather Dipsychus and the Spirit together—take on a representative quality unattained by Hewson or Claude. The treatment of religion and love, of society and the professions, above all of the individual struggling to determine the shape of his own life, bear more closely on the lives of thinking men. These topics are explored in a variety of moods and styles that give the poem the complexity of modern experience: philosophic meditation, social satire (sometimes witty, sometimes sardonic), lyrical outbursts of joy or grief, comedy that is humorous or ironic, and at the end the note of tragedy. But what is most exciting is suggested by Sidgwick's defense of Clough from the charge of failure:

> Clough's literary originality and importance lies precisely in what unfitted him for practical success. He was overweighted with certain impulses, felt certain feelings with a too absorbing and prolonged intensity; but the impulses were noble, at least an "infirmity of noble minds"; they are incident to most fine natures at a certain stage of their development, and generally are not repressed without a certain sense of loss and sacrifice. This phase of feeling is worthy of being worthily expressed.[6]

The intellectual passion for truth and the moral passion for personal integrity and dedicated action can hardly survive the transition from the state of youth, when young men—many young

---

5. In my opinion the arrangement adopted by the 1951 editors is the most satisfactory, and barring their casual treatment of scene IIA, where they have printed "a selection of lines" which seems to them "to preserve the general sense and the best poetry" (*Poems*, p. 533), their text of the poem is a good one.

6. *Miscellaneous Essays*, p. 62.

men—see visions, to the conventional mores and self-centered goals of adult life, social and professional. The struggle to maintain them and their ultimate defeat is the theme of *Dipsychus*. Nowhere else in English poetry, I think, has it been explored with such power and subtlety.

1. Lyric Drama

The poem is a portrait of Dipsychus, indeed a self-portrait, in a series of soliloquies. (There are dialogues with the Spirit, but the Spirit is a voice from his own consciousness.) In form, therefore, it is similar to Arnold's "Empedocles on Etna," begun a year earlier and quite possibly active in Clough's creative mind. For besides being their authors' major efforts to "analyse the modern situation in its true *blankness* and *barrenness*," they are both dialogues of the mind with itself.[7] Or, in another terminology, they are monodramas in which only one person is unmistakably real and the other figures and incidents exist merely as occasions for self-expression or as a means of objectifying what is essentially an internal action. In this sense, the lyric drama is simply an expanded version of the dramatic ode developed by the Romantics to embody subjective experience. In both cases the movement of mind is progressive. It is by and through a process of introspective meditation, combining the setting with autobiography and abstract ideas (religious, social, and moral), that the protagonist reaches in the end a fresh or deepened understanding of himself—of who he is and what he believes and how he is to live.[8] In the course of both poems, Empedocles and Dipsychus come to see the ultimate pattern of their lives. They discover through a series of self-revelations the necessity, respectively, to commit suicide and to submit. Indeed, one could say that the more "romantic" Empedocles chooses death in order to avoid submission.[9]

In the pattern of Clough's life, *Dipsychus* (1850) represents a

---

7. Arnold, *Letters to Clough*, p. 126, and preface to *Poems* (1853), opening paragraph.
8. I am indebted here to Robert Langbaum, *The Poetry of Experience* (New York, 1957), pp. 63–64, 191, 199.
9. See my "Arnold's 'Empedocles on Etna,'" *Victorian Studies*, *1* (1958), 326–31.

return to the subjective poetry of his earlier years and a reversal of the direction adopted in *The Bothie* (1848) and partly followed in *Amours de Voyage* (1849). But Claude's soliloquies in Rome point forward to those of Dipsychus in Venice a year later, and the three poems may be viewed as a progressive movement from objective to subjective art—or, in temper of mind, from gaiety, to ennui, to something like despair. That would parallel Clough's own history from 1848 to 1850. Certainly in the summer of 1850 he was perhaps more introverted and depressed than he had ever been before. "*I* could have gone cracked at times last year with one thing or another," he said in 1851, and some of the things are known. He was past thirty and still unmarried, much against his desire, and having found University Hall as intolerant as the cloisters of Oxford and pedagogy a "crambe repetita" of doubtful use, he was preoccupied and baffled by the question of what he was to do and the kind of life he was to lead—or have to lead.[10]

This is not to say that Dipsychus *is* Clough, or that the poem is autobiography. On a conscious level the Romantic and Victorian poets imagined characters more or less like themselves in order to embody more or less of their own experience. They cast themselves in dramatic roles and created a series of personae. Anne Clough wished that "we knew more about the time when Dipsychus was written" (she meant of Clough at the time when *Dipsychus* was written).[11] But I doubt if that would help. We know enough now to understand why he wrote a lyric drama in which youthful ideals were subjected to the pressure of common sense and the way of the world. Beyond that we have to examine not the poet but the personae—both of them, Dipsychus and the Spirit.

2. *Dipsychus*

Like Empedocles, Dipsychus is the modern, highly educated intellectual, with the same deep desire to preserve a kind of high integrity from contamination, whether by society or the exigencies of human existence. But Empedocles is a philosopher preaching

---

10. *Correspondence, 1*, 274, 278–79, 290. Arnold's *Letters to Clough,* pp. 85, 130, reflect Clough's indecision.
11. MS. life of her brother (above, Chap. 2, n. 74).

a new creed, largely Stoic, partly Epicurean, to take the place of a superstitious religion, and a poet struggling against the destructive force of intellectualism. Dipsychus is simply an older and more introspective Claude, concerned like him with the problem of independence or submission, only in a wider and more crucial area than love, and with Claude's double awareness intensified and made central to the character. Dipsychus is Di-psychus, the man of two minds or two natures, the "double self."

It might seem at first that one self was the other character in the poem, the Spirit, especially since there are lines which suggest that he may be, or can be, a segment of Dipsychus's personality.[12] But apart from the verbal difficulty of this interpretation, requiring "the two-natured man" to talk with his other nature, the text leaves no doubt, I think, that Clough meant Dipsychus himself to be two-psychied. As the latter is arguing the contrary claims of the active and the contemplative life, in what is an inner debate, he suddenly remarks:

> To thine own self be true, the wise man says.
> Are then my fears myself? O double self!
> And I untrue to both.
>
> (X, 62–64)

This is not to suggest that he is divided between the active and the contemplative selves, or between any other polarity. Dipsychus, to speak more strictly, is the double-minded personality, pulled in opposite directions or seeing opposite sides to every question, whether it be love, religion, or the problem of action. In Scene IIA, for example, the primary tension is not between himself and the Spirit, but between his conscience and his sexual impulses:

> many and many a time my foolish foot
> O'ertreading the dim sill, spite of itself
> And spite of me, instinctively fell back.
>
> . . .
>
> Backed, and refused my bidding.
>
> (IIA, 64–66, 72)

---

12. See below, p. 171.

It is quite true that the Spirit is entirely sympathetic with "me," and is ready enough to support the claims of lust and sneer at such ridiculous scruples. But the conflict is within Dipsychus himself, and we feel the marked difference between his sensual passion and the cool cynicism of the Spirit. Scene III begins with Dipsychus's commentary: "Alas, how quietly [we slide]

> Out of our better into our worse selves,
> Out of a true world which our reason knew
> Into a false world which our fancies make.
>
> (III, 3-5)

Though the double-mindedness is a trait of character and not a polar opposite, in most cases the two points of view fall into two categories, and Clough's hero has something of the dual personality of Goethe's Faust. The latter explains to Wagner:

> Two souls, alas, cohabit in my breast,
> A contract one of them desires to sever.
> The one like a rough lover clings
> To the world with the tentacles of its senses;
> The other lifts itself to Elysian Fields
> Out of the mist on powerful wings.[13]

Since Dipsychus was first called Faustulus (and the Spirit Mephistopheles), the conception of his character may have had its source in this speech. Clough, however, made his hero an idealist (conceived of not as a dreamer but as a man striving to live by higher values than those of the world), but an idealist well aware of certain earthy instincts and worldly standards in himself which might have their own validity. This awareness keeps the character human and provides an enemy within the gates prepared to welcome the Spirit.

Through the first part (Scenes I–VII) the idealist is conspicuous, stepping in "to arrest my ingress" at the door of the prostitute; exalting "the sweet domestic bonds, the matrimonial sanctities"; condemning the hypocrisies of society, and its dependence on

---

13. Part I, lines 764–69, in the translation by Louis MacNeice (New York, 1951), p. 40.

"hungry brothers" for gaieties and luxuries; refusing in the spirit of the Gospel to fight a duel; questioning the Utopian dream of life; and reacting with dismay to the lawlessness of a world without God. In the second part (Scenes VIII–XIII) he sets up a life of "noble deeds" and, with reservations, one of contemplation in opposition to the usual goals of men. But being a dipsychus, he is able to feel the attractions, and to recognize the wisdom, of the world he condemns.

3. *The Spirit*

What I take to be the shaping plan of the poem occurs in a letter Clough published in the *Balance* for February 13, 1846. There he said:

> The relation in which the moral and spiritual element stands, in our age, to the business-like and economic, reminds one of a traveller on the continent, who, much to his discontent, and not without continual but futile interference, is yet obliged, by his ignorance of language and customs and character, to surrender the conduct of his journey to an experienced and faithful, but somewhat disreputable and covetous-minded companion.

He then went on to define "the moral and spiritual element" in phrases that suggest the idealism of his hero: "Simplicity, a freedom from display, a quiet homely life, we, indeed, believe to be the healthiest for all men—'plain living and high thinking.' "[14] Four years later when *Dipsychus* was written and Clough himself was personally involved, the tension between the elements had increased, and the ambivalent nature of the companion was more sharply conceived.

On the disreputable side the Spirit is the *homme moyen sensuel*, entirely free of moral principles, taking things as he finds them and not bothering his head about fine distinctions of right and wrong, or highfalutin questions about the reality of God or the nature of truth:

---

14. Page 50. For Clough's authorship, see *Correspondence, 1*, 169.

> Enjoy the minute,
> And the substantial blessings in it;
> Ices, *par exemple;* evening air;
> Company, and this handsome square;
> Some pretty faces here and there;
> Music! Up, up; it isn't fit
> With beggars here on steps to sit.
> Up—to the café! Take a chair
> And join the wiser idlers there.
>
> (I, 50–58)

For such a life,

> *Orandum est,* one perfect prayer
> For *savoir-vivre, savoir-faire.*
>
> (VIII, 71–72)

But *savoir-penser* is silly: indeed, it is "useless trying to explain things," religious or profane. Best to trust only one's "business-wits." The worldly spirit, scornful of both reason and imagination, relies on common sense.[15]

It tells one, first and last, to conform: to believe what everybody believes and do what everybody does—everybody that *is* anybody. To be sincere at the cost of being unconventional would be stupid or quixotic:

> Men's business-wits the only sane things,
> These and compliance are the main things.
>
> (VII, 45–46)

Skepticism and moral neutrality make the hypocrisy of conformity natural and easy.

Acting on these assumptions, the Spirit is the tempter, bent on persuading Dipsychus to take his pleasure where he will, irrespective of religious sanctions or social justice, and to abandon the life of lonely contemplation for a smart marriage and a successful ca-

---

15. The last phrases quoted are in Scene VII, 43–45. For my account of the Spirit, I am partly indebted to W. H. Hudson's fine essay on Clough's thought in *Studies in Interpretation,* pp. 124–25.

THE SPIRIT

reer—in a word, to sell his youthful idealism for a mess of worldly pottage. The Spirit even describes himself as

> This worldly fiend that follows you about,
> This compound of convention and impiety,
> This mongrel of uncleanness and propriety.
>
> (XI, 48–50)

He means, "as you would say," but he does not deny it; he only claims that he, too, has his *"grandes manières"* and can speak "high sentiment"—of what kind we can imagine.

In this act of branding himself, the Spirit shows that he is also a compound of candor and self-perception, and our judgment is suddenly complicated. Indeed, the Spirit is so winning in some respects, and comes so close to capturing the role of hero—like Milton's Satan—that he almost persuades us to forget his real character. We come to feel, as Clough told his uncle, that "perhaps he wasn't a devil after all. That's the beauty of the poem; nobody can say." The qualification of "perhaps" is significant, for the Spirit *is*, at heart, an evil spirit, "hateful unto God."[16] But the remark justifies our ambivalent impression.

Being a man of the world, the Spirit has the manners of a gentleman. He is affable, urbane, superbly poised, and completely conservative in taste and politics. " 'Tis sad," he says,

> to what democracy is leading;
> Give me your Eighteenth Century for high breeding;
>
> (III, 101–02)

and also, he might have added, for neoclassical art. In these and other respects he reminds us of Clough's uncle, who is later to remark that much of what the Spirit said was "sensible enough."[17] Both are educated men and critics of poetry; and the Spirit can quote not only Scripture, as he should, but Béranger, Butler, and Juvenal, and refer brightly to Strauss or to Kant's "Antinomies of

---

16. In the Epilogue, *Poems,* p. 294, and Scene XIII, 71.
17. Epilogue, *Poems,* p. 294. For their anti-Romantic and neoclassical taste, see the Prologue, *Poems,* p. 222; Scenes IV, 204–23, and XI, 146–49.

the Moral Sense." He has a sense of humor that keeps the poem lively, and a sharp satiric wit that is by no means always pointed, not directly at least, against idealistic attitudes. Its purpose is sometimes to expose the underside of things (to show things "as they are," as Byron said of a similar poem called *Don Juan*), or to look at human nature in the dry light of common sense.[18] This may lead to a cynical or cranky reduction of the ideal to the selfish or stupid, as it sometimes does, but it can also be an honest and shrewd recognition of what idealism ignores.

In Scene V the Spirit has just finished a characteristic plea for religious conformity (" 'Tis proper once a year or so to do the civil thing and show") when he sings a famous lyric:

> "There is no God," the wicked saith,
>   "And truly it's a blessing,
> For what he might have done with us
>   It's better only guessing."
>
> "There is no God," a youngster thinks,
>   "Or really, if there may be,
> He surely didn't mean a man
>   Always to be a baby."
>
> "There is no God, or if there is,"
>   The tradesman thinks, " 'twere funny
> If he should take it ill in me
>   To make a little money."
>
>   .   .   .
>
> But country folks who live beneath
>   The shadow of the steeple;
> The parson and the parson's wife,
>   And mostly married people;
>
> Youths green and happy in first love,
>   So thankful for illusion;
> And men caught out in what the world
>   Calls guilt, in first confusion;

---

18. The last phrase is in Scene IX, 169–70.

> And almost every one when age,
> Disease, or sorrows strike him,
> Inclines to think there is a God,
> Or something very like Him.
>
> (V, 154-65, 174-85)

Far from being an object of satire, the Spirit is here a satirist himself, striking at the secular motivations of belief—half-belief at that—and unbelief. In a similar way his criticism of Dipsychus, normally redounding to his own discredit, can unexpectedly become valid. When he taunts him for what we ourselves, with all our sympathy for the man and his dilemma (which is our dilemma, too) find simply exasperating—the perpetual self-analysis, the endless search for more and still more pros and cons, the always postponed decision—we dare not say a word.[19]

In short, Clough gave his Spirit the common sense he recognized in the world of action and underscored its neglected value—neglected by the dipsychuses but not by the Robert Walpoles:

> He [Walpole] delighted in clearing young men's minds of cant; that for example of professions of honesty & patriotism, which he called "school-boy flights"; he himself, he said, was "no saint, no reformer, no Spartan. . . ."
>
> The master quality of his mind was common sense. He estimated things very much at their real value: & if he put them a little below the right figure, it was only because he thought that the safer extreme. Confronting the ordinary facts of a very ordinary age & having set himself to carry on the government of the country for the practical best, he took things as they were, or as nearly as he could guess they were, treated men according to their positive actions & not their very doubtful professions & aspirations.

With the change of only a few words, this character of Walpole, from a lecture of Clough's on Swift, could be that of the Spirit. Its

---

19. Scenes X, 97-133, and XI, 107-89.

limitation, however, is not overlooked: its "low-principle," Clough goes on to say, is "gross & offensive."[20]

As we might expect, the Spirit also has the qualities of mind which Clough so much admired in the eighteenth-century philosophers: the stress on "plain matter of fact," the "abhorrence of illusion," the "rejection of the vague, the untested, the merely probable," and the "resolute, upright purpose, as of some transcendental man of business, to go thoroughly into the accounts of the world." These were virtues, Clough said, that claim "more than our attention," claim "our reverence"; and they must not be lost, however precious we consider "Shakespeare's intellectual, or Milton's moral sublimities."[21] It is against this background that the Spirit tells Dipsychus he has been "making mows" too long to the blank sky:

> 'Tis time you learn
> The Second Reverence, for things around.
> Up, then, and go amongst them; don't be timid;
> Look at them quietly a bit: by-and-by
> Respect will come, and healthy appetite.
>
> . . .
>
> Why will you walk about thus with your eyes shut,
> Treating for facts the self-made hues that float
> On tight-pressed pupils, which you know are not facts?
> (XI, 115–19, 124–26)

And he goes on to insist that one must see

> what *is*,
> And will be too, howe'er we blink, and must
> One way or other make itself observed.
>
> (XI, 131–33)

Though he is scarcely fair to Dipsychus, whose "sublimities" he cannot understand, the Spirit is here at his best, taking the highest

---

20. I quote from the copy at Harvard University, bMS. Eng. 1036 (7), fol. 27. Another copy is in the Bodleian. In his review of F. W. Newman's *The Soul*, written in 1849 or 1850, Clough also praises common sense: *Poems and Prose Remains*, *1*, 297, 298, 300.

21. *Prose, 1*, 350–51, or pp. 347–48.

ground available to common sense and striking at the fastidious superiority to "things around" which is the intellectual's vice.

This reverence for facts, in the absence of any higher reverence, makes possible a kind of honesty and candor which is difficult for the idealist to achieve. Since the Spirit does not profess to believe in "spiritual" values, he can frankly celebrate the "low" pleasures the idealist despises, and can even imply that the idealist enjoys them too, behind his disingenuous profession of plain living and high thinking. In *"Spectator ab extra"* the Spirit gayly chants:[22]

> As I sat at the café, I said to myself,
> They may talk as they please about what they call pelf,
> They may sneer as they like about eating and drinking,
> But help it I cannot, I cannot help thinking
>   How pleasant it is to have money, heigh ho!
>   How pleasant it is to have money.
>
> I sit at my table *en grand seigneur,*
> And when I have done, throw a crust to the poor;
> Not only the pleasure, one's self, of good living,
> But also the pleasure of now and then giving.
>   So pleasant it is to have money, heigh ho!
>   So pleasant it is to have money.
>
> . . .
>
> They may talk as they please about what they call pelf,
> And how one ought never to think of one's self,
> And how pleasures of thought surpass eating and drinking—
> My pleasure of thought is the pleasure of thinking
>   How pleasant it is to have money, heigh ho!
>   How pleasant it is to have money.
>   (IV, 130–41, 190–95)

What a miserable standard of value and what a despicable person! And yet, come to think of it, it *is* rather pleasant to have money, as *"they"* ought to admit, and would admit if they were as honest as the Spirit. The satire, we see, is double-edged; and once we sense the right tone, we modify our first reaction. Take the Spirit's

22. For the title, see *Poems,* p. 539.

remarks about the poor. Only a moment before he has seen Dipsychus spoil his pleasure in a gondola ride by thinking of "our slaving brother set behind" and is now flaunting his own superiority to such trivial scruples.

> I drive through the streets, and I care not a d—mn;
> The people they stare, and they ask who I am;
> And if I should chance to run over a cad,
> I can pay for the damage if ever so bad.
>   So pleasant it is to have money, heigh ho!
>   So pleasant it is to have money.
>
> (IV, 148–53)

The raffish tone is unmistakable. We see the raised eyebrow and the flicker of a smile. The Spirit, it appears, is not "entirely serious"; he is being deliberately, almost outrageously facetious.

That one Victorian critic should have called this subtle and complex passage the portrait of a wealthy parvenu "destitute alike of feeling and of education, to whom years of money-making and labour-cheapening, has given a heart of stone and the brain of a calculating-machine," is another illustration of what Clough was up against in his own time.[23] Most Victorian readers were quite unprepared for this ambivalence (villains are black and what they say is bad) or this alliance of levity and seriousness (attitudes are simple and linear: you cannot joke and be in earnest; and you must not joke about serious things).

A more flexible reading, however, must not tempt us to neutrality. After all, "they" *are* right. And we must not forget that for all his wit and satire, his candor and his common sense, the Spirit is compounded of convention and impiety. He is the Enemy. No less than Milton's Satan, who also had his virtues and was plausible enough to impose on Blake and Shelley, he is "The Power of this World! hateful unto God!"[24]

---

23. Samuel Waddington, *Arthur Hugh Clough*, p. 238.
24. Scene XIII, 71. An extreme example of misunderstanding is in H. W. Garrod, "Clough," *Poetry and the Criticism of Life*, p. 125: "The moper and the mocker, Mephistopheles and the Muff, Dullness and the Devil—these are the two souls in one person to which the poem owes its title. All along the line the Devil has the best of the argument, and the sympathy of the reader."

THE SPIRIT

The question of how to conceive of the Spirit (as distinct from defining his character) is raised by Dipsychus himself at the start of the play:

> What is this persecuting voice that haunts me?
> What? whence? of whom? How am I to detect?
> Myself or not myself? My own bad thoughts,
> Or some external agency at work,
> To lead me who knows whither?
>
> (I, 17–21)

Later on he adds some historical facts:

> I have scarce spoken yet to this strange follower
> Whom I picked up—ye great gods, tell me where!
> And when! for I remember such long years,
> And yet he seems new come. I commune with myself;
> He speaks, I hear him, and resume to myself;
> Whate'er I think, he adds his comments to;
> Which yet not interrupts me.
>
> (VIII, 28–34)

From these texts it might appear that the Spirit is simply an alter ego which has been externalized for dramatic purposes. Symonds called him "that second self which usage with the world and the unnumbered centuries of human tradition have imposed upon the soul."[25] It may be so, but there are times when it is all but impossible to suppose that Dipsychus could be speaking. In Scene I we have no trouble identifying the Spirit's philosophy,

> Enjoy the minute,
> And the substantial blessings in it,
>
> (50–51)

with the unideal side of Clough's hero. This could be his "own bad thoughts." But earlier in the scene, after Dipsychus quotes his (that is, Clough's) "Easter Day," with its refrain, "Christ is not risen," the Spirit's comment is his own:

25. *Last and First*, p. 110.

> I thought 'twas in the Bible plain,
> On the third day he rose again.
>
> .   .   .
>
> Having once happened, as we know,
> In Palestine so long ago,
> How should it now at Venice here?
>
> (17–18, 36–38)

No "side" of Dipsychus could speak those words. And though he might have agreed to send his wife and servants to church, as the Spirit later demands, he could not have added, "No infidelity, that's flat."[26] The two psyches of a dipsychus must form a credible personality.

But even so, we need not attribute these speeches to an external agency in the literal sense. If they are not what Dipsychus would say, they are what he can imagine the world would say. The Spirit is best viewed, therefore, as the voice of that worldly philosophy which the double-minded man can hear within himself, sometimes with sympathy, sometimes not; a voice he welcomes by moments (and thus makes his own) or by moments merely listens to, unhappily.

4. Background

Although the conflict represented by Dipsychus vs. the Spirit has a long history, it was aggravated in the later eighteenth century, and still more so in the nineteenth, by a noticeable increase of worldliness, which in turn provoked an increase of asceticism. The growth of naturalism in the age of reason and the emergence of bourgeois society as the dominant culture (upon the arrival of the industrial and democratic revolutions) created an environment that was conspicuously secular. The importance of wealth and social position became more pronounced and more within the reach of men who had the energy and ambition to pursue them. Idleness and luxury on the one hand, and, on the other, intense and some-

---

26. Scene VIII, 60–65.

times unscrupulous competition could not help but breed standards of value and samples of human nature that were ugly.[27]

It was these developments, so patently irreligious, that provoked the Puritan or Evangelical revival. Starting with Wesleyanism and spreading to the "higher classes" under the leadership of William Wilberforce in the 1790s, it succeeded a generation later in influencing the ethics of Thomas Arnold, Carlyle, and J. H. Newman, and through them in establishing the Victorian ideal of moral earnestness. The goal of life became a Christlike character from which not only sinful thoughts but all selfish desires for pleasure, wealth, or success would be rooted out, and the moral will, under the control of a strict or "tender" conscience, would strive for purity of mind and the strict performance of every duty, public and private. At Rugby, Arnold's sermons, denouncing the sins of "selfish extravagance ... idleness ... excess in eating and drinking," and calling for a life of Christian warfare against evils within and without, were constantly presenting his pupils with the supreme choice between two paths—"the path which may lead most readily to worldly wealth and honour, or that in which they may best and safest follow Christ!"[28]

Both paths were conspicuously present in the school, for Rugby was still in the process of being reformed. One boy described by Clough was "tormented by the very obvious contradiction between the evangelical exhortations given him at home [and in the school chapel], and the common school-boy view of life and conduct, distracted between conscientiousness and sociability."[29] If this was not himself, it could have been. Clough felt the same tension at Oxford, for there the two paths were even more conspicuous, and there Arnold's attack on worldliness was reiterated with greater stress by Clough's tutor, and for some years his intimate friend, W. G. Ward. Besides protesting strongly against "the elements of preferment-hunting, of ambition for success, of measuring things

---

27. See *Victorian Frame of Mind*, pp. 191–95, and for the next paragraph, pp. 218–22, 228–31.

28. Thomas Arnold, *Christian Life, Its Course, Its Hindrances, and Its Helps* (5th ed. London, 1849), Sermons XIV, p. 151, and XI, p. 115.

29. *Poems and Prose Remains, 1,* 296, from the review of F. W. Newman's *The Soul,* written in the year of *Dipsychus* or a year earlier.

practically by a worldly standard," he talked of worldliness as a false friend and dangerous foe:

> Worldliness, under the specious appearance of knowledge of the world, or under the plea of common sense, would often obtain a footing which might afterwards grow until the spirit of this world had altogether expelled the Spirit of God. He spoke of it as "the circumambient poison," and waged against it a hearty and uncompromising war.[30]

Even without Clough's Epilogue, with its reference to Dr. Arnold and its description of the religious movement "beginning with Wesleyanism, and culminating at last in Puseyism," we could feel sure that *Dipsychus* was rooted in the Evangelical struggle to check the secular spirit, and that Arnold and Ward had had their share in its conception. But we might have missed the important clue provided by another remark in this Epilogue. Clough has just told his uncle that what is represented "is the conflict between the tender conscience and the world" when he adds, reflecting his new ability in the late forties to view moral earnestness with some detachment, "Now, the over-tender conscience will, of course, exaggerate the wickedness of the world."[31] That exaggeration shows itself mainly in the extreme terms in which the conflict is presented: purity *vs.* contamination. (Ward's reference to the "circumambient poison" of the world is right to the point.)

Clough and Matthew Arnold thought of man as possessing something within himself enormously precious, and at the same time highly delicate and fragile. It may be called the Palladium dwelling high in the mountains, or the "good in the depths of thyself," or "the buried world below"; sometimes it is simply the "individual" or "our individuality"; but most often and perhaps most appropriately, because of its moral and spiritual connotations, it is called the soul. Whatever the name, it must be guarded with intense care from any contact with the world if its purity is not to be contami-

---

30. Wilfrid Ward, *William George Ward and the Oxford Movement* (London and New York, 1889), pp. 69–70.

31. *Poems*, pp. 294, 296. The overtender conscience is also attacked on p. 295, and in the review of F. W. Newman's *The Soul* (above, n. 20), *1*, 300.

nated. We can only "possess our souls in resistance"; one "must subsist in ceaseless opposition . . . that the world win no mastery over him." One should fly all contact, like the scholar-gipsy, lest he be "infected" with the "disease of modern life"; and, as Mrs. Clough remarked in her discussion of *Dipsychus,* any "contact with the world" will mean "the almost necessary loss of ideal purity."[32] This is demonstrated in "Jacob," where the poet had his father, the cotton merchant of Liverpool and Charleston, at the back of his mind.[33] Under the necessity of battling with selfish men, Jacob has had "to lose, almost to shun, the thoughts" he loved, has had to forfeit "the antique pure simplicity . . . the dower of innocence and perfectness of life" which he had inherited, and has been forced to adopt

> the stony-hard resolve,
> The chase, the competition, and the craft
> Which seems to be the poison of our life
> And yet is the condition of our life!

Written a year later in 1851, that is *Dipsychus* in miniature. Exactly ten years earlier the same theme had been treated differently in "Blank Misgivings . . ." (Poem no. X):

> I have seen higher holier things than these,
>   And therefore must to these refuse my heart,
> Yet am I panting for a little ease;
>   I'll take, and so depart.
>
> Ah hold! the heart is prone to fall away,
>   Her high and cherished visions to forget,
> And if thou takest, how wilt thou repay
>   So vast, so dread a debt?
>
> How will the heart, which now thou trustest, then
>   Corrupt, yet in corruption mindful yet,
> Turn with sharp stings upon itself! Again,
>   Bethink thee of the debt!

---

32. Arnold, *Poetical Works,* pp. 236, 235, 199, 437, 261; Clough, *Poems,* pp. 30, 241, 199; Mrs. Clough, in *Letters and Remains,* p. 146.

33. See above, Chap. 2, n. 74.

—Hast thou seen higher holier things than these,
And therefore must to these thy heart refuse?
With the true best, alack, how ill agrees
That best that thou wouldst choose!

This is more confident (the next stanza speaks hopefully of viewing the Summum Pulcrum in heaven), but the same tension is at the core of *Dipsychus*.

No doubt there is something fastidious about the whole attitude. References to "the base crowd" or "men of the crowd" who make life "hideous, and arid, and vile," leave one a little uncomfortable; and though Arnold's remark about himself and Clough "agreeing like two lambs in a world of wolves" is not to be read as solemn statement, it suggests that they could overstate their own virtue as well as the world's wickedness.[34] On the other hand, they were far from being aesthetes. They were simply young men whose upbringing had been "so unworldly, so sound, and so pure,"[35] that they were specially conditioned to see the ugly aspects of society at a moment when these were particularly virulent—to see them clearly and to see them magnified. Both "seeings" were combined in *Dipsychus*.

To say the least, the creative task was formidable. The reader had to be made to see the truth in Dipsychus's view of the world while he realized its exaggeration; he had at once to sympathize with the judgment and to criticize its imbalance. Clough achieved his goal partly, as we shall see, by the imagery of pollution and disease with which Dipsychus describes reality, and partly by a masterly distinction between his hero's estimate of the Spirit and the reader's. Though on one occasion Dipsychus admits he likes the Spirit's sense of humor, it is his only compliment. "Ill spirit," "cursed spirit," "this filthy Belial," this "imperious fiend," "the Power of this World! hateful unto God" represent his attitude fairly enough. But not ours. Because Clough himself had come to recognize at Oxford that the world had its charm—the urbanity,

---

34. Clough, *Dipsychus*, Scene VI, 94; Arnold, "Rugby Chapel," lines 155–58, and his *Letters, 1848–1888*, ed. G. W. E. Russell (2 vols. London and New York, 1901), *1*, 6.

35. Arnold's *Letters*, *1*, 22–23. Cf. *1*, 36, on "a deep desire for truth, purity, and goodness"; *1*, 38, on the " 'pure in heart.' "

the poised detachment that meant freedom from fanaticism, the sophistication of the capital, the value of common sense—he could give the devil his due. And because in the later forties, partly a result of this, partly a cause, he had reacted against "father" Arnold and the rigidities of moral earnestness, and adopted a more liberal and flexible judgment, he *did* give the devil his due. Indeed, on one occasion he allowed the Spirit to defend himself in a tone of voice commanding respect. He was pleading with Dipsychus for "the Second Reverence, for things around," and went on to insist:

> To use the undistorted light of the sun
> Is not a crime; to look straight out upon
> The big plain things that stare one in the face
> Does not contaminate; to see pollutes not
> What one must feel if one won't see.
>
> (XI, 127–31)

5. *The Action: Scenes I–VII*

Though undesignated, the drama falls into two parts. In the first, Scenes I–VII, the question raised by the tension between the protagonists is whether or not Dipsychus is to adopt the standards of the world and the conduct they condone or require. His moral dilemma is centered in turn on sensuality, "good society," the aesthetic dream, religious skepticism, the fighting of duels, and religious conformity. In the second part, Scenes VIII–XIII, the question is whether Dipsychus is to adopt a worldly vocation and devote his life, not to noble deeds or to study and art, but to a professional career. The second question is simply a special case of the first, since by worldly standards noble deeds and intellectual pursuits are dubious. The Spirit's chant in Scene X applies, therefore, to both parts:

> Submit, submit!
> For tell me then, in earth's great laws
> Have you found any saving clause,
> Exemption special granted you
> From doing what the rest must do?
>
> . . .

> 'Tis Common Sense and human wit
> Can find no higher name than it.
> Submit, submit!
>
> (X, 163–67, 192–94)

One aspect of this conflict between independence and submission is given special emphasis: the preservation or the loss of purity.

What may be called the first movement of the poem, Scenes I–IIA, opens with Dipsychus realizing that Venice is no different from the Naples he described (Clough described) last year on Easter Day. He repeats in agonized tones:

> "Through the great sinful streets of Naples as I past,
> With fiercer heat than flamed above my head
> My heart was hot within; the fire burnt, and at last
> My brain was lightened when my tongue had said,
>   Christ is not risen!"

At this point he is interrupted:

> *Spirit*
> Christ is not risen? Oh indeed!
> Wasn't aware that was your creed.
>   *Dipsychus*
> So it goes on. Too lengthy to repeat—
> "Christ is not risen."
>   *Spirit*
> Dear, how odd!
> He'll tell us next there is no God.
> I thought 'twas in the Bible plain,
> On the third day he rose again.
>   *Dipsychus*
> Ashes to Ashes, Dust to Dust;
> As of the Unjust also of the Just—
>   Yea, of that Just One too!
>
> (I, 7–21)

THE ACTION: SCENES I-VII   179

The Spirit's jaunty wit and empty profession of faith clash with striking incongruity against the solemn, momentous statements of Dipsychus. The battle could not have been joined more dramatically.

The subject of these scenes, however, is not religion but the "sinful streets" and the most elemental of moral dilemmas. Dipsychus is tempted to spend the night with one of the "Venetian pets" he sees in the Public Garden, a desire he has often felt before but never dared indulge. At first the Spirit, playing the traditional role of tempter, adopts the obvious strategy:

> 'Tis here, I see, the custom too
> For damsels eager to be lovered
> To go about with arms uncovered;
> And doubtless there's a special charm
> In looking at a well-shaped arm.
> In Paris, I was saying—
>
> (II, 49–54)

to which Dipsychus answers with a passionate invocation to the "clear stars above" to "steep my brain in your essential purity," and to the great Alps, seen at a distance, to "lead me with you—take me away; preserve me."[36] A moment later, under fresh provocation from the Spirit, he speaks the very language of the Victorian ethic of purity, which included the protective exaltation of women as angels.[37]

> O moon and stars forgive! And thou, clear heaven,
> Look pureness back into me. O great God,
> Why, why in wisdom and in grace's name,
> And in the name of saints and saintly thoughts,
> Of mothers, and of sisters, and chaste wives,
> And angel woman-faces we have seen,
> And angel woman-spirits we have guessed,
> And innocent sweet children, and pure love,
>
> (IIA, 1–8)

---

36. Cf. Arnold's "Switzerland," Poem 2.
37. I describe the ethic of purity in *Victorian Frame of Mind*, pp. 353–56, 359.

why did he ever "lend chaste ears" to "parley with this filthy Belial," this toad "sly-sitting at Eve's ear" and whispering his "poisonous" dream?

    The sensual temptation having failed, the Spirit changes tactics, and speaking as a man of the world who knows the truth and is free of school-boy illusions, plays the whole thing down. This second and more insidious appeal, common as it is in life, has rarely been expressed in English poetry.

> O yes, you dream of sin and shame—
> Trust me, it leaves one much the same.
> 'Tisn't Elysium any more
> Than what comes after or before:
> But heavens! as innocent a thing
> As picking strawberries in spring.
>
>   .   .   .   (IIA, 12–17)
>
> I know it's mainly your temptation
> To think the thing a revelation,
> A mystic mouthful that will give
> Knowledge and death—none know and live!
> I tell you plainly that it brings
> Some ease; but the emptiness of things
> (That one old sermon Earth still preaches
> Until we practise what she teaches)
> Is the sole lesson you'll learn by it—
> Still you undoubtedly should try it.
> "Try all things"—bad and good, no matter;
> You can't till then hold fast the latter.
>
>   .   .   .   (20–31)
>
> Briefly—you cannot rest, I'm certain,
> Until your hand has drawn the curtain.
> Once known the little lies behind it,
> You'll go your way and never mind it.
> Ill's only cure is, never doubt it,
> To do—and think no more about it.
>
>   (36–41)

The voice of worldly common sense could be more candid but it could hardly be more persuasive.

When it fails because Dipsychus calls on the protective image of "matrimonial sanctities" (for which he must be undefiled), the Spirit proposes an alternative: to lead his friend into "good society" where he may make "a virtuous attachment formed judiciously" and learn the way of the world. This is easier for Dipsychus to reject:

> To herd with people that one owns no care for;
> Friend it with strangers that one sees but once;
> To drain the heart with endless complaisance;
> To warp the unfashioned diction on the lip,
> And twist one's mouth to counterfeit.
>
> (III, 34–38)

That is to "base-alloy the ingenuous golden frankness of the past" and "lose one's youth too early." With something like the anguish of prescience, he cries out: "Oh, not yet, not yet I make this sacrifice." And when the Spirit argues that wheat must have its tares, Dipsychus insists that in our "needful mixture with the world," it is quite enough that with the rising sun each day

> Our rising heart, fresh from the seas of sleep,
> Scarce o'er the level lifts his purer orb
> Ere lost and sullied with polluting smoke—
> A noonday coppery disk. Lo, scarce come forth,
> Some vagrant miscreant meets, and with a look
> Transmutes me his, and for a whole sick day
> Lepers me.
>
> (III, 69–75)

This has a note of unreality, and in contrast to the incisive attack on social convention, it seems captious. The explanation is clear: the imagery of pollution and disease betrays the exaggeration that Clough recognized in Dipsychus's view of the world.

Scene IV is a masterpiece of organization. The central subject, admirably symbolized by the action (an excursion in a gondola), is the Utopian dream of idyllic life. But the idealist in Dipsychus, who is not the dreamer, is quick to expose the facts that fantasy would conceal; to remind himself, so to speak, of the harsh realities. The Spirit, of course, has no use for such disturbing thoughts, and opposes them with his own version of life at its best. This triple point of view is explored in a series of disparate speeches that function in a manner that is more symbolist than Victorian; for though the separable parts are less deviously related than they are in a poem like "The Waste Land," they work in the same way, by juxtaposition and symbolic implication.

The scene opens with Dipsychus singing:

> How light it moves, how softly! Ah,
> Could life, as does our gondola,
> Unvexed with quarrels, aims, and cares,
> And moral duties and affairs,
> Unswaying, noiseless, swift, and strong,
> For ever thus—thus glide along!
> How light we move, how softly! Ah,
> Were all things like the gondola!
>
> (IV, 11–18)

If they were, one could live a life of aesthetic enjoyment at a safe distance from the shore:

> In one unbroken passage borne
> To closing night from opening morn,
> Uplift at whiles slow eyes to mark
> Some palace front, some passing bark;
> Through windows catch the varying shore,
> And hear the soft turns of the oar—
> How light we move, how softly! Ah,
> Were all things like the gondola!
>
> So live, nor need to call to mind
> Our slaving brother set behind!
>
> (IV, 27–36)

And the uneasy dream is shattered! The social conscience, with its particular "aims, and cares, and moral duties," makes it impossible to forget certain facts. But the Spirit laughs at such a ridiculous scruple (we pay him, don't we?), and Dipsychus is provoked into a contrasting song beginning,

> Our gaieties, our luxuries,
>   Our pleasures and our glee,
> Mere insolence and wantonries,
>   Alas! they feel to me;

and ending with the Blakean stanza:

> The joy that does not spring from joy
>   Which I in others see,
> How can I venture to employ,
>   Or find it joy for me?
>
> (IV, 43–46, 51–54)

The exasperated Spirit, asking, "Who's to enjoy at all?" and "What's . . . he to us?", calls for a return to easy gaiety, picking up the initial refrain with a significant modulation:

> How light we move, how softly! Ah,
> Tra lal la la, the gondola!
>
> (IV, 61–62)

For him a life of enjoyment—of sensual enjoyment—is not a contrary to fact condition, but the only rational thing to live for. Tra lal la la, enjoy the minute, and the gondola in it!

Ignoring the protest, Dipsychus holds up the aesthetic dream in a new form with a new moral criticism.

> Yes, it is beautiful ever, let foolish men rail at it never.
>
> .   .   .
>
> Life it is beautiful wholly, and could we eliminate only
> This interfering, enslaving, o'ermastering demon of craving,
> This wicked tempter inside us to ruin still eager to guide us,
> Life were beatitude, action a possible pure satisfaction.
>
> (IV, 63, 66–69)

These lines, and the next speech about beholding people "consorting and coupling," are transplanted from another poem which

Dipsychus (Clough) made last year in Italy (this time at Rome),[38] but they grow naturally here, in the Venetian soil of the Public Garden. What shocks the Victorian idealist with his code of purity is precisely what the Spirit identifies with love, though at the moment he only laughs at the versification. What, then, *should* one love and behold? Dipsychus sings:

> O let me love my love unto myself alone,
> And know my knowledge to the world unknown;
> No witness to the vision call,
> Beholding, unbeheld of all;
> And worship thee, with thee withdrawn, apart,
> Whoe'er, whate'er thou art,
> Within the closest veil of mine own inmost heart.
>
> (IV, 82–88)

Thus divinely inspired, Dipsychus sees the Spirit's life as an ugly piece of deception:

> Better it were, thou sayest, to consent,
> Feast while we may, and live ere life be spent;
> Close up clear eyes, and call the unstable sure,
> The unlovely lovely, and the filthy pure;
> In self-belyings, self-deceivings roll,
> And lose in Action, Passion, Talk, the soul.
>
> Nay, better far to mark off thus much air
> And call it heaven, place bliss and glory there;
> Fix perfect homes in the unsubstantial sky,
> And say, what is not, will be by-and-by;
> What here exists not, must exist elsewhere.
>
> (IV, 89–99)

That is better far because it is less destructive of the soul. But it, too, is Utopian deception; and the wiser Dipsychus concludes:

> But play no tricks upon thy soul, O man;
> Let fact be fact, and life the thing it can.
>
> (IV, 100–01)

---

38. *Amours de Voyage*, Canto III, 173–81.

The Spirit, thinking of the stanza addressed to him (lines 89–94), pretends to find it worthy of Malebranche or Berkeley because, he implies, Dipsychus is identifying reality with appearance, claiming that the world is simply how it appears to him, namely, filthy and unlovely. So it is *he* who is deceiving himself and playing tricks. With witty irony the Spirit disposes of such a subjective metaphysic (which Dipsychus had not, in fact, adopted), and is happy to defend the objective reality of good wine and the female body:

> These juicy meats, this flashing wine,
>   May be an unreal mere appearance;
> Only—for my inside, in fine,
>   They have a singular coherence.
>
> This lovely creature's glowing charms
>   Are gross illusion, I don't doubt that;
> But when I pressed her in my arms
>   I somehow didn't think about that.
>
> (IV, 106–13)

Truth is, we cannot understand the world; all we know is that "God won't, and we can't mend it"—not even the crazy idealists. So,

> Being common sense, it can't be sin
>   To take it as we find it;
> The pleasure to take pleasure in;
>   The pain, try not to mind it.
>
> (IV, 118–21)

The next speech, in which Dipsychus suddenly asks, "Where are the great, whom thou woulds't wish to praise thee?" seems unconnected, but it may be viewed as a fresh variation on the pattern of Utopian dream vs. the hard facts. Where are those who are above the pleasure-seekers?

> Where are the great . . .
> Where are the pure . . .
> Where are the brave?

But as the "where" is repeated with increasing stress of mind, the skeptical implication keeps growing until the dreamer is forced to abandon these ideal images. One must seek the heroic virtues in himself, Dipsychus concludes—only to add, with mocking irony,

> submit to find
> In the stones, bread; and life in the blank mind.
> (IV, 126–27)

Ignoring the interruption, the Spirit celebrates the pleasures of good living, including "the pleasure of now and then giving" a crust to the poor, through a dozen amusing stanzas, ending with a return to the key symbol:

> A gondola here, and a gondola there,
> 'Tis the pleasantest fashion of taking the air.
> To right and to left; stop, turn, and go yonder,
> And let us repeat, o'er the tide as we wander,
>   How pleasant it is to have money, heigh ho!
>   How pleasant it is to have money.
> (IV, 198–203)

In the final evolution of Scene IV, the Spirit's preference for the clarity of neoclassical architecture over Gothic tricks of "light and shade" leads to another variation of the opening lyric, this time by Dipsychus, referring to the Gothic Palace of the Doges:

> How light we go, how soft we skim,
> And all in moonlight seem to swim!
> The south side rises o'er our bark,
> A wall impenetrably dark;
> The north the while profusely bright.
> The water—is it shade or light?
>
>   .   .   .
>
> O sight of glory, sight of wonder!
>
>   .   .   .
>
> How light we go, how softly! Ah,
> Life should be as the gondola!
> (IV, 236–40, 252, 256–57)

But the moonlight that makes Venice the more beautiful to Dipsychus is only "moonshine after all" to the Spirit, who finds

> It goes against my conscience really
> To let myself feel so ideally.
>
> (IV, 264–65)

No one shall make *him* repose on "things so deucèd unsubstantial." Even Dipsychus cannot do so for long; and after urging the gondolier to go more slowly, he realizes that to continue would be impossible:

> On to the landing, onward. Nay,
> Sweet dream, a little longer stay!
> On to the landing; here. And, ah,
> Life is not as the gondola!
>
> (IV, 302–05)

Given certain inescapable facts—like moral duties, quarrels, and cares, sexual passion, the lack of heroism—life cannot be beautiful truly or aesthetic enjoyment possible for long. The dream vanishes, the ride ends. Only for a moment is Venice under moonlight. But moonlight, not moonshine, for this is not to denigrate the aesthetic sensibility. As they land, the Spirit blandly inquires where they should go for some *limone* or *gramolata persici,* that is, for something more nourishing than a vision of beauty.[39]

Scene V opens with a new dream, a nightmare, followed by a new excursion, to the Lido. With the conclusion of Scene IV still echoing in our ears, we hear Dipsychus saying:

> I dreamt a dream; till morning light
> A bell rang in my head all night,
> Tinkling and tinkling first, and then
> Tolling; and tinkling; tolling again.
> So brisk and gay, and then so slow!

39. Cf. Henry Sidgwick, *Miscellaneous Essays,* p. 66: "His yearning for the ideal he never tried to quench or satisfy with aught but its proper satisfaction; but meanwhile the claims of the real, to be accepted as real, are paramount. He clings to the 'beauty of his dreams'; but—two and two make four."

> O joy, and terror! mirth, and woe!
> Ting, ting, there is no God; ting, ting—
> Dong, there is no God; dong,
> There is no God; dong, dong!
>
> (V, 7–15)

This antiphony of sound and rhythm, in which the brisk and gay "tings" are set off against the slow, despondent "dongs," is the formal projection of the advantages of atheism set against its evils—precisely the dual view we should expect from Dipsychus. But as in Scene IV, the idealist is too clear-sighted to fall for a fancy dream. He sees that the pleasures are illusions, and that the mirth and joy are hollow. For in a society without moral or civil law (because without their divine sanction), the unconfined indulgence of the desire for sex and the desire for power is not so satisfying as it might seem.

> Ting, ting, there is no God; ting, ting;
> Come dance and play, and merrily sing—
> Ting, ting a ding; ting, ting a ding!
> O pretty girl who trippest along,
> Come to my bed—it isn't wrong.
> Uncork the bottle, sing the song!
> Ting, ting a ding: dong, dong.
> Wine has dregs; the song an end;
> A silly girl is a poor friend
> And age and weakness who shall mend?
> Dong, there is no God; Dong!
>
> . . .
>
> Ring ding, ring ding, tara, tara,
>
> . . .
>
> From east and west, and south and north,
> Ye men of valour and of worth,
> Ye mighty men of arms, come forth,
> And work your will, for that is just;
> And in your impulse put your trust,
> Beneath your feet the fools are dust.

> Alas, alas! O grief and wrong,
> The good are weak, the wicked strong;
> And O my God, how long, how long?
> Dong, there is no God; dong!
>
> (V, 16–26, 59, 63–72)

With the same ironic praise of the new order and the same despairing comment, Dipsychus speaks of "resentment's rule" and the law of the sword supplanting "merchant justice" and the police. But

> Lawyers are villains, soldiers too;
> And nothing's new and nothing's true.
> Dong, there is no God; dong!
>
> (V, 105–07)

This view of the world as it would be without faith is, in fact, what it largely is *with* "faith." That is why it is also the Spirit's view, but his different reaction breaks sharply across the moral distress of Dipsychus. After arguing the wisdom, nonetheless, of belonging to the Church of England, he picks up the refrain, "There is no God," to explore the psychological motivations—for him the sole motivations—of belief and unbelief, founded on the desires and needs of the moment.[40]

Having arrived at the Lido, Dipsychus plunges with ecstatic abandon into the "grand surge"—while the Spirit complains of the thistles pricking his feet—and comes out refreshed in body and soul. (Maybe the nightmare was only a nightmare, and all is well. Maybe the second "Easter Day" was the right answer to the first—which Dipsychus had quoted in Scene I—arguing that the essentials of Christianity could still be true, philosophically, even though the Gospels proved false, historically:

> Though He be dead, He is not dead.
>   In the true Creed
>   He is yet risen indeed,
>   Christ is yet risen.)

---

40. See above, pp. 166–67.

But any such hope (it is not voiced) is destroyed by the derisive mockery of the Spirit:

> Pleasant perhaps. However, no offence,
> Animal spirits are not common sense.
>
> . . .
>
> They're good enough as an assistance,
> But in themselves a poor existence.
> But you—with this one bathe, no doubt,
> Have solved all questions out and out.
> 'Tis Easter Day, and on the Lido
> Lo, Christ the Lord is risen indeed, O!
>
> (V, 226–27, 230–35)

The ironic praise of atheism for allowing the aristocratic sword to displace the "merchant justice" of civil law is projected into action by Scene VI. When Dipsychus refuses to answer an insult with a challenge, the Spirit jabs at him for acting like a "shopkeeper's son," and insists that the Sermon on the Mount was intended only for the masses, "at best the vulgar bourgeoisie." But Dipsychus is happy to admit,

> I am a man of peace,
> And the old Adam of the gentleman
> Dares seldom in my bosom stir against
> The good plebeian Christian seated there.
>
> (VI, 211–14)

The old Adam stirred enough, however, to make him feel, for a moment at least, that he was "not quite in union" with himself (VI, 123), and to admit that his hesitation might owe something to the "too exclusive fervency" of his early religious life (VI, 186). But his fastidiousness is equally important. He expostulates in characteristic imagery:

> Heaven! to pollute one's fingers to pick up
> The fallen coin of honour from the dirt—
> Pure silver though it be, let it rather lie!
>
> . . .

> To enter the base crowd and bare one's flanks
> To all ill voices of a blustering world,
> To have so much as e'en half-felt of one
> That ever one was angered for oneself!
>
> (VI, 88–90, 94–97)

In Scene VII, the first part of the poem is rounded off by having Dipsychus return to Clough's "Easter Day," which he had quoted in Scene I. Now, after the view of an amoral and antireligious world that has emerged, its account of a godless universe is the more telling; and the lines,

> My brain was lightened when my tongue had said,
>   "Christ is not risen,"
>
> (VII, 14–15)

instantly remind us of the nightmare of Scene V. There too the "lightening" was equally ironic.

Where a space is left in the manuscript, Dipsychus was also to recite at least part of what is now called "Easter Day II," for the Spirit's sarcasms, especially the reference to finding "a strong Strauss-smell about it," apply far more readily to the second ode. With his solid common sense and his neoclassicism, the Spirit is irritated by the complexities and nuances of religious attitude in the poem (a creed should be simple and explicit); and his skepticism, which he neatly purports to derive from the respectable Bishop Butler (with some truth), finds the effort to explain things simply ridiculous. The moral is clear:

> At any rate, this rationalistic
> Half-puritano-semitheistic
> Cross of Neologist and Mystic
> Is, of all doctrines, the least reasonable—
>
> (VII, 55–58)

and since *no* doctrines are provable, compliance is the only wisdom:

> Take your religion as 'twas found you,
> And say no more of it—confound you!
>
> (VII, 64–65)

6. The Action: Scenes VIII–XIII

To this point in the poem, Dipsychus has been victorious. He has resisted every temptation, whether from the Spirit or from elements in himself friendly to the Spirit. Sensuality, "good society," the Utopian view of life, the appeal of atheism, personal vengeance, and hypocritical conformity—each has been rejected in turn. This victory is immediately reflected at the start of Scene VIII, "The Academy." After finding the portrait of Byron drawing his sword in the "brave cause" of Greek independence more moving than Titian's "Assumption of the Virgin," Dipsychus makes a clear affirmation: If we must live, it must be "not for profit, not for fame, and not for pleasure's giddy dream"; it must be for "noble deeds." A moment later, therefore, he feels strong enough to look the world in the face. In the past he has heard the Spirit's comments and sometimes answered them, but he has never recognized him or asked him what he wanted. Now, however,

> we'll be definite, explicit, plain;
> I can resist, I know; and 'twill be well
> To have used for colloquy this manlier mood,
> Which is to last, ye chances, say, how long?
>
> (VIII, 40–43)

But this question, taken with the preceding dismissal of youthful poetry as nothing worth,

> Unless to make maturer years content
> To slave in base compliance to the world,
>
> (VIII, 26–27)

inject a note of ominous foreboding. And when the Spirit comes to Dipsychus's call

> With something of an exultation too, methinks,
> Out-peeping in that springy, jaunty gait,
>
> (VIII, 47–48)

we see the end in sight. The defeat is implicit in Dipsychus's moment of triumph. Indeed, the very phrasing of the address, protesting so vigorously that the whole matter is purely academic, reveals the lurking presence of the enemy within, ready to betray the idealist:

> Should I, my follower,
> Should I conceive (not that at all I do,
> 'Tis curiosity that prompts my speech)—
> But should I form, a thing to be supposed,
> A wish to bargain for your merchandise,
> Say what were your demands? what were your terms?
> What should I do? what should I cease to do?
> What incense on what altars must I burn?
> And what abandon? what unlearn, or learn?
>
> (VIII, 50–58)

With these explicit queries, the battle begins (within himself no less than with the Spirit), and the crisis of his life is at hand. For the question is no longer whether Dipsychus will do this or do that, but whether he will live his own life or submit to "serve as other servants do; and don the lacquey's livery of the house" (IX, 138–39). In a very real sense his soul is at stake.

This accounts for the difference in form between the two parts. Because the first was planned as a series of isolated engagements in which Dipsychus was to resist a series of particular temptations, one by one, the action could be staged at the Piazza, the Public Garden, in a Gondola, and so on. But in the second, only Scenes VIII and X have any locale; the others are soliloquies and dialogues, somewhere in Venice. This absence of setting and incident makes the second part less attractive, less good theater, but it is completely defensible artistically, for the central struggle of Dipsychus's life, brought on by the external events of the first part, is now abstract and internal. It may even be argued that the second part is more dramatic than the first, not less, since now the issue is life or death, held in the balance as we wait for Dipsychus to conquer or submit.

As usual, the struggle between abstract principles is joined on a concrete question: in this case, whether to act or not to act. Dipsychus is not opposed to action in itself. On the contrary, he longs for "noble deeds" or "some not unworthy work," and is ready even to drudge for an end that is "one's choice and the correlative of the soul."[41] But that is not what the Spirit means at all, or what the world has to offer, as Dipsychus realizes:

> Action is what one must get, it is clear,
> And one could dream it better than one finds,
> In its kind personal, in its motive not;
> Not selfish as it now is, nor as now
> Maiming the individual.
>
> (IX, 147–51)

Therefore, if one *must* act, perhaps the only available course is to accept the Spirit's proposition: to marry (and at the Spirit's choice, of course, so that the woman will exert the right social and political influence) and to enter a profession—"if not the Church, why then the law."

In Scene IX, the proposition is considered in a long soliloquy, opening with an immediate reply by the tender conscience to specific demands:

> The Law! 'twere honester, if 'twere genteel,
> To say the dung-cart. What! shall I go about,
> And like the walking shoeblack roam the flags
> With heedful eyes, down bent, and like a glass
> In a sea-captain's hand sweeping all round,
> To see whose boots are dirtiest? Oh, the luck
> To stoop and clean a pair!
>
> (IX, 1–7)

And as for marriage, since he still believes that "heart can beat true to heart," he will not "seat some alien trifler on the throne a queen may come to claim." And yet love is "so rare, so doubtful, so exceptional," perhaps it should not be "an item in the reckonings of the wise." (And if not, then he might as well marry at the Spirit's choice.) This oscillating movement of mind characterizes the long soliloquy that follows, where the pros and cons of action are ex-

---

41. Scenes VIII, 20, 107, and IX, 115–17.

plored in a succession of debates that leave the problem unresolved. The decision is made on the most elemental grounds:

> He that eats
> Must serve; and serve as other servants do.
>
> (IX, 137–38)

To live is the prime necessity that ultimately forces the idealist into the world.

If the hostile view of action that continues through the later scenes is not to be dismissed as escapism or fastidious detachment, it must be read with historical imagination. There is justice, no doubt, in some of the Spirit's caustic remarks about timidities and vanities, but basically the reader is invited to understand the dilemma and to sympathize with Dipsychus's deep reluctance to act.

The dilemma was implicit in the Puritan tradition: the world, like the flesh and the devil, was evil, and yet one must not live in sinful idleness. One must serve God by serving his children; he must work in a vocation. The tension was resolved by saying that one was to be *in* the world but not *of* it. There are vestiges of this Evangelicalism in both Clough and Matthew Arnold; and Dipsychus can talk of a life of study and art as sometimes seeming "all ignoble."[42] But this ethic of action rested on various assumptions that were breaking down in the nineteenth century: that the work one does is itself good, that it will not contaminate the doer, and that it fits the individual's ability and character.

The very effort of the Evangelical leaders from Wilberforce to Arnold to Ward and Newman to check the growth of worldliness by making the conscience more critical and alert, more "tender," could make pursuits which less earnest generations had innocently followed seem distasteful, if not outright immoral, with the result that all the greater stress was laid on the nobility of action. But unhappily noble deeds seemed harder and harder to find in a commercial environment (a connection between the rise of industrialism and the decline of heroism was often suggested), and by noble

---

42. Scene X, 70; cf. IX, 85, 89.

standards ordinary deeds could seem tawdry. Speaking of "a state of things that offers but little opportunity for elevated *action*," Clough went on to remark, in a letter to his fiancée, that "to live in domestic comfort, toiling in some business not in itself of any great use, merely for the sake of bread for the household, does look at times a little ignoble, or at any rate unchivalrous."[43]

Even apart from any high morality, Puritan or heroic, the increasing size of factories and offices in an expanding economy had a depressing effect on the value of work. It could belittle the job, and make the substitute for noble action all the more repellent:

> At the [huge] members of the vast machine,
> In all those crowded rooms of industry,
> No individual soul has loftier leave
> Than fiddling with a piston or a valve.
> Well, one could bear that also: one could drudge
> And do one's petty part, and be content
> In base manipulation, solaced still
> By thinking of the leagued fraternity,
> And of co-operation, and the effect
> Of the great engine. If indeed it work,
> And is not a mere treadmill! Which it may be;
> Who can confirm it is not? We ask Action,
> And dream of arms and conflict; and string up
> All self-devotion's muscles; and are set
> To fold up papers. To what end? We know not.
>
> (IX, 120–34)

Small wonder Dipsychus goes on to say that at any rate we are paid for it and that he who eats must serve. Once work loses its "goodness," it is undertaken only from necessity.

And at what cost to the individual? In the face of increasing luxury in the upper classes and increasing mammonism in the middle classes, one might well wonder if he *could* be in the world and not of it; and if *of* it, then contaminated by it. That fear, rooted

---

43. *Prose, 1,* 172, or p. 178. Cf. *Correspondence,* 2, 380. The background is suggested in *Victorian Frame of Mind,* pp. 285–86, 317, 339–40.

in the commercial spirit and the Evangelical revival,[44] was stimulated by the Romantics:

> To fly from, need not be to hate, mankind:
> All are not fit with them to stir and toil,
> Nor is it discontent to keep the mind
> Deep in its fountain, lest it overboil
> In the hot throng, where we become the spoil
> Of our infection, till too late and long
> We may deplore and struggle with the coil,
> In wretched interchange of wrong for wrong
> Midst a contentious world, striving where none are strong.
>
> . . .
>
> Is it not better, then, to be alone,
> And love Earth only for its earthly sake?
> By the blue rushing of the arrowy Rhone,
> Or the pure bosom of its nursing lake.

This is Byron, but in sentiment it might be Wordsworth or Senancour or Amiel, to mention only Romantics whom Arnold or Clough admired; indeed, the "Stanzas in Memory of the Author of Obermann" come immediately and relevantly to mind.[45]

The difficulty of acting has another source that is peculiarly Victorian—and modern. In a revolutionary period in which traditional beliefs and social structures are being questioned and transformed, the individual is unsure of himself. He does not know where he stands or how he fits into the scheme of things. What should he do? No doubt what suits his nature. But what *is* his nature? In fact who *is* he? In this way the problem of action came to involve the problem of identity. Arnold, who was "sick of asking what I am, and what I ought to be," told Clough in 1849 that his "one natural craving" was not for profound thoughts or spiritual workings, "but a distinct seeing of my way as far as my own nature is concerned." A few years later, however, after he had married

---

44. See above, pp. 172–76.
45. *Childe Harold*, Canto III, stanzas lxix and lxxi; in "Obermann," see especially lines 137–60.

and settled down into an inspectorship of schools (mainly, it seems to me, by coming to terms with the Spirit), he could speak sternly when Clough betrayed the same uncertainty:

> You ask me in what I think or have thought you going wrong: in this: that you would never take your assiette as something determined final and unchangeable for you and proceed to work away on the basis of that: but were always poking and patching and cobbling at the assiette itself—could never finally, as it seemed—"resolve to be thyself"—but were looking for this and that experience, and doubting whether you ought not to adopt this or that mode of being. . . .[46]

In that state of mind, one might well adopt this and that and another mode of being, none of them "right," with a resulting sense of disunity. Arnold should have included himself and quoted "The Buried Life":

> And we have been on many thousand lines,
> And we have shown, on each, spirit and power;
> But hardly have we, for one little hour,
> Been on our own line, have we been ourselves.
>
> . . .
>
> And long we try in vain to speak and act
> Our hidden self, and what we say and do
> Is eloquent, is well—but 'tis not true!

For this "we," Dipsychus is another persona. He too is "not quite in union" with himself, and finding no end that is the "correlative" of his soul, feels that to act at all, "I must sluice out myself into canals." In Scene X the question of personal identity is explicit. No doubt one should be true "to thine own self," but what if he has a "double self"? Is he the contemplative man or is he the man of action? By moments he is sure that the first is right and feels his "soul secure in place." But there are hours when the life of study and art seems unsatisfactory, and yet when the alternative life of action seems dangerous, so that he feels

---

46. "Self-Dependence"; *Letters to Clough*, pp. 110, 130. The problem of identity is also discussed above, pp. 57–58.

THE ACTION: SCENES VIII–XIII

> Bewildered, baffled, hurried hence and thence,
> All at cross-purpose ever with myself,
> Unknowing whence from whither.[47]
>
> (X, 77–79)

Scenes IX and X are distinguished by a change of emphasis. In IX, Dipsychus is exploring what can be said in favor of action in the world and trying to meet it with counterarguments. This debate continues in X, but here it centers on the inactive, contemplative life he is now living, a life of

> love, and faith, and dear domestic ties,
> And converse with old friends, and pleasant walks,
> Familiar faces, and familiar books,
> Study, and art, upliftings unto prayer,
> And admiration of the noblest things:[48]
>
> (X, 65–69)

and, he could have added, the fascination of observing the sheer flow of existence (X, 28–29), which is symbolized by the wide view from "the Campanile's top" (X, 80). But for all its rewards, such a life can sometimes seem ignoble because selfish (X, 70) or seem limiting and confining:

> Hints haunt me ever of a More beyond:
> I am rebuked by a sense of the incomplete,
> Of a completion over-soon assumed,
> Of adding up too soon.
>
> (X, 31–34)

Thus, he also feels the fascination of breaking out into the world of action. And yet, "to leave the habitual and the old" (X, 48) is not only frightening in itself, it must also deprive him of a way of life which, if not perfect, has brought him the deepest satisfaction.

47. Scenes VI, 123; IX, 107, 116; and X, 62–63, 74.
48. Cf. Francis Palgrave's "Memoir" of Clough, *Poems* (1862), pp. vii–viii, calling him a "poet who walked the world's way as matter of duty, living a life, meanwhile, hidden with higher and holier things, with the friends and books he loved so fondly, with deep solitary thought. . . ."

> Be it enough;
> If I lose this, how terrible! No, no,
> I am contented, and will not complain.
>
> . . .
>
> If this should go,
> If this pure solace should desert my mind,
> What were all else? I dare not risk this loss.
> To the old paths, my soul!
>
> (X, 84–86, 93–96)

But the opening lines of Scene XI make the contrary conclusion almost inevitable:

> 'Tis gone, the fierce inordinate desire,
> The burning thirst for Action—utterly;
>
> . . .
>
>   gone, yet will come again.
>
> (XI, 1–2, 4)

Fierce and inordinate is not the desire to do noble deeds. It is the frantic desire, as the next lines show, to resolve the paralysis of indecision by plunging into activity, any activity, and so gain relief from "twisted thinkings" and the "bewildered, baffled" state of mind.[49]

When this neurotic impulse is added to the necessity to eat, capitulation follows. After imperiously dismissing the Spirit, Dipsychus, alone, surrenders:

> It must be then. I feel it in my soul;
> The iron enters, sundering flesh and bone,
> And sharper than the two-edged sword of God.
>
> . . .
>
> Therefore, farewell! a long and last farewell,
> Ye pious sweet simplicities of life,
> Good books, good friends, and holy moods, and all
> That lent rough life sweet Sunday-seeming rests,
> Making earth heaven-like. Welcome, wicked world,

---

49. The last phrases are in Scenes IX, 146, and X, 77.

> The hardening heart, the calculating brain
> Narrowing its doors to thought, the lying lips,
> The calm-dissembling eyes; the greedy flesh,
> The world, the Devil—welcome, welcome, welcome!
>
> (XI, 73–75, 78–86)

We recognize the characteristic exaggeration but at this moment we can feel only a sense of grim pathos.

Though the back-and-forth debates of Scenes IX–XI may be a little long (Clough's uncle, I am sorry to say, dropped into a doze while Dipsychus "was drivelling through his later soliloquies"),[50] the conflict with the Spirit is adroit and dramatic. The Spirit's role is not to argue the advantages of submission (the self that wills it does that for him), but to command and threaten and ridicule the self that hesitates. Each scene ends with his hypnotic chant:

> Submit, submit!
> 'Tis common sense, and human wit
> Can claim no higher name than it.
> Submit, submit!

And over and over we hear his warning cry to Dipsychus, "Beware, beware," mainly of clinging to "impractical" ideals.

> Devotion, and ideas, and love,
> And beauty claim their place above;
> But saint and sage and poet's dreams
> Divide the light in coloured streams,
> Which this alone gives all combined,
> The *siccum lumen* of the mind
> Called common sense: and no high wit
> Gives better counsel than does it.
> Submit, submit!
>
> (IX, 164–72)

This philistine dismissal of the whole frame of mind that Dipsychus clings to is accompanied by two scathing speeches that are

---

50. Epilogue, *Poems*, p. 294.

calculated to make him utterly ashamed of both his precious intellectual life and his dithering hesitations:

> To moon about religion; to inhume
> Your ripened age in solitary walks,
> For self-discussion; to debate in letters
> Vext points with earnest friends.
>
> . . .
>
>   Oh, no doubt,
> In a corner sit and mope, and be consoled
> With thinking one is clever, while the room
> Rings through with animation and the dance.
>   (X, 97–100, 102–05)
>
> Whatever happen, don't I see you still,
> Living no life at all? Even as now
> An o'ergrown baby, sucking at the dugs
> Of Instinct, dry long since.
>
> . . .
>
>   Methinks I see you,
> Through everlasting limbos of void time,
> Twirling and twiddling ineffectively,
> And indeterminately swaying for ever.
>   (XI, 177–80, 185–88)

There is truth in all this, of course; one shudders to admit it. But the Spirit, we see, is as capable of exaggerating as the idealist. Indeed, in this cruel caricature there is a sadistic note not heard before, which reflects the masochism of the intellectual at moments when his isolation seems nothing but conceited self-defense, and the indecision of the flexible mind becomes intolerable weakness.[51]

The last two scenes, XII and XIII, are complementary studies of Dipsychus in defeat. His pros and cons in Scene XII are nothing but ex post facto arguments designed to justify or palliate the ugly decision already made. In order to attack the world, perhaps

---

51. For other sarcasms of the Spirit, see Scenes X, 106–33, 171–79, and XI, 44–45.

one *must* take service with it. Some one sent him and to do something, surely. To do a treachery? But the thing's done and he's already taken of the pay. Besides, isn't he another Samson whom the Philistines have maimed and blinded and kept to make them sport, but who eventually, no doubt, will destroy them, and himself too, if need be, in some noble action? As the Spirit says, so aptly,

> Could there be finer special pleading
> When scruples would be interceding?
>
> (XII, 85–86)

In the final scene Dipsychus tries to quiet the scruples by denying the completeness of the submission. He can still bargain with the Spirit, he argues, to retain some of his life for himself; and if that fails, well, "I can but render what is of my will, and behind it somewhat remaineth still." But the Spirit laughs at a reservation so purely theoretical, and starts chanting "Little Bo Peep, she lost her sheep. . . ."

The second part of the poem is tied together and its meaning sharpened by a pattern of religious imagery in which Dipsychus is seen as poised and wavering between the two kingdoms. He himself is "a child of heavenly birth," "a kidnapped child of Heaven," who clings to moments of "upliftings unto prayer" when he likens himself to John of Patmos on the Lord's day, or tells his enemy, "I am in higher hands than yours." The Spirit, on the other hand, is the "devil," the "imperious fiend," the "Power of this World! hateful unto God!" He begs Dipsychus to learn the "Second Reverence" ("for things around" and not above), talks "sternly of a something much like duty," and describes his own wisdom as a "revelation."[52]

In this scheme of imagery, the moment of submission becomes the Fall of Dipsychus. The iron, sundering his flesh and bone, is "sharper than the two-edged sword of God"; he bids a long farewell to an Eden of "holy moods, and all that lent rough life sweet Sunday-seeming rests, making earth heaven-like"; goes on to wel-

---

52. Re Dipsychus: Scenes X, 68, 91–92, 141, 183, and XII, 78. Re the Spirit: Scenes XI, 41, 60, 66, 115–16; XII, 32; and XIII, 71.

come, sarcastically, "the greedy flesh, the world, the Devil"; and thinking of the flood that swept over "the world of the ungodly" when Noah was saved, cries out:

> O God, O God! The great floods of the fiend
> Flow over me! I come into deep waters
> Where no ground is![53]

After the Fall, Dipsychus, too, hears a voice, or dreams he does, singing:

> "When the enemy is near thee,
>   Call on us!
> In our hands we will upbear thee,
> He shall neither scathe nor scare thee,
>   Call on us!
>
>   .   .   .
>
> Call, and following close behind thee
> There shall haste, and there shall find thee,
>   Help, sure help.
> When the panic comes upon thee,
> When necessity seems on thee,
> Hope and choice have all foregone thee,
> Fate and force are closing o'er thee,
> And but one way stands before thee—
>   Call on us!
>
>   (XII, 8–12, 18–26)

Since he did not call—or, calling, was not answered—and help is now useless, this promise is replete with ironies. But it can evoke a moment of bravado:

> Not for thy service, thou imperious fiend,
> Not to do thy work, or the like of thine;
> Not to please thee, O base and fallen spirit!
> But One Most High, Most True, whom without thee
> It seems I cannot.
>
>   (XII, 32–36)

---

53. Scene XI, 74–75, 80–82 (the "holy moods" are those of X, 65–69), 85–86, 105–07. For the flood, see Matthew 24:38–39, and 2 Peter 2:5.

To support this dubious proposition, in the desperate effort to justify himself, Dipsychus turns to Luke to argue that out of "the mammon of unrighteousness" we must make friends (which at once recalls the conclusion of the parable, "Ye cannot serve God and mammon"); and after citing, to the same end, the injunction in Genesis that a man leave his parents and cleave to a wife, Dipsychus remarks sardonically:

> O man, behold thy wife, th' hard naked world;
> Adam, accept thy Eve.[54]
>
> (XII, 69–70)

This ironic use of biblical phrasing to expose the perversion of Christian meaning is employed deliberately by the Spirit, proud of preempting the role of his old enemy. Scene IX ends:

> O did you think you were alone?
> That I was so unfeeling grown
> As not with joy to leave behind
> My ninety-nine in hope to find
> (How sweet the words my sense express!)
> My lost sheep in the wilderness?
>
> (IX, 185–90)

And in Scene XI, when Dipsychus calls out in distress as the floods sweep over him, the Spirit speaks reassuringly:

> Fear not, my lamb, whate'er men say,
> I am the Shepherd; and the Way.[55]
>
> (XI, 214–15)

After these passages the full meaning of the Spirit's reference to Little Bo Peep in Scene XIII suddenly emerges, with the added impact of surprise from the fusion of nursery rhyme and Gospel. A few moments later, predicting how pleasant it will be for Dipsychus to become like other people, the Spirit speaks his last line with a mixture of taunt and triumph:

---

54. Cf. Luke 16:9, 13; Genesis 2:24.
55. Cf. John 10:14, and 14:6; 1 Peter 2:25.

> Little Bo Peep, she lost her sheep!
>
> (XIII, 85)

In a tone of infinite weariness, Dipsychus confirms the unspoken conclusion, and ends the play with

> Peace, peace! I come.
>
> (XIII, 86)

7. Emphasis

By stressing the satire of *Dipsychus*, it is possible to view the poem as an attack on the introspective intellectual. Its broad meaning is then suggested by a passage in Clough's "Recent English Poetry":

> There is something certainly of an over-educated weakness of purpose in Western Europe.... There is a disposition to press too far the finer and subtler intellectual and moral susceptibilities; to insist upon following out, as they say, to their logical consequences, the notices of some single organ of the spiritual nature; a proceeding which perhaps is hardly more sensible in the grown man than it would be in the infant to refuse to correct the sensations of sight by those of the touch.

In another passage even more clearly applicable to *Dipsychus*, and written probably in the same year as the poem, Clough insisted that people must "settle the question of reconciling the world and the Spirit" by serving God *in* the world. To do so they had to cultivate "plain sense and worldly wisdom," and not stand "powerless to decide, unable to discern, stimulated by vague enthusiasm, and tortured by overirritable conscience."[56] This critical attitude certainly emerges in Scenes IX–XI and may have been what the poet intended to emphasize. But once he came face to face with submission to the world at all its cost imaginatively realized, Clough

---

56. *North American Review*, 77 (1853), 22, reprinted in *Prose, 1,* 377–78, or p. 372; *Poems and Prose Remains, 1,* 300.

could feel only sympathy for his protagonist and view the event as a tragic necessity.[57]

It is true that *Dipsychus* is not a tragedy in the usual sense. Clough had enough respect for his "villain" and enough distaste for his "hero" to keep the poem free from the suffering and injustice that mark the tragic experience, and from characters that assume tragic proportions. And yet Symonds was right to find here "the deep and subtle tragedy of human life and action—of free souls caged, and lofty aspirations curbed—a vulgar and diurnal tragedy over which no tears are shed in theatres, but which, we might imagine, stirs the sorrow of the angels day by day as they look down upon our world."[58]

[57]. This interpretation is supported by the later fragment, "Dipsychus Continued," for there Clough underlined the tragic implications of the original poem by showing Dipsychus, thirty years later, as a successful judge applauded by "the foolish crowd," but painfully aware of being "the slave and servant of the world" and doing "the justice that is but half just." When the woman he had once called Pleasure returns as a prostitute to confront him, he suffers acute remorse.

[58]. *Last and First*, p. 130.

7

MARI MAGNO

THE GREAT CREATIVE PERIODS of Clough's life were periods of extreme introspection, loneliness, and depression: 1839–41 at Oxford under the shock of seeing the religion of Arnold challenged by both Catholicism and Theism, and 1849–51 at London when the defeat of political liberalism and the disillusionment of finding University College as intolerant as Oxford, made it "the dreariest, loneliest period of his life."[1] In America from November 1852 to July 1853, there was the distraction of social intercourse with Emerson, Norton, and other Bostonians, and at the same time a neurotic depression too deep for creative excitement. Some of the "Songs in Absence" are attractive, but some are scarcely above the level of the Annuals, and the other pieces he wrote in the United States are thin and conventional. His American writing consisted mainly of the translation of Plutarch and half a dozen essays for periodicals. After he entered the Education Office upon his return in 1853, he abandoned poetry entirely until his last illness in 1861.[2]

There is no problem about this eight-year silence. The drudgery of his work and the demands of a growing family (he had married

---

1. *Prose, 1,* 39, or p. 41, for the quotation; cf. a remark made to Blanche Smith on Dec. 31, 1851 (the MS. letter is in the Bodleian Library): "I have been sitting 'among the tombs & in desert places' pretty well two years now." For intolerance, see *Prose, 1,* 164, or p. 170; for his depression in America, see my "Checklist" of Clough's prose, items 50, 51, 54, 56, and his letters to Blanche Smith from Nov. 1852, to June 1853, in the *Correspondence*.

2. *Correspondence, 2,* 608.

in 1854) left him little time or energy for writing,³ but the crucial factor was a pattern of life that destroyed the conditions that had nourished his creative spirit. Mrs. Clough's account of the matter is straight to the point:

> Up to this date we may almost say that he had been too free from active and absorbing employment for his own happiness. . . . The want of definite and continuous occupation left his mind free to deal restlessly with the great insoluble problems of the world, which had for him so true a vitality that he could not dismiss them from his thoughts. After his marriage there was none of this enforced and painful communing with self alone. He had plenty to do; and the close relations into which he was brought with various members of his wife's family kept him actively employed, and tasked his sympathies to the full. All the new duties and interests of domestic life grew up and occupied his daily thoughts. The humour which in solitude had been inclined to take the hue of irony and sarcasm, now found its natural and healthy outlet.⁴

However irritating the complacent tone and the bland assumption that married "happiness" was much superior to the painful self-communing that had been transmuted into poetry, that is the primary explanation. And though we may dislike her account of the change as progress—and suspect it too (one wonders if his "experience . . . at home," as Mrs. Clough goes on to say, "made many perplexed questions . . . clear and simple to his mind")—it is doubtful if Clough himself would have disagreed. Weary of inaction, distressed by the endless dialogue of the mind with itself, suffering from the isolation of the introvert, and plagued by the moral problem of sex, he must have welcomed his new life for the release it brought him. More than that, it meant the fulfilment of half his nature—call it his Rugby nature. He now enjoyed, Mrs. Clough reports, not only "natural repose in the pleasures of a home," but also the opportunity to devote himself "to the service of others,"

---

3. Ibid., 2, 588; *Prose, 1,* 44, 45–46, or pp. 45, 47.
4. *Prose, 1,* 44–45, or p. 46.

including Florence Nightingale. It may be true, too, that this final period was one of "rest and contentment."[5]

But to imagine, as Jowett did, that Clough's marriage was "the real blessing and happiness of his life" is surely mistaken, and a final sign of the indifference to his art that characterized his friends.[6] It was not a blessing for the poet and therefore it was not happiness for the man. Clough was too intelligent not to recognize the cost involved, however willing he was to pay it. Indeed, he had always thought of marriage and literature as incompatible, and had viewed the former almost as a temptation. "I sometimes think," he wrote to Blanche Smith even when they were engaged, "that my course is one that must be walked alone, and that it is altogether too unpleasant and poverty stricken for married happiness"; that by comparison he thought living "in domestic comfort . . . a little ignoble"; that his "ambition" was to live in "a world of abstraction."[7] Nonetheless, like his own Dipsychus, he submitted to the Spirit, and in the event sacrificed literary work for domestic comfort. So he must have viewed it, in wry silence. More than one remark of Mrs. Clough's betrays a state of mind that is scarcely happy. "To a period of wasting thought and solitude [before his marriage] succeeded one of over-strenuous exertion"; he worked not "according to his strength, but according to his will"; "his mind turned more and more to action as its natural relief." When he tried to resume his duties at the Education Office after a leave-of-absence for ill health in which he did some writing, he overtaxed himself instantly—"not by what he did but by *the old anxieties* coming back on him."[8] One of them, surely, was the recognition of having suppressed, by marriage and compulsive work, the one talent which is death to hide.

But the ill health that drove him abroad in 1861 had its compensation, for as soon as Clough was "again at leisure *and in solitude*

---

5. Ibid., *1*, 44, or p. 46.
6. *Correspondence*, 2, 605. Mrs. Clough makes the same claim in *Prose*, *1*, 46, or p. 47. It is only fair to add that later on when Jowett read Clough's poetry with some attention, he recognized (*Letters of Benjamin Jowett*, ed. Evelyn Abbott and Lewis Campbell [London, 1899], p. 177) that "he was a real poet."
7. *Prose*, *1*, 172, 193, 195, or pp. 178, 199–200, 201.
8. *Prose*, *1*, 45, 47, or pp. 47, 49; *Correspondence*, 2, 613, 614. The italics are mine.

... the old fountain of verse, so long dry within him, reopened afresh,"⁹ and in a brief revival of creative life, he wrote his fifth long poem, *Mari Magno, or Tales on Board.*

1. A New Departure

No work of Clough's has met with such divided judgment. For all his high opinion of the poet, Henry Sidgwick called it the "genius of twaddle"; and in our time Morchard Bishop, after praising *Amours de Voyage,* thought *Mari Magno* might be the "most embarrassingly dreadful long poem of the nineteenth century." On the other hand, to J. A. Symonds it was this "ripest product of his mind" that "won [him] a place among the poets of the world"; and more recently H. W. Garrod decided that if *Mari Magno* had been completed, it would have been "Clough's masterpiece" and have made its author a great poet.¹⁰

As these quotations might imply, the critics seem agreed at least on one thing: that the new poem, coming after eight years of silence, was a new departure radically different from his previous work. The point was made explicitly by Mrs. Clough:

> He had to enter on a new line, to create a new treatment of old subjects, to turn them over and bring them out in the new light of his critical but kindly philosophy. This, in "Mari Magno," he had begun to do, and the rapid production of these last poems makes us believe that this new vein would have continued had he lived, and that we should have received a further expression of his views about the daily problems of social life.

These remarks belong in the same context with a statement that follows her description of Clough's release from painful self-com-

---

9. *Prose, 1,* 51, or p. 52. The italics are mine.
10. Sidgwick, *Miscellaneous Essays,* p. 87, though this extreme view is modified in his *Memoir* (above, Chap. 5, n. 23), p. 216; Bishop (above, Chap. 5, n. 6), p. 72; Symonds, *Last and First,* p. 96, and *Cornhill Magazine, 14* (1866), 419 (the authorship of this article is assigned to Symonds on a publisher's list); Garrod, *Poetry and the Criticism of Life,* p. 122. Favorable comments by R. H. Hutton and J. A. Froude are quoted in Lady Chorley, *Clough,* p. 321.

muning: that having "passed from the speculative to the constructive phase of thought," he would, had he lived, have written works of a "more positive and substantial kind."[11]

Certainly, no one can read through the poetry chronologically and not come on *Mari Magno* with surprise; but not primarily for the reason Mrs. Clough gives, that the "new treatment of old subjects" was objective in focus and didactic in purpose. It is true that Clough wanted, now more than ever, to turn away from his inner life and write a series of stories on his old subject of love and marriage, each to be related by a passenger on an ocean liner, and each to illustrate a moral idea. This is substantially what he did. The first tale, for example, centering on a marriage thwarted by the hero's indecision, is a retelling of *Amours de Voyage,* with more story and far less introspective analysis. The third tale, the American's, is a concrete and literal illustration of Claude's speculations, in the same poem, on juxtaposition.[12] Between these two is the second, the Clergyman's first tale, which opens with an obvious description of Clough himself (lines 24–46), and goes on to explore the frustrations of desire in a manner very like *Dipsychus,* but its unexpected denouement and the constructive moral at the end, "Love is fellow-service," hold it to the new line.

The denouement is the accidental meeting of the lovers after their "final" separation five years earlier, followed by the marriage they so narrowly missed. This happy ending is characteristic of *Mari Magno;* for the "new treatment of old subjects," if not optimistic, was at least hopeful, as it was bound to be in a poetry that deliberately avoided the anxieties of introspection and aimed at a moral impression. If a girl stands alone on a Liverpool dock without family or friends to protect her, a kind sea captain marries her out of pity. If a Scotch lassie sails to Australia, persuaded that her Oxford gentlemen has deserted her, she finds there a father for her child, and years later, on a visit to England, makes her lover happy by giving him back his son—who is gladly accepted by the childless

---

11. *Prose, 1,* 41, 45, or pp. 42–43, 47. Cf. *1,* 40, or p. 41: "The 'Ambarvalia' . . . are all poems of the inner life, while the 'Mari Magno' poems deal with social problems, and the questions of love and marriage."

12. See Canto III, letter vi.

A NEW DEPARTURE

wife. Everywhere reparation is made or forgiveness offered for sins that are not very black.

But strictly speaking, of course, the new line of *Mari Magno* was not really new. Thirteen years earlier, Clough had written an objective narrative with a happy ending in which "problems of social life" were also under scrutiny and more than one moral was implied. As a matter of fact, the final tale in *Mari Magno* is a rewriting of *The Bothie,* taking the same situation of a love affair between a "College fellow" and a Highland girl and exploring the results of the opposite possibility, of their *not* marrying. What Mrs. Clough found new in 1861 is simply a return to 1848, and a fresh effort to develop a line that had been largely abandoned in *Amours de Voyage* and entirely so in *Dipsychus.*

What is really new in *Mari Magno* is something quite different, and for a modern reader not only surprising but on first contact disappointing. There are modern analogies that enable us to read *Dipsychus* and *Amours de Voyage* in our stride. But for this poem we do not have the knowledge of George Crabbe and Coventry Patmore that would remove the initial strangeness and forestall an immediate distaste. If we are unprepared, the first lines of the poem can seem appalling:

> "Dearest of boys, please come to-day,
> Papa and mama have bid me say,
> They hope you'll dine with us at three;
> They will be out till then, you see,
> But you will start at once, you know,
> And come as fast as you can go.
> Next week they hope you'll come and stay
> Some time, before you go away.
> Dear boy, how pleasant it will be!
> Ever your dearest Emily!"
>
> (I, i, 1–10)

But the impression would be different, even today, let alone at the time, if we knew the opening lines of Patmore's *Faithful for Ever,* published a year earlier:

> Mother, I smile at your alarms!
> I own, indeed, my Cousin's charms,
> But, like all nursery maladies,
> Love is not badly taken twice.
> Have you forgotten Charlotte Hayes,
> My playmate in the pleasant days
> At Knatchley, and her sister, Anne,
> The twins, so made on the same plan,
> That one wore blue, the other white,
> To mark them to their father's sight.

Clough read *The Angel in the House* in 1855 and liked it; read *Faithful for Ever* in February 1861, and liked it even better. In between, in 1856, he read all of Crabbe, admired his realism, and thought some of his tales of "the highest merit."[13] Though the plan of a series of stories told by travellers came from Chaucer, the idea of domestic tales of ordinary life centering on love and marriage, and told in a conversational, off-hand manner, was suggested by the blended influence of Patmore and Crabbe. The result was something new for Clough, and something which is unfamiliar, or dated, for us.

As always, Clough made his imitations his own. If not so sternly powerful or tragic as Crabbe's, his tales have greater tenderness and more delicate perception, and compared with Patmore, few of the trivial domesticities and almost none of the sentimentalism. Clough's anti-Romantic view of love, which here again is affirmed, saved him from Victorian "woman-worship," and brought a realism into his studies of love and marriage not to be found in Patmore.[14]

Nevertheless, the plain style of *Mari Magno* is uneven and inadequate. Everywhere there are traces of hurried and unrevised composition as Clough felt the pressure of time in the face, if not of death, of imminent return to his life in England: stop-gap phrases and stop-gap lines, words that confuse or destroy the rhythm, bad

---

13. *Correspondence*, 2, 494, 522, 584.
14. In this paragraph I am indebted to Symonds, *Last and First*, p. 95. The anti-Romantic view of love is in Tale II, 136–47, *Poems*, pp. 336–37.

A NEW DEPARTURE 215

or conventional rhymes,[15] and above all passages here and there which no comparison with Crabbe or Patmore can make less banal or awkward than they are:

> Helston, my schoolfellow, but much
> My senior, in a yacht came o'er,
> His uncle with him, from the shore
> Under Worms-head: to take a sail
> He pressed them, but could not prevail;
> Mama was timid, durst not go,
> Papa was rather gruff with no.
>
> (I, i, 127–33)

This is what Sidgwick called "the deliberately *infantile* simplicity of style in which parts of them (especially [the] First Tale) are written."[16]

But the average level is much higher than that, and even in octosyllabics, where he was never at ease, Clough could succeed. After the dance

> the brief sleep of closing night
> Brought a sensation of delight,
> Which, when I woke, was exquisite.
> The music moving in my brain
> I felt; in the gay crowd again
> Half felt, half saw the girlish bands,
> On their white skirts their white-gloved hands,
> Advance, retreat, and yet advance,
> And mingle in the mingling dance.
>
> (I, ii, 118–26)

And his five-foot couplets can be used as effectively for narrative as for introspection.

> Going to his room, one day, upon the stair
> Above him he perceived her lingering there;
> Upon the stair she lingered; at the top,

---

15. Cf. Garrod, *Poetry and the Criticism of Life*, p. 122.
16. *Memoir* (above, Chap. 5, n. 23), p. 216.

> As though till he should follow, seemed to stop,
> And when he followed, moved—and yet looked round
> And seeming as if waiting to be found
> At her half-open chamber door she stood;
> A sudden madness mounted in his blood
> And took him in a moment to the place;
> He stooped, and seeking swift the half-hidden face
> There, with the exultation of a boy,
> Read in her liquid eyes the passion of her joy;
> And went in with her at the fatal door
> Whence he reissued innocent no more.
>
> (VI, 122–35)

Perhaps it is not the style so much as something else, equally new to Clough, that disturbs a modern reader. Though the handling of plot is often skillful, it is often Victorian in its use of melodramatic meetings and surprising coincidences. In three of the stories parted lovers suddenly encounter each other after long separation; in two others, trivial but incredible incidents remind one of Hardy's "Satires of Circumstance"; and in one of the tales the hero, suffering agonies of guilt for a small adultery abroad, is accosted in a London street by a "hapless thing of woe, the occasion of his shame twelve wretched months ago."[17] Sometimes the fault lies in the way the incident is handled. In the first tale, the young man who left the cousin he loved without a proposal is looking idly at the passengers embarking on a steamer at Brienz when suddenly he sees

> A figure full, but full of grace,
> Its movement beautified the place.
> It turns, advances, comes my way;
> What do I see, what do I say?
> Yet to a statelier beauty grown,
> It is, it can be, she alone!
> O mountains round! O heaven above!
> It is—Emilia, whom I love;
> "Emilia, whom I love," the word

---

17. Tale VI, 241–42, *Poems*, p. 363.

> Rose to my lips, as yet unheard,
> When she, whose colour flushed to red,
> Half turned, and soft, "My husband," said;
> And Helston came up with his hand,
> And both of them took mine.
>
> (I, iv, 120–33)

In the last tale, the mother of the hero's illegitimate son, on seeing her former lover again in a London drawing-room, calls next day on his wife:

> "His child is six foot high,
> I've kept him as the apple of my eye,"
> Cried she, "he's riding, or you'd see him here.
> O joy, that he at last should see his father dear!"
>
> (VII, 343–46)

What is wrong with these passages is that neither is natural. Clough is trying to heighten the emotions artificially, and this clashes at once with the ordinary realities of life that are the substance of the tales.

Finally, two of the stories are marred for a modern reader by the assumption of mores that are now dated. Sexual irregularities which hardly seem damnable today are grounds for acute shame, so acute that in one case the fallen hero, though forgiven by his wife, will not return to his home, and does penance for a year in a London garret. But what is hardest to take is the deferential attitude of the Scotch lassie toward her Oxford gentleman. Speaking later of the marriage that did not take place, Christian tells him:

> Though for myself, indeed, I sought it not,
> It seemed so high, so undeserved a lot,
> But for the child, when it should come, I knew—
> O, I was certain—what you meant to do.
>
> (VII, 414–17)

Apropos of his failure to return to Liverpool and of the sacrifice of a small income his marriage would have entailed, she remarks, abjectly:

> O, and myself how willingly I blamed,
> So simple who had been and unashamed,
> And mindful only of the present joy,
> When you had anxious care your busy mind to employ.
> Ah, well, I said, but now at least he's free,
> He will not have to lower himself for me.
> He will not lose three hundred pounds a year,
> In many ways my love had cost him dear.
>
> (464-71)

A word of critical detachment from Clough would have shifted the perspective, but in this area he was still very Victorian. It was radical enough that he viewed affairs of this kind with concern, and that he was willing to tolerate marriage across class lines; but the class lines still seemed to him entirely proper.

2. Distinction

In these various ways, involving style and plot and mores, *Mari Magno* is the most dated and the least successful of Clough's longer poems. But once its "Victorianisms" are recognized as such, the high quality of the best tales is apparent. Their chief virtue is Clough's unique ability—perhaps I should say willingness—to record experiences of daily life. He uses material which almost anyone would pass by as too ordinary and trivial, especially that of adolescence and early manhood, and by treating it with delicacy, he gives it almost the excitement of the strange. To put this another way, he will take situations that most poets would dramatize or romanticize, and handle them with a simple fidelity that illuminates their neglected realities. For this we may partly thank his conviction that poetry should deal with "ordinary feelings, the obvious rather than the rare facts of human nature."[18] But primarily we should trace it to that extreme sincerity which was also by moments an artistic liability. "The good feature in all your poems," Arnold told him (the bad feature, of course, being their

---

18. *Prose, 1,* 360-61, or p. 357.

deficiency in art) "is the sincerity that is evident in them: which always produces a powerful effect on the reader—and which most people with the best intentions lose totally when they sit down to write. The spectacle of a writer striving evidently to get breast to breast with reality is always full of instruction and very invigorating."[19] Though such a criticism of "all" Clough's poems is biased and misleading, it applies fairly well to *Mari Magno*. For there limitations in form are balanced by Clough's description of amatory emotions as they exist outside of "poetry and novels."[20] A commentary on the first tale will indicate the kind of distinction which I also find in the second, and to some degree in the sixth and seventh.

In a five-part structure Clough follows the changing relations of Emily and the narrator from boy-girlhood to a final meeting as friends after her marriage. On his first visit, when he is twelve and she fourteen, an incident occurs on an excursion to Sea-Mew Island:

> And I and Emily out of reach
> Strayed from the rest along the beach.
> Looking into a sort of cave
> She stood, when suddenly a wave
> Ran up; I caught her by the frock,
> And pulled her in, and o'er a rock,
> So doing, stumbled, rolled, and fell.
> She knelt down, I remember well,
> Bid me where I was hurt to tell,
> And kissed me three times as I lay;
> But I jumped up and limped away.
>
> (I, i, 138–48)

Nothing more is said nor need be. Next year they exchange valentines. His is a poem he composed for the occasion, but hers was bought.

---

19. *Letters to Clough,* p. 86.
20. Tale II, 143.

> 'Twas stupid of her, as I thought:
> Why not have written one?
>
> (I, i, 160–61)

Five years later on the next visit (part ii), the young man is amazed to find Emily transformed into a poised young woman who seems to him to have

> Such knowledge in her eyes and brow;
> For all I read and thought I knew,
> She simply looked me through and through.

> She had not studied, had not read,
> Seemed to have little in her head,
> Yet of herself the right and true,
> As of her own experience, knew.
> Straight from her eyes her judgments flew,
> Like absolute decrees they ran.
>
> (I, ii, 41–43, 46–51)

As we should expect, Clough's hero is acutely unhappy and awkward at the country ball. He hates dances. But the next morning dim feelings of delight recall the dancing figures in all their charm, and he concludes:

> The impulse had arrived at last,
> When the opportunity was past.
>
> (I, ii, 127–28)

This incident and the comment are both symbolic; the latter, indeed, might have stood as an epigraph to the entire story. During the rest of his visit the hero cannot regain his confidence. He can only be rude to the girls; look "to their father still with fear of how to him I must appear"; find himself "put to shame when once some rough he-cousins came"; and at last depart, "half glad, half wretched."

A year later (part iii), there was no problem of silence. The Oxford intellectual

> talked in a superior tone
> Of things the girls had never known,
> Far wiser to have let alone;
>
> (I, iii, 22-24)

and "the busy argufying brain of the prize schoolboy" made everyone miserable, including himself. The motives are various, but one

> was the instinctive wish to try
> And, above all things, not be shy.
>
> (I, iii, 40-41)

A word, a jest, a laugh might have restored the old associations, "but nothing came."

When he next meets Emily in Switzerland (part iv), he is returning from a trip to Greece and Rome. Reclining on the Giesbach turf, he muses:

> Travel's a miniature life,
> Travel is evermore a strife,
> Where he must run who would obtain.
> 'Tis a perpetual loss and gain;
> For sloth and error dear we pay,
> By luck and effort win our way,
> And both have need of, every day.
>
> (I, iv, 66-72)

This too is symbolic, for his own loss, out of sloth or error, is almost immediately apparent. When he suddenly sees Emily in a group of tourists and knows at once, at last, that he loves her, he is introduced a moment later to her husband.

The final meeting, which occurs presently in England (part v), is a masterpiece of narrative dialogue in which the speakers pretend to answer questions which they really use as opportunities to say something else, managing all the while to imply the love they will not mention. She begins by urging him not to waste his days in a college: "Fellows grow indolent," and in any case he will wish sometime to marry [which Fellows were not allowed to do in unreformed Oxford]. He seizes on the opening to charge her, obliquely, with having married without love:

> I said, "Emilia, people change,
> And yet, I own, I find it strange
> To hear this common talk from you:
> You speak, and some believe it true,
> Just as if any wife would do;
> Whoe'er one takes, 'tis much the same,
> And love—and so forth, but a name."
>   She coloured. "What can I have said,
> Or what could put it in your head?
> Indeed, I had not in my mind
> The faintest notion of the kind."
>   I told her that I did not know—
> Her tone appeared to mean it so.
> "Emilia, when I've heard," I said,
> "How people match themselves and wed,
> I've sometimes wished that both were dead."
>
> (I, v, 31–46)

For "people" we should read "you and your husband" (on the authority of "both"), though the speaker may not be aware of it. She ignores the implied criticism of "match" and repeats her admonition, dropping the argument of marriage:

> "I know it will be just a crime
> If you should waste your powers and time.
> There is so much, I think, that you,
> And no one equally, can do."
> "It does not matter much," said I,
> "The things I thought of are gone by;
> I'm quite content to wait to die."
>
> (I, v, 56–62)

This complements line 46. The tone that had been bitter is now weary, with a touch of self-pity (he is asking to be comforted), and neither reference to death is to be taken literally. Emily is roused at first to scorn and then to still higher praise, encouraging him with a gesture of self-abasement as she foresees a time when he may look back on her and her sisters with disdain; and if this happens,

> So you your rightful place obtain,
> That will to me be joy, not pain.
>
> (I, v, 88–89)

When they part next day he thinks she would have kissed him (the earlier kiss when he hurt himself in the cave is now recalled with irony), but he turns away, saying to himself, " 'Twas better not to have it so," which reverberates with meaning. The story ends a year later with a revealing remark: although he had not valued her judgment (it was only her words that had had power to touch him),

> Strangely still,
> It had been cogent on my will.
> As she had counselled, I had done,
> And a new effort was begun.
>
> (I, v, 107–10)

The best commentary on this story and the next, as well as on the last two—indeed, on most of Clough's narrative art—was made by J. A. Symonds in 1868:

> He is able to see men and women as they are, very imperfect in their affections, often too weak even to love without an *arrière pensée*, letting priceless opportunity slip by, and killing the flower of one part of their nature by the drought and dryness of the other part.[21]

The piteous waste of possibility with its frustration of the heart or of the soul, and the response it evokes—never rebellious or bitter, simply a quiet joylessness as of a burden borne without complaint and without hope—this is the persistent quality of Clough's vision. It is recorded most poignantly in *Dipsychus* and *Amours de Voyage*. But even in the hopeful *Mari Magno* we find the same somber view, for on second scrutiny the happy endings are seen to be so accidental as to suggest the one-in-a-million, and they scarcely obliterate the previous suffering. In the second tale, the lost opportunity would have continued to reduce two human

---

21. *Last and First*, p. 96.

beings to a minimal existence but for a chance meeting five years after parting, when by good luck they are both still single. In the clergyman's second tale, the guilt of an overscrupulous conscience comes close to wrecking the lives of a whole family, and the misery of husband and wife is ended only by the accidental illness of a daughter, calling the father to his home again. The final story has the same kind of "happy" ending—hardly more than a release from unhappiness—and Clough called it "a tale of human suffering and tears." He was thinking of the painful separation of the lovers, the anxiety of the unwed mother, her new grief at leaving her son with his father, and the father's cry at the end,

> O love, love, love, too late!
>
> (VII, 510)

One remembers the refrain of the *conducteur's* song in "My Tale," though written in a lighter key: "Adieu, gay loves, it is too late a day."[22] Always the saving opportunity lies in the past, thwarted by accident or indecision; nothing comes to fruition. In some lines written in 1851, Clough's deepest wisdom is embodied in masterly form:

> But that from slow dissolving pomps of dawn
> No verity of slowly strengthening light
> Early or late hath issued; that the day
> Scarce-shown, relapses rather, self-withdrawn,
> Back to the glooms of ante-natal night,
> For this, O human beings, mourn we may.[23]

22. *Poems*, p. 348.
23. Ibid., p. 395.

A FINAL WORD

THAT CLOUGH WAS A FAILURE because he was not an artist, that he should have written in prose, that he wrote only one memorable poem ("Say not the struggle nought availeth")—this long injustice at long last is dying. It cannot survive, we see, a fresh and sensitive scrutiny of his work. In a score of shorter poems, and especially in *The Bothie, Amours de Voyage* and *Dipsychus,* Clough's success is demonstrable. I will not argue that he was a major poet and not a minor one; the terms are loose. I will only claim that for us he belongs with Tennyson, Browning, Arnold, and Hopkins, intrinsically and relevantly. No doubt he wrote nothing so impressive as "In Memoriam," "The Ring and the Book," "Empedocles on Etna," or "The Wreck of the Deutschland." But his three masterpieces emerge today as superior, I think, to "The Princess," "Maud," and most of the "Idylls," to "Pippa Passes" and "In a Balcony," to "Balder Dead," "Sohrab and Rustum," or "Tristram and Iseult."[1] In an essay written in 1882, R. H. Hutton placed Clough among his peers:

> For my own part, though I should not assert that Clough is the great poet of our age, I should agree heartily with Mr. Lowell that he will in future generations rank among the highest of our time, and that especially he will be ranked with Matthew Arnold, as having found a voice for this self-questioning age—a voice of greater range and richness even, and of a deeper pathos. . . .[2]

1. Arnold himself told Clough (*Letters to Clough*, p. 147) that when, in *The Bothie* and *Amours de Voyage*, he used the manner later adopted by Tennyson in "Maud," he used it with "far more freedom vigour and abundance than he [Tennyson] does."

2. *Brief Literary Criticisms*, ed. Elizabeth M. Roscoe (London and New York, 1906), pp. 305, 306. The essay first appeared in the *Spectator* for Nov. 25, 1882.

It is true that Clough lacked the variety of Tennyson, Browning, and Arnold, and the originality of Hopkins. His refusal to utilize medieval legend and classical myth, the limited scope of his characters, the predominantly subjective and skeptical nature of his poems, and the plainness of his style give his work less diversity than that of his major contemporaries. But on a second or third reading, with special attention to the narrative poems of 1848–50, one comes to recognize an unexpected range and depth. Clough was amazingly aware of both himself and his age, and alert to the newest developments of thought that spring up at the point of intersection. His notation of anti-heroism and the loss of identity was not only early but perceptive: he saw most of the causes. No one struck more forcefully at the amoral character of a worldly society. But Clough's major insight was psychological. He explored subtleties of feeling that included paradoxical emotions, followed the devious twistings of inner debate, and knew the dumb sense of thwarted effort and lost opportunity. His range of observation is reflected in his range of form: satire, comedy, and romance; sensuous description; philosophical lyric; and the dialectic of reason. And he created a style equal to his need. His control of syntax, denotation, and tones of voice, especially the tone of irony—all in natural idiom and flexible rhythms—was skillful enough to project his complex experience. He did not succeed, perhaps, as often as Tennyson, Browning, and Arnold, but he left behind him a distinguished body of work.

In addition to its intrinsic virtues, Clough's poetry has the further attraction of contemporary relevance. We welcome his special capacity, so rare in his own age, for double vision. He could see at least two sides to every question. (He could even see two sides to seeing two sides of every question.) He could sympathize with Hewson, Claude, and Dipsychus, admire them and praise them, and at the same time allow the critical spirit to expose their limitations. Here, as in shorter poems like "Is it true, ye gods, who treat us," "That there are powers above us I admit," or—significant title —"Thesis and Antithesis," he had the ability attributed by Eliot to the metaphysicals, and by inference to the moderns, of recognizing, "implicit in the expression of every experience . . . other kinds of experience which are possible."[3] This gift of dipsychian vision saved him from both the simplifications and the didacticisms of his contemporaries, and now makes him a living poet in the 1960s.

His modernity has broader foundations. In 1869 Henry Sidgwick described the emergence of what might be called "the modern spirit" in terms that sound surprisingly contemporary today, and traced its first manifestation to Clough:

> His point of view and habit of mind are less singular in England in the year 1869 than they were in 1859, and much less than they were in 1849. We are growing year by year more introspective and self-conscious: the current philosophy leads us to a close, patient, and impartial observation and analysis of our mental processes. . . . We are growing at the same time more unreserved and unveiled in our expression; in conversations, in journals and books, we more and more say and write what we actually do think and feel, and not what we intend to think or should desire to feel. We are growing also more sceptical in the proper sense of the word: we suspend our judgment much more than our predecessors, and much more contentedly: we see that there are many sides to many questions: the opinions that we do hold we hold if not more loosely, at least more at arm's length: we can imagine how they appear to others, and can conceive ourselves not holding them. We are losing in faith and confidence . . . and we are gaining in impartiality and comprehensiveness of sympathy. In each of these respects, Clough, if he were still alive, would find himself gradually more and more at home in the changing world.[4]

He would be even more at home today when these characteristics are built into our frame of mind.

Clough did not use the tightly integrated form or the condensed image packed with implication which are now so much in vogue. But nevertheless, like Byron—the later Byron he preferred to the earlier—he achieved "almost all the virtues of ambiguity and comprehensiveness which may accompany a poetry of synthe-

---

3. From "Andrew Marvell," *Essays* (above, Chap. 2, n. 29), p. 289.
4. *Miscellaneous Essays*, p. 60.

sis"; and he achieved them primarily by using "the ironic juxtapositions" that express "the balanced point of view."[5] When we add to this the intellectual character of his verse and the idiomatic style devoid of sensuous diction and incantatory rhythm, we realize that Clough is not only one of the best of Victorian poets, he is also perhaps the most modern.

5. Ernest J. Lovell, Jr., "Irony and Image in Byron's *Don Juan,*" *The Major English Romantic Poets,* ed. C. D. Thorpe, Carlos Baker, and Bennett Weaver (Carbondale, Illinois, 1957), p. 143. Clough's preference for the later Byron is in *Prose, 1,* 320, or p. 317.

BIBLIOGRAPHY

Arnold, Matthew, *Essays in Criticism, First Series* (1865), London, 1875.
—— *Essays in Criticism, Second Series* (1888), London and New York, 1891.
—— *Letters, 1848–1888*, ed. G. W. E. Russell, 2 vols. London and New York, 1901.
—— *The Letters of Matthew Arnold to Arthur Hugh Clough,* ed. H. F. Lowry, London and New York, 1932.
—— *On the Study of Celtic Literature and On Translating Homer,* New York, 1883. They were first published, respectively, in 1865 and 1861–62.
—— *Poetical Works,* ed. C. B. Tinker and H. F. Lowry, London, 1950. This edition contains the preface to *Poems* (1853).
Bagehot, Walter, "Clough's Poems," *National Review*, 15 (1862), 310–26, reprinted in his *Literary Studies* (1879), ed. R. H. Hutton, 3 vols. London, 1898.
Brooke, Stopford, *Four Victorian Poets: A Study of Clough, Arnold, Rossetti, Morris,* London and New York, 1908.
Carlyle, Thomas, *Critical and Miscellaneous Essays* (1838), 5 vols. in the Centenary Edition of Carlyle's *Works,* ed. H. D. Traill, 30 vols. New York, 1896–1901.
Chorley, Lady Katharine, *Arthur Hugh Clough: the Uncommitted Mind,* Oxford, 1962.
Clough, Arthur Hugh, *The Bothie of Tober-na-Vuolich: A Long-Vacation Pastoral,* Oxford and London, 1848. I have used the later title. The original one was *The Bothie of Toper-na-Fuosich.*
—— *Ambarvalia: Poems by Thomas Burbidge and Arthur Hugh Clough,* London and Oxford, 1849.
—— *Poems . . . with a Memoir* [by Francis Palgrave], Cambridge and London, 1862.
—— *Letters and Remains,* London, 1865.
—— *The Poems and Prose Remains . . . with a Selection from His Letters and a Memoir,* ed. his wife, 2 vols. London, 1869.

——— *Prose Remains . . . with a Selection from His Letters and a Memoir,* ed. his wife, London and New York, 1888. This and the first volume of the previous work are often cited together as *Prose;* where this is done, a double reference is given.

——— *Poems,* ed H. F. Lowry, A. L. P. Norrington, and F. L. Mulhauser, Oxford, 1951. Referred to as *Poems* in the notes.

——— *Correspondence,* ed. Frederick L. Mulhauser, 2 vols. Oxford, 1957.

Clough's MSS. Most of the letters are in the Bodleian Library at Oxford and the Houghton Library at Harvard: see the catalogue in *Correspondence,* 2, 622–49. All of the unpublished prose known to exist is in the same two libraries (see my "Checklist" cited below), except Clough's journals, which are now on loan to F. L. Mulhauser at Pomona College.

Clough, Blanche Smith, (Mrs. Clough), "Memoir of Arthur Hugh Clough," in *The Poems and Prose Remains* (1869), in many later editions of the poems, and in *Prose Remains* (1888).

Garrod, H. W., "Clough," *Poetry and the Criticism of Life,* Cambridge, Mass., 1931, pp. 109–27.

Houghton, Walter E., "The Prose Works of Arthur Hugh Clough: A Checklist and Calendar, with Some Unpublished Passages," *Bulletin of the New York Public Library, 64* (1960), 377–94. Referred to as "Checklist" in the notes.

——— *The Victorian Frame of Mind, 1830–1870,* New Haven, 1957.

Hudson, W. H., "Arthur Hugh Clough," *Studies in Interpretation,* New York and London, 1896, pp. 77–149.

Hutton, R. H., "Arthur Hugh Clough," *Spectator, 42* (1869), 1073–75, reprinted with some changes in *Essays Theological and Literary,* 2 vols. London, 1871, 2, 368–91, and *Literary Essays,* London and New York, 1892, pp. 286–309.

Osborne, James I., *Arthur Hugh Clough,* London, 1919.

Sidgwick, Henry, "The Poems and Prose Remains of Arthur Hugh Clough," *Westminster Review, 92* (1869), 363–87, reprinted in *Miscellaneous Essays and Addresses,* London, 1904, pp. 59–90.

Symonds, J. A., "Arthur Hugh Clough," *Fortnightly Review, 10* (1868), 589–617, reprinted in *Last and First,* ed. Albert Morell, New York, 1919, pp. 63–137.

Waddington, Samuel, *Arthur Hugh Clough: A Monograph,* London, 1883.

INDEX

Abrams, Meyer, 68 n.
Academy, 100 n.
Addison, Joseph, 10
Allingham, William, 39, 55, 99 n., 113, 131
Amiel, Henri Frédéric, 197
Anti-Hero, 128–35, 185–86, 226
Aristotle, 50, 109 n., 113
Arnold, Jane. *See* Foster, Mrs. W. E.
Arnold, Matthew, xii, 2, 3 n., 31, 32, 35, 37, 58, 64, 80, 81, 84, 97, 99, 110, 112–13, 115, 141, 174, 176, 195, 197–98, 225, 226; criticism of Clough's poetry, 1, 2, 3, 5–7, 7–8, 9, 10–11, 17 n., 18, 24, 25–26, 30, 36–37, 44, 96, 99, 118 n., 218–19; poems mentioned or quoted, 5–7, 22, 26 n., 58 n., 64, 69, 97, 99 n., 111 n., 129, 132, 141, 142–43, 159, 179 n., 197, 198, 225; theories of poetry, 7–8, 9 n., 11 n., 14–15, 17, 24, 25, 41–42, 69, 70, 78, 96, 99 n.
Arnold, Dr. Thomas, 13–14, 18, 34, 46, 71, 82, 92, 111 n., 129 n., 131, 173, 174, 177, 195, 208
Arnold, Thomas, Jr., 2 n., 34 n., 100 n., 136
Arthur, King, 129
Atlantic Monthly, 3
Auden, W. H., xii
Austen, Jane, 14, 99

Bagehot, Walter, 18, 22, 81 n., 135
Balance, 72 n., 110 n., 163
Balzac, Honoré de, 99
Barrett, Elizabeth. *See* Browning, Elizabeth Barrett
Bateson, F. W., 41 n.
Beattie, William, 113 n.
Beaumont, Francis, 41
Béranger, Pierre-Jean de, 56, 113, 165

Berkeley, George, 185
Bishop, Morchard, 126 n., 211
Blackwood's Magazine, 4
Blake, William, 170, 183
Book of Common Prayer, 66
Bottome, Phyllis, 34
Bridges, Robert, 42
Brimley, George, 13 n.
British Critic, 14 n., 58–59
British Quarterly Review, 96 n.
Brooke, Stopford, 19 n., 20, 61, 8_
Brookfield, Mrs., 73
Brown, E. K., 24 n.
Browning, Elizabeth Barrett, 95, 99
Browning, Robert, 37, 40, 51, 73, 75–76, 82, 99, 132, 225, 226
Bulletin of the New York Public Library, xii
Bunsen, Chevalier, 70
Burbidge, Thomas, 3, 27
Burke, Edmund, 129
Burns, Robert, 17, 41 n.
Butler, Joseph, 165, 191
Byron, George Gordon, Lord, 9, 17, 29, 39, 56, 71, 82–83, 88, 89, 93, 94, 95, 98, 113, 125, 129, 131, 132, 166, 192, 197, 227

Cambridge Apostles, 13, 46
Carlyle, Thomas, 3 n., 4 n., 13, 36, 69, 71, 72 n., 93–94, 95, 98, 126, 141, 173
Charlemagne, 129
Châteaubriand, François de, 125
Chaucer, Geoffrey, 17, 94, 99 n., 214
Chorley, Lady Katharine, 81 n., 157 n., 211 n.
Clough, Ann Perfect (Clough's mother), 114 n., 115 n., 120
Clough, Anne Jemima (Clough's sister), 51, 77 n., 90, 160

Clough, Arthur Hugh: in America, 2, 82, 157 n., 208; Arnold's poetry in relation to his, 3 n., 15, 24–26, 31, 64, 69–70, 142–43; eighteenth-century philosophy, 44–45, 168; theme of frustration, 154–55, 223–24, 226; limitations as a poet, 15, 30–37, 214–18, 226; on love, 45, 135–55, 183–84, 194, 212, 214; marriage and his writing, 15, 208–10; and metaphysical poetry, 49–55, 64; modern characteristics today, xii, 22–23, 93, 95, 112, 226–28; and neo-classical poetry, 10–12, 25, 38–49, 62; use of the New Testament, 52–53, 61, 65–68, 190, 203, 205; use of the Old Testament, 33, 52–53, 57, 72, 73, 75, 78, 80–91, 175, 190, 203, 204, 205; at Oxford, 2, 6, 20, 24, 46, 70, 77, 80–82, 84, 92, 160, 173, 176; theories of poetry, 38–44, 45–46, 48, 55–59, 68, 82–83, 95, 97–99, 158, 218; religious attitudes in the poems, 60–68, 70, 80, 82–91, 122–31, 184, 188–90, 191; and Romanticism, 38, 45–46, 55–68, 71; at Rugby School, 2, 13, 20, 24, 68, 82, 173; social and political attitudes in the poems, 100–02, 104–06, 109–12, 123–24, 131, 134; his style, 12–13, 17, 114–15, 226 (*see* references just above under metaphysical, neo-classical, and Romanticism); at University College, 40, 82, 208; at University Hall, 2, 160. *See also* under Anti-Hero; Doubt; Evangelicalism; Identity; Purity

———, Poems:
Adam and Eve, 25, 57, 80–91, 92–93
"Ah, what is love, our love, she said," 32–33
Ambarvalia, 2–3, 12, 27, 32, 44, 56, 59, 92, 212 n.
Amours de Voyage, xii, 3, 15–16, 17, 19 n., 20, 25, 34, 56, 72, 95, 96, 100, 119–55, 156, 158, 160, 184 n., 211, 212, 213, 223, 225, 226
"Blank Misgivings of a Creature moving about in Worlds not realized," 31–32, 56, 61, 77, 175–76
Bothie of Tober-na-Vuolich, xii, 3, 5, 7, 15–16, 17, 18 n., 19 n., 20, 25, 26, 56, 80, 82, 92–118, 119, 130, 156, 158, 160, 213, 225, 226
"But that from slow dissolving pomps of dawn," 224
Dipsychus, xii, 16, 17, 25, 40, 45, 49, 56, 58, 61, 72, 82, 87, 95, 132, 155, 156–207, 212, 213, 223, 225, 226
"*Dipsychus* Continued: A Fragment," 157, 207 n.
"Duty—that's to say complying," 72
"Easter Day. Naples, 1849," 38, 58, 64–68, 171, 178, 191
"Easter Day II," 189, 191
"Enough, small room,—tho' all too true," 77
"Epi-Strauss-ium," 38, 50, 52–53
"Genesis XXIV," 78
"Hope evermore and believe," 32
"In controversial foul impureness," 46–48
"In the Great Metropolis," 72
"Is it true, ye gods, who treat us," 27–30, 38, 226
"It fortifies my soul to know," 91
"Jacob," 38, 73–78, 175
"Jacob's Wives," 78
"July's Farewell," 106 n.
"The Latest Decalogue," 38, 56, 72–73
"Look you, my simple friend," 12, 72
Mari Magno, 56 n., 57–58, 70 n., 82, 116 n., 208–24
"The Mystery of the Fall." *See* under *Adam and Eve*
"Natura Naturans," 38, 53–55
Poems, ed. Lowry, Norrington, and Mulhauser (1951), xi, 3 n., 22, 23, 157, 158 n.
"Qua Cursum Ventus," 38, 50
"Qui Laborat, Orat," 38, 43, 44
"Repose in Egypt," 78
Poems in the *Rugby Magazine*, 3
"Say not the struggle nought availeth," 3, 38, 47, 225
"Seven Sonnets," 38
"Sic Itur," 50
"So I, as boyish years went by, went wrong," 77
"Song of Lamech," 76, 78, 91

INDEX

"Songs in Absence," 208
"That there are powers above us I admit," 60–61, 226
"Thesis and Antithesis," 226
"To the Great Metropolis," 72
"To think that men of former days," 130
"Upon the water, in the boat," 50
"Uranus," 38, 62–64
"ὁ θεὸς μετὰ σοῦ," 112 n.
"ὕμνος ἄυμνος," "Hymnos ahymnos," 44 n.
————, Prose:
Essays in the *Balance,* 72 n., 110 n., 163
Checklist of Clough's Prose Writings, by W. E. Houghton, xii, 49 n., 56 n., 71 n.
Correspondence, ed. Mulhauser, xi, 14 n., 22, 23
"The Development of English Literature," 44–45, 168
Dryden, lectures on, 40–41, 42
"Letters of Parepidemis," 115 n.
"Notes on the Religious Tradition," 30 n., 80
"On Language," 48
"Poems and Ballads of Goethe," 139 n., 140 n.
"Recent English Poetry," 15 n., 78, 97–99, 206
"Review of F. W. Newman's *The Soul,*" 80, 168 n., 173 n., 174 n.
"Review of Some Poems by Alexander Smith and Matthew Arnold." See "Recent English Poetry"
Rugby and Oxford Journals, xi
Essays in the *Rugby Magazine,* 68 n., 78
Swift, lectures on, 42 n., 131 n., 167
Undergraduate Essays, 71, 77 n.
Wordsworth, lecture on, 30, 37 n., 41, 56, 82–83, 88
Clough, Mrs. Arthur Hugh (née Blanche M. Smith), 2, 6, 7 n., 25 n., 30 n., 44 n., 45, 80, 81, 92 n., 100 n., 136, 140, 146 n., 151 n., 157, 175, 208 n., 209–10, 211–12, 213; her views of Clough's poetry, 3 n., 4, 15, 18, 53 n., 59 n.
Clough, James B. (Clough's father), 70, 77, 78, 175
Coleridge, John Duke Lord, 46 n.
Coleridge, Samuel Taylor, 10, 11, 24, 25, 57, 68, 140
Collins, Mortimer, 96 n.
Collins, W. Lucas, 4 n.
Columbus, 94
Congreve, William, 107
Conington, John, 12 n.
Contemporary Review, 21 n.
Conybeare, William Daniell, 70
Cornhill Magazine, 4, 211 n.
Cowper, William, 40, 41, 44, 59
Cox, R. G., 39 n.
Crabbe, George, 40, 71, 94, 116, 213–15

Daily News, 4
Dante, 45
Davie, Donald, 44 n., 48 n.
The Decade, 46
Dedalus, 62
Demosthenes, 42
Dickens, Charles, 97
Dickinson, Patric, 23 n.
Donne, John, 9, 49, 50–51, 57
Doubt and ennui, 5 n., 19, 36, 57–58, 65, 68–69, 81–82, 84, 92, 110–11, 125–28, 146 n., 153, 202, 206
Dowden, Edward, 14
Drake, Sir Francis, 94
Dryden, John, 9, 11, 17, 25, 40, 41, 42, 44, 50–51, 56, 59, 60, 61, 64, 115
Duff, Katherine, xi

Edinburgh Review, 39 n.
Eliot, George, 18
Eliot, T. S., xii, 44 n., 47, 48 n., 71, 124, 182, 226–27
Emerson, Ralph Waldo, 16, 92, 95, 115 n., 117 n., 150, 208
Empedocles, 160–61
English, 23 n., 119 n.
English Studies, 83 n.
Etudes Anglaises, 23 n.

Evangelicalism, 18, 33–36, 56, 99, 137, 172–74, 177, 195–97

Fairchild, Hoxie, 1, 37 n.
Flaubert, Gustave, 14
Fletcher, John, 41
Foakes, R. A., 50 n.
Fortnightly Review, 2 n.
Foster, Mrs. W. E., 69 n.
Fraser's Magazine, 12 n., 40 n., 113 n., 114 n., 139 n., 140 n.
Froude, James Anthony, 3, 4 n., 106, 211 n.

Garrod, H. W., 23 n., 170 n., 211, 215 n.
Gell, John, 58, 59, 73 n.
Germ, 96 n.
Gibbon, Edward, 129
Goethe, Wolfgang von, 30 n., 55, 69, 82, 86, 90–91, 93, 94, 95, 98–99, 113, 115, 116 n., 125, 135, 139, 140, 156, 162
Goldsmith, Oliver, 3, 41, 44 n.
Gollin, Richard, 1 n.
Gosse, Edmund, 20
Greene, Graham, xii
Guardian, 16 n.
Guyot, Edouard, 21 n.

Hallam, Arthur Henry, 9 n., 38, 44 n.
Hamilton, A. H. A., 100 n.
Hannay, James, 17 n.
Hardy, Thomas, 216
Hare, Julius, 10
Hawkins, Edward, 81
Heath-Stubbs, John, 23 n., 71
Herbert, George, 3, 49
Herschel, John Frederick William, 70
Homer, 5, 68, 81, 93, 115
Hopkins, Gerard Manley, 33, 42, 115 n., 225, 226
Houghton, Walter Edwards, 1 nn., 49 n., 56 n., 71 n., 77 n., 159 n., 208 n.; *Victorian Frame of Mind*, cited, 13 n., 15 n., 17 n., 34 n., 69 n., 106 n., 125 n., 126 n., 136 n., 173 n., 179 n., 196 n.
Hudson, W. H., 126 n., 164 n.
Hume, Joseph, 44, 129
Hutton, Richard Holt, 18, 81 n., 99 n., 115 n., 136, 141 n., 211 n., 225

Huxley, Thomas Henry, 141

Identity, problem of, 57–58, 92, 93, 197–99, 226

Johari, G. P., 80 n., 85 n.
Johnson, Samuel, 47, 48 n., 49
Johnson, Wendell Stacy, 58 n.
Journal of Aesthetics and Art Criticism, 10 n.
Jowett, Benjamin, 210
Jump, J. D., 23 n., 119 n., 126 n.
Juvenal, 71, 165

Kant, Immanuel, 165–66
Keats, John, 19, 39, 40, 41, 97
Kermode, Frank, 38 n., 44 n.
Killham, John, 102 n.
Kingsley, Charles, 12 n., 113, 114

Laforgue, Jules, xii
Langbaum, Robert, 159 n.
Leavis, F. R., xii
Leopardi, Giacomo, 14
Levy, Goldie, 22 n., 73 n.
Lewes, George Henry, 4 n., 116 n.
Lister, T. H., 39 n.
Living Age, 141 n.
Locke, John, 44, 45, 68
Longfellow, Henry Wadsworth, 99 n., 115 n.
Lovell, Ernest J., Jr., 228 n.
Lowell, James Russell, 4 n., 225
Lowry, Howard Foster, 6 n., 7 n., 22, 25 n., 111 n.
Loyola, Ignatius de, 123
Lucretius, 141, 142 n.
Lynd, Helen Merrell, 73 n.
Lyttelton, A. T., 141 n.

MacCarthy, Desmond, 19 n., 21, 22
Macaulay, Thomas Babington, 68
Macmillan, Daniel, 13 n.
Macmillan's Magazine, 19 n., 40 n., 156
MacNeice, Louis, xii, 162 n.
Malebranche, Nicolas de, 185
Margoliouth, H. M., 140 n.
Maurice, Frederick Denison, 93

INDEX

Medwin, Thomas, 93 n.
Milford, Sir Humphrey, 20, 37 n.
Mill, John Stuart, 9 n., 125
Milton, John, 9 n., 10, 41 n., 45, 55, 112–13, 165, 168, 170
Mozley, John Rickards, 19 n., 126 n.
Mulhauser, Frederick, 23 n., 81 n.
Murray, John, 93 n.

Newman, Francis W., 80, 168 n., 173 n., 174 n.
Newman, John Henry, 14, 116–17, 173, 195
New Statesman and Nation, 23 n.
Newton, Isaac, 45, 68
New York Times Book Review, 23 n.
Nicolson, Harold, 23
Nightingale, Florence, 20, 210
Nineteenth Century, 2 n.
Noah, 203
North American Review, 98 n., 206 n.
North British Review, 16 n., 96 n., 99 n., 114 n.
Norton, Charles Eliot, 49 n., 53, 208

Observer, 23 n.
Osborne, James, xi, 21 n., 81 n.

Palgrave, Francis Turner, 2, 4, 7, 199 n.
Parkinson, Thomas, 23 n.
Patmore, Coventry, 213–15
Persius, 71
Plato, 62–64
Plutarch, 208
Poetry, Victorian conceptions of, 8–19, 27, 36, 93–96, 115–16, 170. *See also* under Arnold and Clough, theories of poetry
Pope, Alexander, 11, 17, 41 n., 43–44, 113, 115
Pound, Ezra, xii
Preyer, Robert O., 10 n.
Price, Bonamy, 73
Prichard, Constantine E., 80, 82
Pritchett, V. S., 22–23
Publications of the Modern Language Association, 80 n., 111 n.
Pugin, A. W. N., 118
Puritanism. *See* Evangelicalism

Purity, ethics of, 174–76, 179, 181, 184, 190–91, 197, 199 n.

Quarterly Review, 19 n., 94, 95 n.

Richards, I. A., xii
Roberts, Michael, 23 n.
Robertson, J. M., 17–18
Robinson, Crabb, 68 n.
Rogers, Frederic, 14, 58–59
Rossetti, William Michael, 19 n., 95–96
Rousseau, Jean-Jacques, 55, 113
Routh, H. V., 24 n.
Rugby Magazine, 3, 68 n., 78

Saintsbury, George, 19–20
Sainte-Beuve, Charles-Augustin de, 14
Sand, George, 14, 99
Sarton, May, 38
Saturday Review, 1 n., 7 n., 116 n.
Scott, Sir Walter, 56, 94, 113
Scrutiny, 39 n.
Sellar, W. Y., 16 n., 96, 126 n.
Senancour, Etienne P. de, 96, 132, 197
Sewanee Review, 21 n.
Shackford, Martha Hale, 21 n.
Shairp, John Campbell, 45, 80, 122 n., 135, 136, 153–54
Shakespeare, William, 10, 14, 41 n., 45, 49, 55, 69, 94, 99 n., 106–07, 112–13, 125, 126, 168
Shelley, Percy Bysshe, 13, 14–15, 19, 39, 40, 41, 170
Sidgwick, Henry, 3 n., 4 n., 7 n., 18, 36, 80 n., 136, 141, 157, 158, 187 n., 211, 215, 227
Smith, Alexander, 41 n., 95, 96 n., 97
Smith, Blanche. *See* Clough, Mrs. Arthur Hugh
Smith, William Henry, 40 n., 156 n.
Socrates, 62
Spasmodics, 26, 95, 96 n. *See under* Alexander Smith
Spectator, 7 n., 225 n.
Spender, Stephen, 1, 23
Spenser, Edmund, 94
Spinoza, Baruch, 53
Stanford, W. B., 50

Stanley, Arthur Penrhyn, 4 n.
Sterling, John, 93, 94, 99, 115–16
Strachey, Lytton, 2, 20, 22
Strauss, David Friedrich, 51, 52–53, 165
Studies in English Literature, 1 n.
Sunday Times, 1 n., 22 n., 23 n.
Swift, Jonathan, 42 n., 131 n., 167
Swinburne, Algernon, xii, 19, 22, 23
Symonds, John Addington, xi, 2 n., 3 n., 16 n., 18, 19 n., 30 n., 81, 126, 136, 156, 157, 171, 207, 211, 214 n., 223

Taylor, Henry, 13, 38–40, 44 n.
Temple Bar, 17 n.
Tennyson, Alfred, Lord, 9 n., 15, 19, 26, 32, 38, 40, 41, 76, 92, 94–95, 96, 99, 109, 115, 132, 225, 226
Thackeray, William Makepeace, 73, 97, 99, 129
Theocritus, 115
Thompson, Lawrance, 23 n.
Thucydides, 111 n.
Tillotson, Geoffrey, 1
Times Literary Supplement, 1, 23 n.
Timko, Michael, 1 n., 8 n., 83 n.
Tinker, Chauncey Brewster, 6 n., 111 n.
Titian, 192
Trawick, Buckner B., 111 n.
Trilling, Lionel, xii, 24, 25

Tuckwell, William, 100 n.

Varnhagen von Ense, Madame Rachel, 69
Veyriras, Paul, 23 n.
Victoria, Queen, 18
Victorian Newsletter, 8 n., 58 n.
Victorian Studies, 23 n., 159 n.
Virgil, 81, 115
Voltaire, 55, 113, 129

Waddington, Samuel, xi, 19 n., 21 n., 81 n., 170 n.
Walpole, Robert, 131 n., 167
Ward, William George, 44 n., 46, 173–74, 195
Westminster Review, 3 n.
Whewell, William, 19 n., 99 n., 114 n.
Whibley, Charles, 20, 21 n., 37 n.
Whitman, Walt, 37
Wilberforce, William, 173, 195
Wilkinson, J. J. Garth, 113 n., 118
Winters, Ivor, 44 n.
Wolfe, Humbert, 22
Woodward, Frances J., 24 n.
Wordsworth, William, 9 n., 13, 14, 30, 33, 37 n., 39, 40–41, 56, 58, 64, 69 n., 70, 82–83, 113, 115, 140 n., 197

Yeats, William Butler, 35